Counseling Adults
in Transition

Nancy K. Schlossberg received a B.A. in sociology from Barnard College (1951) and an Ed.D. in counseling from Teachers College, Columbia University (1961). Since 1974 she has been a full professor at the University of Maryland's College of Education, Department of Counseling and Personnel Services. She has also been on the faculty at Wayne State University, Howard University, and Pratt Institute. She was the first woman executive at the American Council on Education where she developed the Office of Women in Higher Education. Dr. Schlossberg has written extensively on the subject of adult psychology. In addition to lecturing at numerous universities, Dr. Schlossberg frequently presents papers at the American Psychological Association and The American Personnel and Guidance Association. Dr. Schlossberg, who was elected APA Fellow in 1978, is the 1983 APA G. Stanley Hall Lecturer in Adult Development, and she has been selected as a Distinguished Scholar at the University of Maryland for 1983. Currently, she is codirecting a funded project to develop a telecommunication credit psychology course on "The Adult Years: Continuity and Change."

Counseling Adults
in Transition

Linking Practice with Theory

Nancy K. Schlossberg, Ed.D.

Springer Publishing Company
New York

Springer Publishing Company, Inc.
200 Park Avenue South
New York, New York 10003

84 85 86 87 88 / 10 9 8 7 6 5 4 3 2

Library of Congress Cataloging in Publication Data

Schlossberg, Nancy K.
    Counseling adults in transition.
    Bibliography: p. Includes index.
    1. Counseling. 2. Adulthood. 3. Middle-age—Psychological aspects. I. Title.
BF637.C6S325 1984   158′.3   83-19148
ISBN 0-8261-4230-3

Printed in the United States of America

Contents

17685

Preface

For many years I have been intrigued with how adults develop. This interest has led me to study how adults deal with the ordinary and extraordinary process of living, and how to help them do it. In 1965, I was inspired by the work of Bernice Neugarten, who was then professor of human development at the University of Chicago. I undertook a study of a group of 35-year-old male undergraduates at Wayne State University who were changing at an age beyond which people were then expected to change (Schlossberg, 1970). Most of the men had many burdens that might reasonably have deterred their return to school, such as family responsibilities and heavy mortgages. Most were blue-collar workers with nonworking wives. For example, one was a bus driver studying to be a sociologist; another a janitor preparing to be a teacher. Yet their motivation—job advancement, retirement plans, long-range security—overrode the deterrents and supplied the impetus that led them to realize their dreams. Among the most interesting findings of the study was evidence that the drive for competency and full expression can be triggered by many kinds of events, and that support is central for people who dare to dream of change. Out of a total of 420 men, 322 returned questionnaires; and those 322 have served as my inspiration that people can change at any time—given the appropriate balance of motivation, support, and resources.

Since that time, I have planned yearly conferences on adult development, first at Wayne State and now at the University of Maryland. These conferences have enriched others, promoted my own learning experience, and been my inservice training. At each one, approximately one hundred practitioners and I have learned from adult development theorists such as Carol Gilligan, Roger Gould, Daniel Levinson, Michael Maccoby, Bernice Neugarten, Estelle Ramey, Lillian Troll, George Vaillant, Robert Weiss, and others.

As our knowledge about adult development has increased,

counseling psychologists have been able to help adults uncover new options and take that next step in search of growth and change.

This book, which is intended to be a resource text in adult counseling, is a reflection of all that I have learned from theorists and practitioners.

Today university courses in adult development and counseling are springing up in departments of counseling, psychology, higher education, and human development. My own students have been administrators, counselors and counseling psychologists, gerontologists, librarians, home economists, social workers, and religious leaders. This wide variety of students' experience in most courses and training programs—ranging from those who are professionally trained, to those who are quite experienced but not trained, to the very interested but neither trained nor experienced—poses a dilemma. Decisions must be made on what to cover and how to integrate counseling skills with theories of adult development; both aspects are essential. Effective support and understanding for an adult in transition, who often does not understand his or her conflicting, confusing feelings, depends upon the helper's knowledge of adult development and aging.

As an illustration, think of the helper's responses to a woman who says, "My mother-in-law can no longer live alone. If we bring her into our house, the children will have to double up. I feel we should bring her here, yet deep down I do not want to. I know I will have to be the one whose life is really changed. What shall I do?"

Whether the helper is a friend, professional, or paraprofessional, he or she can assist the woman in distress to cope more creatively by providing support: they can link her to others in the same situation and involve the entire family in the decision making. But it is equally important for the helper to provide the woman with a cognitive framework for the issues of parent care and for the feeling of loss of control over her life. It is not necessarily true that individuals whose skills are in helping and comunications can assist any person or any group of persons. It is also not necessarily true that individuals who have a knowledge of aging and gerontology can work successfully with adults in a helping capacity. Both the skills and the knowledge are needed to insure effectiveness.

After providing an overview of adult development theories, I propose a theoretical framework in this book which illustrates the necessity of connecting knowledge of adult development with helping skills. In addition, I suggest connecting the knowledge and the skills with transition theory, which explains the many factors that influence how an adult copes. This theory helps us to understand adults at different times throughout their lives and the framework can point the way to effective help and intervention.

It is important to note that my approach in this book, as well as an individual reader's reaction to it, may signify a particular set of values. Do we believe in the possibility of change? In a discussion of the interplay between change and continuity, Brim and Kagan (1980) state that people simultaneously desire to change and to remain the same. But possibilities for individual change— our own and others'—must be seen in a social context: What change is permitted and encouraged in a particular society? Are characteristics reversible and malleable? Our answers determine the data we collect, the policies we propose, the programs we initiate, and the words we say. We need to keep in mind that different theorists look at the same data and draw different conclusions, and that any single set of facts can prove either the stability or changeability of human characteristics.

Acknowledgments

The writing of this book has been a major transition in my life. For many months it changed my routines; it has also changed my assumptions about myself.

A book is both a solitary activity and a joint enterprise. I was helped enormously by many in putting it together. First, thanks go to my husband Steve who combines advising and nurturing; to my children Karen and Mark, who gave understanding and joy; and to my father, Saul Kamin, who knows how to work, love, and play.

Many close friends, colleagues, and students have been supportive all through the process. Two editors, Barbara Watkins and Lucy Blanton, have given me care and challenge, and Betty Bowers has typed with dedication.

It is my hope that this book will help helpers link theory and practice together so they can help other adults "put it together" and ensure their ability to work, play, and love.

1

The Foundation for Helping: Knowledge of the Adult Experience

Consider the questions and concerns adults articulate to helping professionals, paraprofessionals, and friends:

- We both retired last year. For me it was easy; for my wife it was unbearable.
- What advice can you give someone whose lover is going through an unbelievable crisis?
- My last five years have drained me. My father died after a long, painful bout with cancer. My mother and mother-in-law both live near me and want things all the time. I've had a hysterectomy; my husband a prostatectomy. My son was involved in drugs last year. I'm pulled in all directions—and often I'm angry.
- When Tom was in the factory working all day, I expected him to be tired at night. Now he's been laid off, and he lies around the house all day. I can't stand it.
- I wish being a football star could go on forever. I also wish I didn't have to face what to do after it's over.
- I'm contemplating early retirement, but my job has lots of status, and I'm afraid if I retire I'll lose all my sense of identity and power. Yet I've had two heart attacks, I need to care for

my sick wife, and really, I'm bored with many of my work-related activities.

- Why me? The kids are finally grown and doing well. We've had two years of marriage counseling, and are getting along better than ever. And now, all of a sudden, I have cancer.

- My husband is facing a job threat; my children are preadolescent; and I'm conflicted about my own career.

- My wife has been loyal, a good mother, a good wife. But I'm bored with her. Do I stay and resign myself to a dull, sexless life? Do I continue having affairs? Or do I free myself and start over?

- As head of a major institution, I assumed when I retired that I'd be the elder statesman. When the phone stopped ringing, when my wife and I started arguing and bumping into each other, I realized I was in the midst of a major crisis.

These concerns relate to how adults can explore, understand, and cope with what is happening in their lives.

Add to these the "what if's" and "if only's," the cries of more and more adult men and women of all ages and walks of life who have made basic decisions about education, career, and lifestyle and feel there is no turning back: "What if I had known earlier that women could be women as well as engineers?" "If only I had completed high school!"

Also add to these the questions which ask "where is," "is there," and "what are,"—questions that may indicate little psychic pain and turmoil but are equally urgent to the individual desperately seeking to achieve full development: "Where is a school with part-time training in tailoring?" "Is there an opportunity for women morticians?" "What are the options for someone with my abilities?"

As helpers we are trying to help adults achieve, increase, or maintain their capacity to love, work, and play, although these goals are often talked about in terms of increased competency, maturity, mental health, and other catch-all phrases. Theorists, whose work we will discuss later in this chapter, talk about the capacity to love and work (Smelser and Erikson, 1980; Vaillant, 1977), the capacity to continually invest in life (Fiske, formerly

Lowenthal, 1980), the ability to respond autonomously and creatively (Loevinger, 1976), and the flexibility to cope with the "hassles" of life (Lazarus, 1981a; Pearlin, 1980). Indeed, Smelser and Erikson organized a book around the themes of work and love in adulthood, based on Freud's definition of maturity as the "capacity to love and work."

Note that, to love and work, I add play which is integral. The gods are often pictured playing, though there is no mythological god of play (Huizinga, 1950). I am reminded here of Norman Cousins' successful battle against cancer using massive doses of vitamin C—and laughter (Cousins, 1979).

How can we, as helpers, best help these adults understand, explore, and cope? What will enable us to most effectively help adults change the situations—or the meanings of the situations—that need to be changed and to handle the stress that accompanies the changes?

One of the best ways we can help adults achieve, increase, or maintain a capacity to love, work, and play is to connect the knowledge of adult development to the helping skills. The more counselors and other practitioners know about normal adult development, the more effective will be their responses and programs. By connecting the knowledge base to the skills, we can be more creative, more tuned in, more connected to the "normal" adults we try to help.

Many theorists explain adult development. All provide useful insights, but perhaps it is most useful for helpers to connect with those theorists who address the variability of adult experience, the "fanning out" of adult experience, and particularly those who emphasize transition theory—which explains the variety of ways individuals cope with the inevitable and often unpredictable transitions over the lifespan.

Before we can focus on transition theory and a framework for using adult development knowledge together with helping skills (which we will do in Chapter 4), we need to get an overview of the current major theories of adult development and, further, to identify those salient themes (for example, intimacy and generativity) which are included in most discussions of adult development and recur throughout the lifespan. Thus this chapter serves as the grounding, context, or foundation on which the framework for the necessary connecting of adult development knowledge and the helping skills can be built.

Theoretical Perspectives on Adult Development

Thirty years ago very little material existed on the topic of adult development. Until very recently, the middle years of life were viewed as relatively static. Developmental psychologists concentrated on the early years—infancy, childhood, adolescence—when both biological and psychological change are rapid and highly visible. The assumption was that once the storms of adolescence were over, adults settled into a steady course with their basic values established and with their major decisions for governing their lives made. For an adult to admit uncertainty and discontent, to switch careers or lifestyles, to appear as other than "mature" and "stable," was seen as deviant and even neurotic.

Today, as improvements in nutrition and medical technology have added years to the average lifetime, and as the number of people living into their seventies, eighties, and beyond has increased, researchers have turned their attention to the later years of life. It is now widely recognized that the view of human life as 18 or so years of rapid development followed by a quiescent four decades until the decline into death is erroneous. Rather, adulthood is marked by interior growth and change which merits serious study and consideration.

Many social scientists are now exploring and defining developmental patterns in the adult years. They reach different conclusions and give attention to different points. Much work is still in process, or embryonic, but as already noted, they all offer guidelines for understanding adult behavior which are useful for helpers. Their work is concerned with such questions as these:

- Is biology destiny?
- What is the relationship of age, sex, and/or stage to behavior?
- What is the role of work, family, and self in the life course?
- How do people adapt to the inevitable internal and external transitions?
- What are the recurring preoccupations of adults?
- What is the relationship of age to cognitive development? To physical development? To health?
- Are adulthood and aging a continuation from earlier years? Or does change occur at any time?

- What is the meaning of time—life time, social time, historical time—to adults?
- Are adulthood and aging best understood by looking at commonalities of events and experiences—or at their variability?

The major theoretical perspectives of adult development can be placed on a continuum (Figure 1-1) according to the degree to which predictability or variability in the life course is emphasized and the extent to which development is related to chronological age.

Along this continuum there are three important theoretical orientations: age and stage theories, life events and transition theories, and individual timing and variability theories. It is important to note that although the three conceptual perspectives are shown here as quite separate (for purposes of discussion), in actuality they overlap, interact, and build upon one another.

Age and Stage: Theoretical Perspectives

Most familiar to the lay public are theoretical perspectives emphasizing the sequential nature of adult development. Stage theories of development can be categorized into three types: those based on age (Levinson, 1978); those based on issues that precipitate new development (Erikson, 1950; Vaillant, 1977; Gould, 1978); and those related to the unfolding of ethical and moral development (Kohlberg, 1970; Gilligan, 1982), cognitive development (Perry, 1970), or ego development (Loevinger, 1976). Stage theories assume some universality of age-specific experience; that is, people pass through similar experiences at similar ages.

Based on age. At the left-hand end of the continuum, Levinson (1978) focuses on relatively universal, age-linked developmental periods that unfold in an orderly sequence, with stable (structure-building) periods alternating with transitional (structure-changing) periods. Through intensive biographical interviews with a sample of 40 men (hourly workers, corporate executives, academic biologists, and novelists)—who at the beginning of this longitudinal study in 1969 ranged in age from 35 to 45—Levinson and his associates have so far explored in depth six distinct periods, each closely linked to age: the Early Adult Transition, or Leaving the Family (which begins in late adolescence), Entering the Adult World (ages 22 to 28), the Age-30 Transition (ages 28 to 33), Settling Down (ages 33 to 40), the Midlife Transition (ages 40 to 45), and Entering Middle

AGE AND STAGE PERSPECTIVES	LIFE EVENT AND TRANSITION PERSPECTIVES	INDIVIDUAL TIMING AND VARIABILITY PERSPECTIVES
Levinson • Invariant sequence of development • Life structure • Dream, mentor • Polarities **Erikson, Vaillant** • Unfolding of life and resolving of inner issues • Identified hierarchical stages **Gould** • Release from childhood assumptions • Tinkering with inadequacies **Perry, Loevinger, Kohlberg, Gilligan** • Hierarchical sequence • Sequence in ego, moral, intellectual development • Sex differences	**Brim, Kagan, Dohrenwends, Danish** • Perspective not theory • Opposed to life stages • Study impact of events and mediating variables • Opposed to early life seen as a determiner of adult behavior **Pearlin, Lazarus** • Impact on life is key to well-being • Coping not life events, are central • Classification of life strains • Classification of coping responses **Lowenthal (Fiske), Chiriboga, Thurnher** • Stage not age • Look at transitions • Balance of resources to deficits • Perceived stresses • Sex differences	**Neugarten** • Fanning out • Psychology of timing • Social clock and bias **Vaillant** • Early trauma not predictive of later behavior **Kohn** • Individual learning capacity related to health, social class and substantive complexity of work **Pearlin, Leiberman** • Differential distribution of strains

Figure 1–1. A Continuum of Adult Development Theoretical Perspectives (Copyright © 1983 by N. K. Schlossberg)

Adulthood (ages 45 to 50). Later periods have been tentatively identified and will be examined more thoroughly as the sample population grows older.

Each period is characterized by its own "developmental tasks." For instance, during the Settling Down period a man is concerned with establishing his place in society (that is, affirming his own integrity and becoming a full-fledged adult) and with "making it" (that is, advancing toward the goals he has set).

Levinson's formulations, which allow individual variation within the overall pattern, emphasize sequentiality and similarity. His findings show "relatively low variability in the age at which every period begins and ends." The seasons of the year are a central metaphor in the theory: The life course unfolds in the inevitable series of "definable forms," each with its own special character—just as spring has a character that is distinct from the character of autumn—and each has its necessary place in the whole.

Based on precipitating results. Another view of adult development is embodied in theories which assert that human beings pass through an invariable sequence of developmental stages, though these stages are not necessarily linked exactly with chronological age; that is, some people move through the stages faster than others, and some people may become arrested at one stage and never move on. Erikson (1950), for instance, postulates an eight-stage progression in ego development, each characterized by a crucial issue that must be successfully resolved before the individual can move on. The adult stages involve the issues of identity (versus role diffusion), intimacy (versus isolation), generativity (versus stagnation), and ego integrity (versus despair).

Erikson's work provided the backdrop for Vaillant's analysis of advantaged men in his longitudinal study of Harvard students (1977). He found that these men had the potential to progress through the basic stages identified by Erikson as well as an additional stage which he labeled *career consolidation*. He also found that those men who were able to achieve intimacy were then able to deal effectively with their careers, which in turn led to the achievement of generativity and integrity. Vaillant examined another set of longitudinal data based on inner city men in 1940 and again in 1976. He found the same progression through Erikson stages, though the external circumstances and details of life looked very different (Vaillant, 1982).

Erikson's views relate to those of Gould (1978), another stage theorist who sees adult development as a struggle for freedom from the internal constraints of childhood, as a sequential process of fluctuations defining the posturing of self in relation to its inner and outer worlds. These fluctuations happen over time, but are not necessarily age specific. Gould perceives people at all ages as being and feeling "stuck," and feels they can be helped to develop "previously underdeveloped aspects of self."

The notion of the struggle for freedom from childhood constrictions and the notion that mellowing and maturity arrive after age 50 are reminiscent of Erikson's view of successful aging as a matter of resolving crucial issues. While Erikson sees the resolution of each crisis as the completion of a stage that is an entity unto itself, Gould believes that at any time most adults are tinkering with some aspect of themselves. This tinkering with inadequacies can be the prod for further growth.

Related to ethical, moral, cognitive, or ego development. Another group of theorists, still classified as stage theorists, sees individuals as moving through an invariant sequence of stages each of which is characterized by a qualitative difference in the way the world is processed or viewed.

One of these theorists, Perry, postulates a model of cognitive develpment based on empirical work with several cohorts of Harvard undergraduates (1970). In interviews at the end of each year, the students were asked a broad general question about what had "stood out" for them during the year and were then questioned in more detail. Their responses were found to reflect attitudes about the nature of knowledge and thinking, the function of educational institutions and teachers, and the responsibility of the learner. Perry defined a set of hierarchical stages, which are as follows:

- *Basic duality.* The world is seen in terms of polarities such as good/bad, right/wrong. Knowledge is absolute, and an "authority" (the teacher) has the "right answer," which will be duly revealed to the hard-working and obedient student.

- *Relativism.* All knowledge and values, including those of authority, are contextual and relativistic.

- *Commitment.* Although absolute certainty is impossible, some kind of personal commitment or affirmation is needed. As this commitment develops, the student affirms his or her own identity.

In addition, Perry's model resembled Kohlberg's (1970) theory of moral development and Loevinger's (1976) theory of ego development in that all three view development as progression from the simple to the complex; from an external orientation (where the individual is dependent on authority or on the judgment of others) to an inner orientation (where the individual takes responsibility for the consequences of his or her own actions); from absolutism and dogmatism to increasing tolerance for ambiguity and uncertainty; from a tendency to perceive those outside one's own immediate group in stereotypic terms to increasing awareness of individual differences and greater empathy with others; and from a strong self-focus to a posture of conformity to the group and then to a mature focus on interdependence with others.

Loevinger describes ego development as a "master trait . . . determining an individual's responses" (Weathersby & Tarule, 1980, p. 26). The earliest stage, labeled *self-protective*, applies to someone who follows rules and thinks in stereotypes, a conformist. At a higher, *self-aware* level, an individual "develops an increasing self-awareness and the ability to think in terms of alternatives, exceptions, and multiple possibilities in situations" (Weathersby & Tarule, p. 29). Most mature is the *autonomous* stage, in which the adult makes commitments, tolerates ambiguities, and incorporates opposites.

These concepts enable us to differentiate among a group facing the same transition—for example, among the newly married, new mothers, or newly retired. Adults at the same transition will process that experience differently—some in a simplistic either/or way, others in a more complex autonomous manner.

Similarly, Kohlberg has developed stages of moral development comparable to Perry and Loevinger: Adults move from obeying rules and laws because they are motivated by fear of punishment to conforming to society and, finally, to being principled and autonomous (Kohlberg, 1970, p. 25).

Gilligan, who seems to agree that there are qualitative differences in the way people process and interpret the world, has nevertheless challenged such definitions of the stages because they are based solely on studies of men. In discussing both Levinson's and Vaillant's work, she shows that both "convey a view of adulthood where relationships are subordinated to the ongoing process of individualization and achievement . . . on the other hand, there is observation that among those men whose lives have served as the model for adult development, the capacity for relationships is in some sense diminished and the men are constricted in their emotional expression" (1982, p. 154). Through interviews with women, she has identified different issues as central in their development: the issues of attachment and interdependence. "Thus there seems to be a line of development missing from current depictions of adult development, a failure to describe the progression of relationships toward a maturity of interdependence" (p. 155). She also states:

> Male and female voices typically speak of the importance of different truths, the former of the role of separation as it defines and empowers the self, the latter of the ongoing process of attachment that creates and sustains the human community.
>
> Since this dialogue contains the dialectic that creates the tension of human development, the silence of women in the narrative of adult development distorts the conception of its stages and sequence. Thus, I want to restore in part the missing text of women's development . . . in focusing primarily on the differences between the accounts of women and men, my aim is to enlarge developmental understanding by including the perspective of both of the sexes.

Life Events and Transition: Theoretical Perspectives

The next major group on the continuum are those theoretical perspectives based on life events and transitions, such as the approach taken by Lowenthal [now Fiske], Thurnher, and Chiriboga in *Four Stages of Life* (1975). This longitudinal study involved four groups of men and women in the San Francisco area—graduating high school seniors, newlyweds, middle-aged parents, and preretirement couples. Each group was on the threshold of a major transition at the start of the study. The researchers found that the groups differed considerably in their general outlook on life, the stresses they faced, and their attitudes toward those stresses, and concluded that it is less important to know that a person is 40 years old than that the person is 40 with adolescent children, recently divorced, about to retire, and so on. Men facing retirement after they have had an active social life, for example, encounter many of the same problems whether they retire at age 50, 60, or 70. Newlyweds of any age are engaged in similar tasks of bonding, discovery, and negotiation. In short, life events—transitions—are more important than chronological age in understanding and evaluating an individual's behavior.

Other theories in this group are labeled *life-span development approaches* and *life-events frameworks*. Brim and Kagan, quoting Baltes' statement that a life-span approach is "a general orientation to the study of behavior" rather than "a specific theory or collection of theories," describe their life-span development approach as "an emergent intellectual movement, responsive to the possibility of change, currently trying to select its major premises, to gather new facts, and to conceptualize the developmental span without using chronological age categories." This is in distinct opposition to theories involving adult stages, for such "stages cast development as unidirectional, hierarchical, sequenced in time, cumulative, and irreversible—ideas that are not supported by commanding evidence" (1980, p. 13).

Other researchers who take this approach include Baltes and Danish (1980), Brim and Ryff (1980), and Dohrenwend, Krasnoff, Askenasy, and Dohrenwend (1978). Many of them acknowledge the role of critical life events as markers, milestones, or transition points. This "critical life-events framework" plays a pivotal role in individual development, giving shape and direction to the various aspects of each individual's life. Those who take this approach tend to reject the notion that childhood experiences (especially traumatic experiences) determine the course of the individual's life.

Pearlin is another theorist who emphasizes transitions. He studied the strains in people's lives and their ways of coping (which depend on whether they are rich or poor, male or female), and concluded that the romance with the study of life events is wearing thin because it tells us nothing about how lives are structured (1982). He instead asserts that change is inevitable and has developed a framework for analyzing the changes brought about by life events as well as the mechanisms adults have for coping with these changes. Lazarus has also studied the everyday hassles and uplifts in life and describes ways of coping (1981a).

The work of these life events and transition theorists is, as already noted, particularly important in connection with the helping skills. This will be discussed in detail in Chapter 2's description of an organizing framework for connecting adult development knowledge to the helping skills.

Individual Timing and Variability: Theoretical Perspectives

On the right-hand side of the continuum are the theorists like Neugarten, who throughout her work emphasizes variability—which she calls *individual fanning out*—by pointing out, for example, that 10-year-olds are more similar to each other than 60-year-olds. "As lives grow longer, as the successive choices and commitments accumulate, lives grow different from each other" (1976).

Evidence supporting this position on variability comes from the Grant Study, which covers 35 years of the lives of more than 200 men (most of them with high ability and from high socioeconomic backgrounds) beginning when they were college sophomores. According to Vaillant:

> When the Grant Study was started, the hope was that it would allow prediction, that once all data were in college counselors could interview sophomores and tell them what they should do with their lives. This was not to be. The life cycle is more than an invariant sequence of stages with single predictable outcomes. The men's lives are full of surprises (1977, p. 373).

Another important finding to emerge from this study was that "it is not the isolated traumas of childhood that shape our future, but the quality of sustained relationships with other people" (Vaillant, 1977, p. 29). (Vaillant's work provides a good illustration of how the continuum's three theoretical perspectives actually overlap and interact. He discusses the sequential nature of stages of maturity, and also sees the possibility of surprise and change.)

Variability through generational differences and the social clock. Neugarten (1976) gives considerable attention to generational differences and distinguishes among three kinds of time: historical time (calendar time), life time (chronological age), and socially defined time (the social clock which relates to age norms and expectations). She says that if we are to understand a particular life history, we must view it in a historical context, and, as historical times change, the prescriptions on age-appropriate behavior are lessening. It is noteworthy that changes over the past several decades have drastically affected individuals. For example, because people are living longer, the postparental period has lengthened considerably; at the same time, however, "economic maturity" for many young people is being delayed as a larger proportion attend college and go on to graduate or professional school. Further, patterns for women in general have changed drastically: More young women are now employed full time; more middle-aged women are returning to the labor force after their children leave home; and child-rearing practices are changing as younger fathers share responsibility with their working wives.

Although each of these and other historical trends have, in turn, an impact on the chronological and social norms relating to what is considered to be age-appropriate behavior, in adulthood there seems to be little biological necessity for our behavior, as Neugarten points out. The most dramatic biological change after puberty is the menopause, which has become surrounded by many emotion-charged myths. But Neugarten suggests that even menopause is not a particularly salient event to most women experiencing it, who are often more concerned about the possibility of their husbands' death, of cancer, and of aging in general.

Nonetheless, despite the fact that there are few major biological punctuation marks for adulthood, most of us continue to have rather rigid notions about what constitutes appropriate behavior for people at different ages, even though the "prescriptive timetable for the ordering of major life events" that decrees the age at which people should, for example, take jobs, marry, have children, retire (or else suffer the consequences of being "off time" in their behavior) is in the process of revision. The extent to which these notions govern our thinking has been demonstrated by Neugarten and her associates in studies which found that at least four in five of their sample of "normal, middle-class Americans" believed that the best age for marriage for men is between 20 and 27 and for women between 20 and 22 and that people should retire between 60 and 65 (Neugarten, Moore, & Lowe, 1965). Such norms as these can be said to constitute our social clock. Because studies were focused on the middle class and are now dated, they are subject to criticism; but we need to be aware of how the social clock may affect those we are helping as well as ourselves. For example, when counselors working in college and university counseling centers were surveyed (Troll & Schlossberg, 1971), it was assumed that these helpers would be less bound by age-appropriate stereotypes than the general population. But the findings showed that those counselors were just like Neugarten's "normal middle-class Americans." Apparently, since most counselors are middle class and not yet sensitized to age as an issue, they may automatically make assumptions about their clients. If a 60-year-old comes to a 30-year-old counselor and states, "I'm thinking of changing careers," there is the possibility that the 30-year-old counselor may assume that the 60-year-old is too old to consider such a change. Thus adults live with a paradox: No biological reason exists for adults to behave in any particular way; yet many adults control their behavior by means of social norms and constraints.

In view of the increasing number of adults returning to school, changing careers, and planning new careers after retirement, it becomes increasingly necessary for us to continue to revise and reevaluate our social clocks, especially since, as Neugarten postulates, this "prescriptive timetable for the ordering of major life events" is in flux. Helpers need to be aware that many adults have built-in social clocks by which they judge whether they are on time in particular life events, and to be off time—whether early or late—may precipitate feelings of uncertainty, inadequacy, anxiety. To be widowed at age 30 may be more traumatic than to be widowed at age 60, and to have a first child at age 40 may create more difficulties than a first child at age 20.

Variability in life strains. Further documentation of the variability dimension stems from the work of Pearlin and Leiberman (1979), who demonstrate how life strains are differentially distributed according to age, sex, and socioeconomic status. They found that most frequently—and disproportionately—life strains are concentrated in young women of lower socioeconomic groups. Clearly, the adult experience differs according to whether an individual is a man or woman, black or white, young or old, rich or poor, healthy or ill. Unfortunately, to date much of the work on adult development is based on data that describe middle-class adults, particularly middle-class males. Helpers need to note that it is fallacious to assume that such data will apply, for example, to clients from low-income groups, new immigrants, clerical workers, homosexuals, or members of other subgroups.

Variability in learning capacity. Assessment of an adult's learning capacity is of central importance. Few people today subscribe to the notion that "you can't teach an old dog new tricks," although the conventional wisdom seems to be that intellectual functioning slows down with age. For instance, Cattell (1963) differentiates *fluid intelligence* (the ability to process information rapidly in problem solving) from *crystallized intelligence* (stored information such as vocabulary and general knowledge). The former seems to decline with age, whereas the latter seems to remain stable and even to improve (Gallagher, Thompson, & Levy, 1980, p. 23). Endocrinologist Estelle Ramey (1981) points out that despite the fact that brain cells are continually being destroyed as a person ages, there are more than enough active brain cells to ensure adequate intellectual functioning in most men and women until they die, except in cases of illness in which, for instance, the circulation to the brain is disturbed. This excess of brain cells may be described as "surplus capacity," as Ilene Siegler did in a recent conversation. She also pointed out that most research on intellectual capacity has so far focused only on the young and the elderly (1981). Adults in the middle years have been ignored.

Willis and Baltes (1980), in reviewing issues connected with the study of adult intelligence, conclude: "Chronological age per se accounts for a relatively modest amount of the variance observed in intellectual aging during late adulthood up to the sixties or early seventies" (p. 263). Instead, three sets of influences must be taken into account, each of which has both biological and environmental correlates:

• *Age-graded influences.* Those biological and environmental determinants which are correlated with chronological age. "Their occurrence, timing, and duration are fairly similar for all individuals of a given set of aging cohorts" (Willis & Baltes, p. 267).

• *History-graded influences.* Those biological and environmental events correlated with historical change. "Their degree of generality and predictability varies. Some of them, however, are fairly normative, in that they apply to most members of a given set of aging cohorts in similar ways" (p. 267). For instance, people who grew up during the Great Depression may differ in consistent ways from people who grew up in the post-World-War-II era of economic expansion, and these differences may be reflected in their cognitive functioning. Similarly, intergenerational differences in labor force participation or family life may result in intergenerational differences in intellectual development.

• *Nonnormative critical life events.* Those events in the life of the individual which are relatively idiosyncratic—for example, unusual opportunities for learning, illness, unemployment, or bereavement. Such events may affect intellectual development directly (as in the case of disease that results in brain damage), or indirectly (through stress).

Willis and Baltes maintain that investigators must give greater attention in their research designs to history-graded influences and nonnormative critical life events if they are to arrive at an understanding of intellectual development over the life span.

Substantive complexity. In a study that throws some light on the conditions under which learning capacity may improve over time, Kohn (1980) identified more than 50 job dimensions or occupational conditions. Twelve of the dimensions have significant effects on psychological functioning, after all other pertinent factors are statistically controlled. The most important is substantive complexity, which may be defined as "the degree to which the work, in its very substance, requires thought and independent judgment. Substantively complex work, by its very nature, requires making many decisions that must take into acount ill-defined or apparently conflicting contingencies. . . . The index of substantive complexity that we have generally employed is based on the degree of complexity of the person's work with things, with data, and with people" (p. 197). Kohn further asserts that substantive complexity is a central structural characteristic of the work experience; that it is related to a wide range of psychological factors including job satisfaction, occupational commitment, self-direction, self-esteem, authoritarian conservatism, and intellectual flexibility; and that the causal relation is reciprocal; that is, adults' psychological functioning affects the substantive complexity of the work they do, and the substantive complexity of the work they do affects their psychological functioning. Looking in particular at intellectual flexibility, as indicated by performance and behavior on tests and during interviews, Kohn states:

> If two men of equivalent intellectual flexibility were to start their careers in jobs different in substantive complexity, the man in the more complex job would be likely to outstrip the other in further intellectual growth. This, in time, might lead to his attaining jobs of greater complexity, further affecting his intellectual growth. Meantime, the man in the less complex job would develop intellectually at a slower pace, perhaps not at all, and in the extreme case might even decline in his intellectual functioning. As a result, small differences in the substantive complexity of early jobs might lead to increasing differences in intellectual development (p. 203).

Moreover, similar results emerged from a study of 269 employed married women, who (as the researchers point out) are "especially likely to be subject to actual and potential conflicts among occupational, conjugal, and maternal roles" (Miller, Schooler, Kohn, & Miller, 1979, p. 80). Those women whose work was substantively complex and, in addition, nonroutinized (that is, they were involved in a variety of unpredictable tasks) demonstrated greater intellectual flexibility than those women performing relatively simple, routine work. Thus, those women who have been continuously exposed to stimulating and complex environments which demand that they exercise their problem-solving abilities may be more intellectually flexible—and thus more likely to benefit from learning activities—than those women who live and work in stultifying environments in which they perform only routine and repetitive tasks. In addition, although the research of Kohn and his associates has been limited to employed adults, it also indicates that many women who do not hold outside jobs may nonetheless perform work—in the home and in the community—of considerable substantive complexity. Further, those women who do play occupational as well as conjugal and maternal roles may live substantively complex lives even if their jobs are relatively low level.

Factors muting variability. The importance of looking at factors muting variability is asserted by Neugarten, Kohn, and others. Many of these factors reside in age bias, that is, the degree to which different types of behavior are ascribed on the basis of age. Three types have been described by Troll (1982):

- Age restrictiveness, or the setting of age limits for any behavior.
- Age distortion, or the misperceiving of behavior or characteristics to fit age stereotypes.
- Ageism, or negative attitudes toward any age group.

Although the internalization of age-appropriate behavior which determines social clocks is decreasing, adults behave as if controlled by biology when, in fact, it is their own set of assumptions about age-appropriate behavior which determines their behavior. Neugarten asks, can we move to a world in which age is irrelevant?

In a work setting, age distortions may manifest themselves in personnel practices that work to the detriment of the individual employee and ultimately of the organization itself. In a survey undertaken to determine the extent to which age bias and age stereotypes are reflected in administrative decisions, Rosen and Jerdee (1977) found that because older workers are viewed as "relatively inflexible and resistant to change," as well as deficient in "creativity, mental alertness, [and] capacity to deal with crisis situations," managers often fail to give them feedback that might improve their work performance, to support their career development and retraining, and to offer them opportunities for promotion.

The distortion by the media of older Americans has become an important area of study. For example, Gerbner and his research associates (Gerbner, Gross, Signonelli, & Morgan, 1980) have developed a method to examine the "aggregate system of messages" that the media communicate about adults. Among the distortions uncovered were that nearly half of elderly television characters were likely to be victimized and that the old—and the young—were stereotyped.

Sex Differences: Theoretical Perspectives

Sex differences are an essential ingredient in understanding adult development. Although adult development theories are positioned here along the continuum according to their predictability/variability and how they construe development as related to chronological age, it is important to note that sex differences—differences in behavior and maturity that are ascribed to men and women—are often more striking than stage differences—differences in timing, order, and recurrence.

These differences are highlighted in several studies. Gilligan (1982a) asserts that maturity for women is different than for men and that this difference must be built into developmental models. Lowenthal, Thurnher, and Chiriboga (1975) found that the women in their sample generally had less positive self-images than the men, felt less in control of their lives, and were less likely to plan for transitions. At the same time, their affective lives were richer and more complex, and they had a greater tolerance for ambiguity. The lifestyles of the men in their study became less complex as they grew older and shed roles and activities, but the pattern for women was simplistic for high school seniors and middle-aged women and complex for newlywed and preretirement women, who played many roles and engaged in many activities. Highly stressed men in the older groups tended to deny stress, while women tended to be preoccupied with stress. Men anticipated placing more value on expressive and interpersonal goals as they grew older, while women expected to direct their interests outward and to become more concerned with contributing to society and doing good in the world. The "criss-crossing trajectories" of men and women at successive stages reflect differing types of developmental changes, as well as different scheduling.

Sex differences are also visible in recent research on how men and women are viewed in the workplace. Management students were asked to rate both the attractiveness and unattractiveness of men and women in relation to their applications for both managerial and nonmanagerial jobs. "No matter which level, attractiveness was an asset for men. For managerial jobs, unattractive women were rated highest. Why should this be? . . . Attractive men were judged to be more masculine and attractive women to be more feminine than their unattractive counterparts. . . . The evidence in the study indicates that stereotypic thinking links femininity with indecisiveness, passivity, emotionality, and other traits antithetical to successful performance in such roles" (Heilman, 1980).

A related finding is that while men tend to turn inward as they grow older (becoming more concerned with interpersonal relations and with expressive rather than instrumental goals, becoming more "feminine"), women tend to turn outward, becoming more involved in the external world, moving from a passive to an active stance (Gutmann, 1977). The implication seems to be that some older women are at least as well suited as older men to positions that demand executive ability.

Further, the social clock schema shows sex differences, although many aspects of variability theories may encompass these differences. Sex differences, however, must be seen in historical perspective, and our view of them may change as new cohorts are studied. Today new research is underway which identifies sex differences (for example, how men and women are differentially treated) and challenges the very content of theories based on male models. For example, Gilligan has challenged Kohlberg's content; others are challenging Perry, Vaillant, and Levinson. These challenges demonstrate that "normal" differs depending on the researcher and the sample. Those engaged in this work will be in the forefront during the next decade.

Overview

The continuum of theoretical perspectives on adult development illustrates that the theorists, while providing us invaluable insights, do not see eye to eye, that indeed theorists like Levinson and Neugarten have diametrically opposing views on the question of predictability and variability in the life course. But the conclusions of the researchers whose work is discussed here depend, to some extent, on the samples studied and the methodologies used. Levinson and his associates studied a small sample of men within a narrow age range, most of them strongly career-oriented and working in high-status jobs (though so far these researchers have not looked in detail at periods beyond the late forties). Lowenthal and her colleagues studied a family-oriented sample that included women and had a much greater age range. Their report, *Four Stages of Life,* is cross-sectional in nature, comparing the four groups. Neugarten studied a variety of samples at a single point in time but focused on historical trends and social shifts over time through her analysis of connections between historical time, chronological age, and socially prescribed time.

Our overview also illustrates that the new work on adulthood has thoroughly challenged the older ideas that adulthood—in contrast to childhood, adolescence, and youth—represents stability and certainty. No theorist assumes that those who are over age 30 have made their important decisions and settled into a steady pattern of living untroubled by the doubts, conflicts, and upheavals that mark earlier years. Instead, our overview makes clear the agreement that adults continuously experience change—transitions—in themselves, their personal lives, their family lives, and their work and community lives, even though the theorists do not agree as to the predictability and variability of change.

There are also recurring themes in the work of all the theorists. For example, the theorists agree that just when an adult thinks he or she has achieved a sense of self, or an intimate relationship, or a fresh sense of competence, situations and people change and their identity, intimacy, competency become elusive. Adults are forever solving their internal and external problems only to find that the solution becomes part of a new thesis, which then needs reexamining—though there is no agreement as to the predictability and variability of these events. The next section provides an overview of the important recurring themes.

Recurring Themes

The themes of adulthood, which most adults are continuously working on throughout the life course, are like the point and counterpoint of a fugue. The themes are also like the dialectical process occurring through the adult years as described by Riegel (1973) who "sees development as moving from simple to complex through the progressive integration of previously inconsistent or contradictory experiences. Change occurs only when a person in an existing condition (thesis) is confronted by a conflicting or opposite situation (antithesis). A successful resolution of this conflict would induce a higher order new state (synthesis) which reconciles both elements of the conflict. This new synthesis becomes, in turn, the thesis to a new antithesis" (Schlossberg, Troll, & Leibowitz, 1978, p. 27).

Even when the view is held that individuals are highly variable in their development and become increasingly differentiated as they grow older, it is still possible to identify what seem to be universal themes in life. Neugarten, the theorist who most strongly emphasizes that development does not unfold in predictable, age-linked stages and that the life course changes in response to social and cultural trends, speaks of "regularities and continuities" from one generation to the next.

Moreover, even as most people grow psychologically as they adapt to various transitions and change their interests, goals, and values as the result of experience, it is still possible to trace themes that recur in their lives, themes that crop up again and again—though in slightly altered form—at different ages and stages.

The work of Erikson contributes an important framework for looking at the life course's recurring themes. He postulates an eight-stage progression in ego development over the lifespan, each with its own critical issue to be resolved. These issues (or themes, as I prefer to call them) are not resolved once and for all and then put aside forever; they recur throughout the individual's life. They are not sequential, rather recurring and overlapping with no regularity.

The themes discussed here include five of those which Erikson describes: identity, intimacy and/or attachment, integrity (renamed here autonomy and satisfaction), generativity, and industry (renamed here competency). The sixth theme is belonging versus marginality. This relates to role changes, and is of special importance in transitions.

If we are able to help adults deal with these themes, we will increase their capacity to love, work, and play. Our understanding of these themes, which underlie most of the concrete concerns adults have, will be an important part of the framework (presented in the following chapters) for helping adults better explore, understand, and cope.

Identity

Underlying all the other recurrent themes is that of identity. According to Erikson, the crisis of identity occurs in late adolescence; young people must establish a sense of self and find a place as individuals in the adult world. If they fail to achieve identity, they are left with "role diffusion" and cannot develop further. In a broader sense, we can say that the crisis of identity is reawakened whenever the individual experiences a major transition. To give an extreme example: A man whose sense of identity is grounded in his career—who defines himself in terms of his work role—will be severely stressed if he suffers a setback in his career or does not progress as rapidly as he had initially expected. For such a man, retirement from the world of work will constitute a severe trauma. Similarly, the woman whose sense of identity derives from her role as wife will find the very foundations of her life shaken if she faces divorce or widowhood.

"Mead distinguished two parts of the *self:* the *I* and the *me.* The *I* is the core or center; it unifies diverse feelings and experiences as well as past, present, and future. . . . The *me* . . . is the part of the *self* that results from interaction with others. . . . It includes a wide variety of individual characteristics from temperament to need for achievement" (Troll, 1982, pp. 228–229).

Thus people confront themselves—who they are when stripped of all roles. They also confront themselves through their work, their families, and their leisure.

Several theorists look at changes in identity over the life course. Neugarten describes three shifts that normally occur in the middle years:

- *Increasing interiority.* People become more introspective, more preoccupied with the inner life of the self, and consequently less involved with and responsive to the outside world.

- A *reversal in directionality.* People think "in terms of time left to live rather than time since birth," and they become increasingly aware that "time is finite."

- *Personalization of death.* People come to see death as something that will happen to them.

But the middle years also have their positive side. In interviews with 100 "well-placed" men and women in the 40 to 60 age bracket, Neugarten was impressed by their heightened sense of competence, their greater self-understanding, and their confidence in their own abilities and expertise (1976, p. 17).

In short, whether the reassessment of the self and the world that usually accompanies a major transition (at whatever age it occurs) leads to greater self-confidence or diminished assurance, the result is a renewed assertion of identity.

Levinson and his colleagues at Yale University (1978) identified a number of "relatively universal . . . age-linked developmental periods." Their theory, linked to changing identity over the life course, focuses on six transitions in the lives of adult men. Each stage has its own developmental tasks in relation to life structures and the self. In late adolescence the individual is developing a new home base and leaving the family. In his twenties, he works to link himself to the wider adult world and establishes occupational direction. In his early thirties he settles down deeply into work, family, interests, and goals, balancing order and ambition, security and striving, control and mobility. In the late thirties, settling down is completed, and the high point of adulthood is reached "as he strives to be affirmed by society in the roles he values most" and what lies beyond begins.

The midlife transition, usually in the early forties, means questioning life structures and modifying or drastically changing those structures as well as recognizing mortality. Restabilization follows as new life structures take shape in a period which includes both possibilities for developmental advance and great threats to the self. Levinson and his associates are still in the process of studying the several forms this restabilization may take for adult men.

Trigger events. Other theorists do not see changes in identity as age-linked but rather as linked to some trigger event or nonevent, particularly during the midlife period, which, depending on the individual's experience, seems to last about ten years (though not tied directly to a particular starting and stopping age). Everything the person has done thus far is put into question: Work life, home life, dreams, and aspirations are critically examined and more often than not are found wanting. It is during this period that time perspectives shift: People see time until death rather than time since birth, which often leads to panic that they will never become any more than they are, that they might never have that spark of excitement again that accompanies a new love. Life is envisioned as more lines and wrinkles, graying hair and sagging skin, less rewards and less fun. But at the same time these midlife people also have contradictory feelings that anything and everything is possible, and they begin to formulate new dreams. Vaillant traces the lives of 98 men from their early twenties to their early fifties and concludes "at age 40—give or take as much as a decade—men leave the compulsive, unreflective busywork of their occupational apprenticeships and once more become explorers of the world within" (1977, p. 220).

Those who do not link a specific age to midlife agree that not everyone encounters these feelings, this soul searching. But a number of changes can occur which often have an impact on the way people see themselves—for example, changes in the body such as an illness, a heart attack, cancer, a slipped disk. An internal or external event can occur which, had it happened at another age, would not have the impact it does now. These marker events trigger what Gould (1978) calls questioning—they push an individual to question the very foundation on which he or she has built his or her life; they put into question the very assumptions people have about themselves.

Differences between two retired football players interviewed on a television show illustrate this point (Schlossberg & Leibowitz, 1980b). One of the men had assumed he would be a football player forever. A knee injury, which forced him to retire, shook him deeply and triggered soul searching and questioning. His wife said, "It's really been hard. I come home after a day at the law library, and then I have to go to work again picking up David's shattered ego." The other football hero had planned all along for a second career. In fact, he had just about finished law school. For him, retiring from football was not a trigger for a midlife crisis.

Four women, returning to college after raising their families, were contrasted with these men. All saw the empty nest period as full of promise, a time that would force them to deal with "who am I?" questions. One woman described how important this rethinking of who she was and where she was going was to her because her husband had recently died.

The following exerpts from an interview with a man illustrate this identity search:

> I'm a man about halfway into his life, and so I've reached that point where—I'm no different from any other man—I've started giving a great deal of thought to who I am, where I've been, where I'm at, and where I'm going from here. I never received or got a whole lot of formal education. I was born and raised in West Virginia, and I never particularly liked school so I never finished. But it wasn't very long after I got out of school that I realized that I wasn't going to go very far, and I didn't particularly want to do for the rest of my life what I was doing at that time. One thing led to another, and I wound up eventually working here, but during all the years in the back of my mind I had planned on going back to school and finishing; but once a

man makes a commitment, particularly a rather large commitment to marriage, and responsibilities start piling up, it becomes more and more difficult, and you reach a point of no return or at least a point where its very difficult to turn about. So I am very acutely aware of how I've been limited and how far I can go.

After I reached 40 or thereabouts, I started visualizing myself being an older man and still sitting on a bench and doing the things a technician does. So I got a chance to go into programming, software as opposed to hardware, in the programming field; and this was a natural step and I grasped it. And I'm happy as a programmer, but what concerns me and what I'm concerned with naturally is my future, you know. I give more thought as to what I'm going to do in the second half of my life, and this bothered me at first. Why should I be worrying about these types of things? But after talking to friends and acquaintances, I found out that this is a rather common thing. It's a natural thing at this point in my life to start thinking about things that I've been concerned with.

The dream. Much of the reappraisal of ourselves and our lives revolves around our dreams. The dreams—our imagined possibilities of what may be—are a key to our identity. Do women submerge their dreams for their husbands? Does the midlife transition become a crisis if an individual realizes his or her dream has been submerged? The reevaluation of the dream occurs at marker times, like retirement or death of a loved one. Levinson et al. found that the men in their study spent a great deal of energy building life around a dream (1978). This means, of course, that as an individual pursues one line of work, one lifestyle, other options—other jobs, other women—are ruled out. As time goes on, there is a creeping consciousness, a grieving over lost opportunities, and a process of disillusionment sets in, complete with "what if's" and "if only's": "What if I had taken that job in Oshkosh?" "If only I had gone to college . . ." "What if I had followed that advice and done such-and-such?" In other words, it is a time of questioning and of regrets, a time of thinking almost obsessively about what might have been. This questioning leads us to consider the role others play, such as parents, who often directly try to influence the course of their children's dreams.

Both Gould and Levinson discuss the role of an individual's spouse in the realization of his or her dream. Does a person select a spouse who encourages or sabotages his or her dream? An Australian movie, *My Brilliant Career,* portrays a heroine who refuses to marry the man she passionately loves for fear of losing her dream, which is to become a great writer. She was afraid he would unwittingly sabotage her dream. Levinson points out that if women lose their own dreams by supporting those of their husbands, deep resentment will creep in.

A word more about women, at least those who are married. They not only reappraise their own dream but the dreams they had for their husbands. If their own lives are not everything they thought they would be, they suffer. But they also suffer in terms of their husbands' lives. Most women have a dream for their husbands: that he should be the biggest and best contractor, doctor, lawyer, policeman; as they are reappraising their own dreams they are also relooking at their husbands' dreams and wondering, Is this what it is all about?

Many also discover that there is a gap between where they are and where they secretly dreamed of being (Brim, 1976). Whether the individual is at the top of his or her field, or the best parent, the individual often feels he or she has fallen short. Often these thoughts are induced by a "marker event"—an outside happening. Two examples come to mind. One woman, who opted happily to make her full-time career as a mother, faced great agony when her 26-year-old son committed suicide. She said, "I am 52 and don't know who I am. Has my life been in vain?" In another case, a man, recently fired at 58, said, "I can't believe that this could happen to me—I've been loyal to the organization and now what do I have left?" However, this aspiration/achievement gap may not result from an external event. A man at 45 suddenly realizes he will never be promoted to vice president. A man or woman is passed over by younger people, and suddenly realizes that he or she is not going to the top. The "top" is defined differently by different people. Let me again quote from an interview with a man in his early forties:

> Well, I really don't—I really don't know where to begin, I don't know what I am going to say to you. I just got this feeling that I'm kind of just dead end, you know? I've got a job, it's all right, but there is no future. And I see younger men getting ahead of me. Here I have a house, a mortgage, I don't have the freedom to move as they do, but yet I get passed over for promotion. I've got a good job, but it is going nowhere; it's just absolutely becoming part of my life that I don't like. I come to work, I do my job, I go home—there's no challenge. It's just kind of humdrum, I've done it many times before. But if I saw someplace I could move, someplace I could go, someplace I could get ahead, do some of the things I really wanted to do when I started in this organization. . . . That's what I want. I don't know where to turn, I don't know what I can do with my life at this particular juncture.

This man is a full professor and head of his department. Most people would define him as successful. Yet he is feeling temporarily unsuccessful.

Career consolidation. The issue of "who am I?" often becomes intertwined with what Vaillant labels *career consolidation.* Vaillant (1977) points out that the Grant Study confirms the adult life patterns outlined by Erikson, but between the decade of the twenties—the stage of intimacy—and the forties—the stage of generativity—Erikson left an uncharted developmental period. Vaillant calls this an intermediate stage of career consolidation, a period during which individuals translate their hobbies and ambitions into occupational terms. Successful resolution of this period results in commitment, contentment, and valuing of the individual's work.

These issues of commitment, contentment, and valuing of work crop up periodically over the lifespan. People are constantly starting over, constantly realizing that as their identity shifts, so does their career commitment. In today's economy, with an increasingly aging work force, there are fewer places at the top. We are now witnessing a new phenomena: the plateaued employee. From the organizational point of view, this is someone who will remain in his or her current job for the remainder of his or her worklife. From the individual point of view, this is someone who feels subjectively boxed in, stuck, bored, and sees no career options for the future. Thus, issues of career commitment come and go, ebb and flow, and relate to that part of an individual's identity which is expressed through work.

Commitments. Using cluster analysis of selected adjectives from a checklist, Fiske and her colleagues have identified four clusters of value commitments: interpersonal, altruistic (including ethical, philosophical, and religious allegiances), mastery (competence, autonomy, creativity), and self-protective (including concern for physical, economic, and psychosocial survival and well-being). These commitments "may be brought into play in any or all of the changing arenas of the adult life course. A work setting, for example, may provide the arena for interpersonal, altruistic, or self-protective intentions as well as those relating to mastery or competence" (Fiske, 1980, p. 245). Indeed, Fiske believes that rigid dichotomies such as work versus leisure are more confusing than helpful; few people compartmentalize themselves in this way.

Initial assessment of the value orientations of the subjects revealed differences by sex as well as by life stage (Thurnher, 1975, pp. 176–200). Moreover, some subjects exhibited a diversified pattern (that is, equally strong commitments in more than one area), whereas others "put nearly all of their eggs into one commitment basket" (Fiske, 1980, p. 250). Followup studies of the subjects indicated not only that individual commitment changed over time but—surprisingly, given the socioeconomic homogeneity of the sample and the fact that members of each of the four groups experienced the same kind of transition—that there was considerable variability in the patterns of change.

Among the women in this middle-class and lower middle-class sample, the occupational setting was generally less important than the home. Both their interpersonal and their altruistic commitments tended to be directed toward raising their children. Fiske says that "for such women, a midlife conflict may be triggered by a sense of failure of mission as mother or by the realization that their child-rearing days are over. The subsequent struggle, for many, is between what they may view as a moral imperative to settle for being a good wife, and their growing awareness of a need for new arenas outside the confining sphere of the family, where their commitments—interpersonal, instrumental, altruistic, or self-indulgent—may find expression" (p. 247).

Fiske had expected to find that those who have deep commitments to work and love would continue to have them. Instead, those who sustained complex commitments "became more despairing, anxious, and sometimes ill" as they aged. (This finding challenges many studies which equate complex satisfying lives in early adulthood and middle age with later life satisfaction.)

Achievement. Also related to identity is achievement. A group of researchers have developed a model which identifies three major achieving styles, that is, preferred strategies that individuals use to get things done, characteristic ways they approach tasks or goals: direct, relational, and instrumental (Lipman-Blumen & Leavitt, 1976). "Direct achieving styles are characterized by direct confrontation of the achievement task . . . through an individual's personal efforts" (Lipman-Blumen, Handley-Isaksen, Leavitt, 1983, p. 99). Relational achievers can be characterized as team players. They contribute to others' achievement, or they are vicarious achievers, that is, they meet their achievement needs through the accomplishments of others—parents, spouses, or children.

Instrumental achievers use an aspect of the achievements in one area to lead to other achievements. For example, the football hero uses his status to promote products which will lead to more

money, or an individual develops what seems to be social friendship but for ulterior purposes like business.

People do not use one type of achieving at all times; rather
they assume different or a combination of styles on different occasions. The researchers, however, have looked to see if certain
groups use one style more predominantly than others. (From a life
course perspective, it would be interesting to see whether there are
gross differences for men and women; and further, whether men
and women shift their predominant style in certain circumstances.)

Achievement styles are learned. They can be identified by a
self-scoring instrument, the L-BLA Achieving Styles Inventory.
Training to increase an individual's repertoire is underway so that
people can be helped to use a variety of styles, depending on the
situation.

Summary of the theme of identity.   Identity has characteristics
of stability and change. With changes in perspective, changes in
circumstances, or changes in roles, the identity theme reemerges.
Identity has two major parts: the *I* that is not related to others and
the *I* that is interdependent with friends, family, work. Theorists
like Neugarten, Vaillant, and Levinson look at identity over the
life course. Formerly identity for men was couched in occupational
terms, for women in family terms. How individuals achieve their
goals also varies. Women have traditionally achieved their identities through others. As Steinem reports in her review of the ten
years of *Ms* magazine, women have become the men they married
(1982). Instead of marrying a doctor or a carpenter, they now become the doctor or carpenter.

Erikson's terms *ego identity* and *role diffusion* may be stated as
follows:

- *Identity.* "Has strongly defined social roles; feels at home in
  work, family, affiliations, sex role; . . . is definite about self and
  who he or she is; feels continuity with past and present."

- *Role diffusion.* "Is ill at ease, lost in groups and affiliations; . . .
  may make radical switches in work or residence without meaning or purpose" (Troll, 1982, p. 18).

Intimacy

According to Erikson's stage theory, the crisis of intimacy occurs in
the early twenties. The critical task is to form a relationship characterized by mutuality. Failure to achieve such a relationship re-

sults in isolation and loneliness. The term *intimacy* covers a wide range of close human ties: spouse, lover, parents, children, friends. Intimacy is marked by free interchange and disclosure, by reciprocal expressions of affection, by mutual trust, empathy, and understanding. Weiss (1982), however, describes the ebb and flow of attachment throughout the lifespan.

The importance of such close interpersonal relationships can hardly be exaggerated. Not only do they constitute a strong source of support in times of stress, but they also add color and warmth to what otherwise might be a drab and flat existence. As Lowenthal and Weiss put it: "In the absence of overwhelming external challenges, most . . . men and women find the energy and motivation to live autonomous, self-generating, and satisfying lives only through one or more mutually supportive and intimate dyadic relationships" (1976, p. 11). Indeed, people with no attachment figures are identified as risk populations; those with attachment and intimacy can cope more effectively with transitions and change (Parkes, 1982, p. 299).

Men and women seem to differ markedly in their ability to form such relationships. American men in particular tend to shy away from intimacy. Their friendships are based on common interests and activities rather than on vital involvement with and affection for the other person. In *Four Stages of Life* (Lowenthal et al., 1975), the researchers found that the women were more complex and affectively rich.

The difficulty that men in our society seem to have with intimacy takes its toll. Lowenthal and Weiss (1976) indicate that the death of a spouse is usually more traumatic for men than for women because men are less likely to have formed close ties beyond the marital relationship; when they lose their wives, they literally lose their best friends. Their relative inability to form close relationships with other people may also contribute to their shorter life expectancy.

Gilligan (1982a) points out that "women . . . define themselves in a context of human relationships" while men "have tended to devalue that." For men, maturity is related to autonomy, but for women it is related to attachment or intimacy. Developing the concept further, Gilligan writes, "Attachment and separation anchor the cycle of human life. . . . The concepts of attachment and separation that depict the nature and sequence of infant development appear in adolescence as identity and intimacy and then in adulthood as love and work" (p. 151). She points out that "this reiterative counterpoint . . . tends to disappear" in those developmental models which equate development with separation in a "linear" fashion. In short, intimacy—as seen by Vaillant (1982) is the "archway" to maturity. In the linear model attachment is left out and autonomy put in.

Gilligan also points out that Levinson's concept of the dream and the special woman's role in that dream are tied to achievement; thus attachments are utilitarian. As Gilligan reiterates, "In all these accounts the women are silent. . . . Thus there seems to be a line of development missing from current depictions of adult development, a failure to describe the progression of relationships toward a maturity of interdependence" (Gilligan, 1982a, p. 155).

When separation is recognized as the key to maturity, women are seen as not meeting the criteria of adulthood. But if we change the content of maturity to reflect women's experience, then interdependence and connectedness—not autonomy—can be the steps through which individuals progress in order to achieve meaningful, enduring relationships.

This type of conflict was expressed in a recent counseling workshop by two women who were committed equally to family and work roles—a double commitment which produced feelings of being pulled in too many directions. A male director of a nursing home expressed his similar conflict between the demands of his job, which included "too much human relations with staff and patients," and the pull from home, with three teenage boys. The counseling advice to all three was to think through their priorities. However, the women were advised to consider family first, and the man, his job. With Gilligan's views (on attachment in many areas of life as legitimate) fresh in my mind (as expressed in *In a Different Voice*, 1982a), I felt it essential to make the point that if prioritizing were in fact necessary, the direction need not be related to gender.

Thus, there are two conceptual issues here. One relates to the possibility of double commitments being "mature" and the other relates to the content of those commitments and whether gender and content need be related.

The forms of intimacy/attachment. What forms may attachment take? What are the networks in which adults operate? Kahn discusses the individual's "convoy" of social support throughout the life course and its importance for happiness and well-being (Kahn & Antonucci, 1980). He sees the convoy as the system of relationships which supply affection and love, affirmation, aid, and feedback. At various times in life, parts of the convoy are interrupted by death, moving, or change. In Kahn's view, the important issue is not an individual's age, but his or her convoy.

The needs for intimacy, affection, affirmation, and feedback have traditionally been met by a family living in one household. But as Troll points out, we need to study friendships over the lifespan and family relations across generations as well as non-family living in the same household. Her textbook on adult development includes a section on new forms of marriage: sexual monogamy, swinging, intimate networks, ménage à trois, group marriage, homosexual partnerships, and communes (1982, pp. 333–335). The presence or absence of intimacy throughout a person's life is more important than the specific form the relationship takes. When loss of an intimate relationship occurs—through death, divorce, a change in commitment, and so on—the crucial issue is whether an individual can reinvest.

Summary of the theme of intimacy. Again, as in the theme of identity, a summary of opposites is helpful.

- *Intimacy.* "Has close intimate relationships with spouse, children, and friends, sharing thoughts, spending time with them, expressing warm feelings . . ."

- *Isolation.* "Lives relatively isolated from friends, spouse, children; avoids contact . . . ; is . . . absorbed in self or indiscriminately sociable." (Troll, 1982, p. 18)

Autonomy and Satisfaction in Adult Life

Erikson defines autonomy as having our own attitudes and ways of doing things and not being afraid to hold our own opinions or do what we want to do.

The concept of control is central to all areas of an individual's life: work, family, friendship, community. Rotter hypothesizes that a person's "locus of control" determines the way that person shapes his or her life (1966). The locus of control can be either internal or external. People with an internal locus of control perceive themselves as having power over their own destiny; they believe that what they do makes a difference in what happens to them. They are actively involved in making decisions about jobs as well as about other events in their lives. At the other extreme, people with an external locus of control feel like puppets on a string; they believe they are controlled by other people, by impersonal social forces, or by fate. Thus, they are passive, apathetic, and unwilling to make decisions because they feel that such decisions are not relevant to what happens to them.

The feeling of helplessness associated with an external locus of control can be related to profound psychological discomfort, even to severe illness and death. Laboratory animals and human beings have been known to die from no observable physiological cause when they find themselves in situations where they feel completely helpless. Many "psychosomatic" disorders may be related to severe stress accompanied by hopelessness. There appears to be a "giving up" complex.

In one study, it was found that women generally had a lesser sense of control over their lives than men, that younger people were only slightly more likely to feel themselves in control than were older ones, and that middle-aged parents were most likely of all four groups to experience helplessness. The authors conclude that the most important of the pretransition conditions is the sense of inner control, for it is strongly associated with both a positive attitude toward the transition and the ability to plan for it (Lowenthal, Thurnher, & Chiriboga, 1975).

Generativity

Erikson places the crisis of generativity at midlife; failure to resolve the crisis results in stagnation, the feeling that life is static, that one is "in a rut." Stagnation, which other theorists say recurs at irregular intervals over the life course, represents a kind of death in life; one feels boxed in, frightened about the future. Many factors may contribute to a feeling of stagnation. Perhaps one is being passed over frequently for job promotions. Someone in a boring, repetitive situation at home or at work will feel stagnated. One example is a 42-year-old male associate professor who has assumed responsibility for his mother-in-law; she now lives with his family in small quarters. He sees no fun or privacy for the foreseeable future; he feels like the "enemy and outsider"; he knows he is doing the right thing but nevertheless feels angry and trapped. He has no time to write, no time for fun. Another example is a 52-year-old female secretary at a university who is working hard in a job she dislikes. Her husband is moderately successful, but they have three children in college and a mother to support. She has lost the joy in her life and feels she has no fun anymore.

Generativity includes renewal, which is more than the biological process that assures survival of the species and grants individuals a kind of immortality through the existence of their children. Generativity also refers to the contribution to future generations through creativity and productivity in areas such as the arts and science. Such achievements give life meaning, and enable the individual to feel that he or she has done something worthwhile that will leave a lasting mark in the world. Indeed, generativity relates to the theme of identity; it constitutes an affirmation of the self.

Levinson suggests by the very title of his work—*The Seasons of a Man's Life* (1978)—his orientation to recurring stagnation and renewal. "To become generative, a man must know how it feels to stagnate—to have the sense of not growing, of being static, stuck, drying up, bogged down in a life full of obligations and devoid of self-fulfillment. . . . The capacity to experience, endure, and fight against stagnation is an intrinsic aspect of the struggle toward generativity in middle adulthood" (p. 30).

Fiske suggests that another way to understand stagnation and renewal is to examine changing commitments over the life course. As a result of her examination of people's work and nonwork, "themes, denoting meaning, which is the essence of commitment" (1980, p. 249), she finds that the individual's value hierarchy or commitments do not remain constant over the life span, that contrary to expectation, major changes or orientations in commitment may occur.

An additional aspect of generativity, which Levinson (1978) discusses, is mentoring—whereby an older person takes responsibility for the growth and development of a younger adult. Combining "authority and mutuality," the mentor is a "mixture of parent and peer," usually older than the protégé. Mentoring usually takes place in a work setting, although it is also common in academe, especially at the graduate level, where a teacher, advisor, or senior researcher may take a particular student in hand as an apprentice. Levinson adds, however, that "mentoring is defined not in terms of formal roles but in terms of the character of the relationship and the functions it serves." Thus, an older friend, a senior colleague, or a relative can function as a mentor.

The mentoring relationship is most visible among men. None of the 40 male subjects in Levinson's sample reported having a female mentor, although "in theory a mentor may be either the same gender or cross-gender." The ·shortage of female mentors in the world of work is unfortunate from the standpoint of both younger men (who could benefit from cross-gender mentoring) and younger women (who may find that potential male mentors either do not take them seriously or are afraid of becoming involved in too close a relationship with a young woman).

Another point to be made about the mentoring relationship is that it changes over time. Often, it simply cools off, evolving into a more casual friendship. Not uncommonly, however, it terminates in conflict and bitterness as the former protégé—striving to become independent—rebels against the mentor. In either case, the relationship—while it lasts—is beneficial both to the younger person, who is given practical guidance and psychological support through the difficult period of initiation into the adult world, and to the mentor, who is given an opportunity for rejuvenation, revitalization, and regeneration.

Competence

The theme of competence is identified by White (1976), who believes that most theories of human motivation overlook the constant striving of individuals to become more fit, more competent. White sees this tendency not as a negative drive whose sole purpose is to relieve tension, but rather as a positive force, akin to a child's compulsion to explore and manipulate the environment. It is the expression of a universal need to expand boundaries, investigate the world, and achieve mastery over it. White distinguishes between *competence* (in the objective sense of fitness or ability) and *sense of competence* (a subjective state), which is the more crucial construct in explaining human behavior. We all know people who are competent in a particular area (such as academic study) and yet feel themselves to be incompetent; it is often vitally important to their well-being that they become aware of their strengths and abilities.

The validity of White's view was dramatized at a presentation by Gould at which he first asked the members of his audience to identify the personal issue which currently concerned them most. By means of a lecture and a demonstration counseling session with a volunteer from the audience, Gould showed that these personal issues related to an aspect of their lives with which they were tinkering, and furthermore, this tinkering was an attempt to overcome childhood prohibitions and to "change one's boundaries of self definition." Pointing out that people in the process of change are often preoccupied with feelings of their own inadequacy and incompetency, Gould emphasized that these feelings should be welcomed as an opportunity to confront deficiencies. Such a confrontation can serve as a stimulus for growth, of "franchising oneself as a competent person," free from parental strictures (1978). Thus, White's concept of an inherent human drive for greater competence and Gould's concept that recognition of incompetence is the first step in actualizing this goal are complementary.

The move from incompetency to competency is usually made in two primary ways: by changing oneself and by pursuing and learning new activities. The process can be tortuous. Gould (1981), noting that people are extremely vulnerable at times of transition and change, found that they often protect themselves from changing by catastrophizing. For example, a 55-year-old woman was afraid that if she took up writing as a serious career it would kill her husband. Frequently, when people tinker with incompetency and try to forge new patterns, they are afraid that if they think and behave differently the sky will fall in. According to Gould, "The catastrophe prediction phenomenon guarantees a slow rate of change and a dialectic stability when it operates as a healthy dynamic. When it operates in an exaggerated fashion as an unhealthy phenomenon, it causes people to be 'stuck,' paralyzed and unable to grow by integrating their new experiences in life" (p. 45).

Gaining competence often occurs through new learning. A recent study of the learning habits of half the 126 million adults 25 years old and over revealed that life changes or transitions may trigger new learning activities. The authors, Aslanian and Brickell (1980), found that there is an almost universal need for adults to become competent at something that they could not do before in order to succeed in the new status. Among the most notable findings to emerge from this survey were the following:

- Close to half the sample indicated that they were engaged in some kind of learning activity at the time of the survey or had been so engaged during the previous year.

- Over four in five of the learners (83 percent) said that they were motivated to learn by some transition in their lives; only 17 percent were learning simply for the sake of learning.

- Of those who said that some life transition had motivated them, 56 percent cited career transitions, 16 percent cited family transitions, and 13 percent cited leisure transitions.

- Sex differences in reasons for learning were evident: 71 percent of the men, but only 42 percent of the women, mentioned career transitions. Twice as many women (21 percent) as men (10 percent) mentioned family transitions. Women were also more likely than men to mention transitions in the areas of leisure, health, religion, art, and citizenship. In short, women show greater variation in their reasons for learning.

A broad perspective on learning motives is offered by Kuhlen (1963), who suggests that adult behavior in general is impelled by two "meta-motives": The first is a positive drive for expansion and growth; the second is a self-protective drive, based on anxiety and insecurity, to compensate for perceived inadequacies. Obviously, both motives may be present in the pursuit of education; that is, adults may seek to improve their social skills and interpersonal relations, or simply to expand their knowledge of the world; or they may be "pushed" by the fear that without further education they will lose their jobs, their friends, or their cognitive powers. Cross (1981) has developed a model explaining participation in life-long learning. She incorporates the individual's drive for competency with the opportunities or barriers the individual faces when attempting to express this need for competency (p. 124), thus suggesting that the psychological need for competency must be seen in a larger context.

In this area of mastery/competence, the sexes seem to shift in different directions. Many midlife men, having peaked occupationally, lose interest in instrumental values and turn instead to interpersonal relations and altruism, whereas many midlife women begin to put more emphasis on mastery and less on interpersonal and altruistic commitments. Several researchers have also noted this apparent crossover of the sexes. According to Fiske (1980), it often produces marital discord since women are not able to move easily into the "outside" world. Instead "they stay home and become increasingly assertive there . . . not only in their relationships with their husbands but, unfortunately, with their adult children as well" (p. 248).

But the drive for competence is lifelong. Both White and Kuhlen believe people continually need to expand, explore, and achieve mastery over the world and over themselves. As they grow older, they continually try out new coping mechanisms that will facilitate "successful transaction with the environment." Empirical support for this view comes from a study of the wives of coal miners (Giesen & Datan, 1980), women between the ages of 47 and 62 who had fewer resources than most women in this age group.

Despite the stereotype of older women as "dependent, passive, incompetent, and generally unable to deal with the problems and crises of life" (p. 57), this study found that most of the women interviewed were evidently able to "interact effectively with the environment" and "cope with and solve problems" (p. 60). Moreover, most of them felt they had gained in competence and were better able to handle life than they had been at a younger age. Similarly, a study of women who led complex lives found that those who were satisfied with their multiple roles also showed gains in competence and in sense of well-being (Baruch & Barnett, 1980).

Erikson discusses competency in two of his stages which he labels *initiative versus guilt* and *industry versus inferiority*. These may be summarized as follows:

- *Initiative.* "Takes pleasure in planning and initiating action; plans ahead."
- *Guilt.* "Lets others initiate action; plays down success or accomplishment."
- *Industry.* "Likes to make things and carry them to completion; strives for skill mastery; has pride in production."
- *Inferiority.* "Is passive; leaves things undone; feels inadequate about ability to do things or produce work." (Troll, 1982, p. 18.)

Belonging Versus Marginality

A seesaw is the best metaphor for the ever-moving relationship between belonging and marginality. Every time an individual moves from one role to another or experiences a transition, the balance of the seesaw changes. The larger the difference in role and the less knowledge beforehand about this role, the more marginal that individual will feel. The first women executives faced such a problem by having no norms, no ways to anticipate their pioneering role. Geographical moves affect the balance and often evoke mourning. People who belonged in one situation may feel marginal in another. Those who migrate to a new culture represent the extreme case.

As more people live longer, they are often required to move into untested roles. Without clear-cut expectations in many areas of their lives, older people may frequently feel confused by the shifts from inclusion to marginal. Further, as Fiske (1980) notes in pointing to the interplay between personality and the social system, if society restricts older people from work and love and allows only play, there are clearly fewer outlets for those with strong commitments. She concludes that it "is regrettable . . . indeed that the more self-generating . . . among the great middle class . . . become, as they reach late middle and old age, deprived of the arenas in which they could serve as role models" (pp. 240–241).

Summary

The theoretical perspectives, all of which include transitions, and the recurring themes in adult development provide important knowledge for helpers as they try to interpret and explain adult experience to their clients—always with the goal of helping in view. This goal can be defined as follows: the achievement, increase, or maintenance of the capacity to love, work, and play in adults. Some would call this maturity. This goal is supported, for example, by Smelser, who writes:

> On the psychological side, the adult years mark the development and integration of cognitive and instrumental capacities that enable people to reach whatever heights of purposeful, organized mastery of the world they are capable of reaching. Too, the adult years are those in which people are able to reach their maximum of mutually gratifying attachments to other individuals. . . . On the sociological side, society . . . has constructed some of its major institutions to specialize in work and love (1980, p. 4).

This definition of maturity—the capacity to continuously invest oneself in working, loving, playing—does not suggest any one way of working, loving, playing. Rather it emphasizes the individual's ability (and necessity) to invest, reinvest, and renew commitments as life circumstances change.

But what does it take to encourage individuals to invest, reinvest, and renew commitments? Vaillant, in his report of the longitudinal study of Harvard graduates writes, "the full life cycle can unfold only when humans are provided both the freedom and opportunity to mature" (1977, p. 202). He identifies four key variables as central to this process:

1. Opportunities—including societal and economic opportunities—to implement one's goals are available.
2. Individuals make investments on their own behalf; in short, they are motivated.

3. Sources of support and guidance are available to help individuals cope.

4. The individual has personal resources, including good health, adequate finances, and mature defense mechanisms.

The men in the Grant Study had both motivation and opportunities. What differentiated their life trajectories, according to Vaillant, were variables 3 and 4: their support and their resources. As Vaillant points out, "the available sources of support and guidance made a big difference to the men" (p. 203). Further, examination of the early lives of the least and best adapted in this study challenged the thesis that adult maturity is predetermined in childhood. Instead it was the experiences in adulthood, especially the availability of love and support, that turned some of the less mature into more open, adapted people. These findings underline the importance of helping: Helpers, by providing both support and resources, are able to turn around an individual's opportunities and to assist individuals to mature and cope successfully.

Thus, the work of many theorists in adult development encourages the view that adults can be helped to mature, to achieve, increase, and maintain their capacity to love, work, and play—and explore, understand, and cope—by developing intimate relationships, continuing to generate, reevaluating themselves, gaining new competencies, and combining autonomy with commitment.

The next chapters contain a framework for helping helpers help adults to grow, mature, and renew commitments. This framework connects the knowledge of adult development outlined in this chapter with the helping skills.

2

A Framework for Helping: Transitions

Much of the writing today on adult development is permeated by the notion that adults of similar ages experience similar stages, or are expected to perform similar tasks. If we adopt this view, we would logically connect helping to specific stages in life, as delineated in the age and stage theories. A new text on adult counseling does this quite creatively (Van Hoose & Worth, 1982). Still, there remain those individuals who do not fit into the particular stages of life described in these theories.

Gilligan clarifies the difficulties of analyzing women according to a male model (1982b). Neugarten explains the difficulties of applying stage theories to both men and women. Neugarten has also, on numerous occasions, pointed out two related problems: The adult development field is still too young to have a unified theory; and further, a stage or sequential approach does not reflect the fact that "as lives grow longer, as the successive choices and commitments accumulate, lives grow different from each other" (1979).

Helpers might easily agree with the notion that adults need to be viewed and portrayed as individuals—some of whom are healthy, some unhealthy; some sexually alive, others dead; some happy, some sad; some productive, others disintegrating; some coping, some collapsing. More difficult is the development of a framework for helpers which incorporates the notion that adult behavior can neither be predicted from early childhood (Vaillant, 1977) nor categorized by age or stage—and which, at the same time, insures that helpers do not need to approach each situation anew.

In essence, we need to put into operation the notion of variability. We need a framework for examining what we know about adults in transition, and we then need to connect this framework to what we know about helping roles so that we can best help adults in transition explore, understand, and cope.

The transition framework presented here has three components: The transition itself must be looked at in terms of its type, context, and impact. The transition process must be examined in relation to the ways the individual reacts to and appraises the situation over time. The coping resources that individuals have—which include variables characterizing the particular transition, the particular individual, and the particular environment—need to be examined to determine the balance of present and possible assets and liabilities. Certain assumptions based in adult development theory and the helping skills influence the framework and the way it will be connected to the helping skills (in Chapter 4). These assumptions are:

- Adults in transition are often confused and in need of assistance. Adults can identify the issues which concern them—for example, being "burned out," divorced, having to change jobs. These issues often relate to the ability to love, work, and play. If these adults can explore the issue more fully, understand its underlying meaning, and develop a plan, they will eventually be able to cope effectively and resolve the problem.

- Friends, coworkers, and professional and paraprofessional helpers can learn about issues of major concern to most adults, listen to the adult in transition in a way that facilitates exploration, provide a framework so that the adult in transition can better understand his or her situation, and, finally, influence the adult to cope more creatively. Basically, the helper, friend, or colleague can approach any issue which is brought up by thinking, Can I help him or her explore the problem more fully, understand the issue in all its complexity, and resolve it creatively?

- To help adults explore, understand, and cope, helpers need to increase their knowledge of communications skills, counseling skills, and adult development. Further, they need to integrate this knowledge. That is, helpers need to be able to weave in skills and knowledge at each phase of helping—whether it is exploring why the individual can or cannot love, work, or play; understanding the underlying reason for the issue; or developing strategies to cope more effectively with life.

In this chapter, the transition and the transition process are described in detail. The next chapter will discuss the clusters of variables pertaining to particular transitions, particular individuals, particular environments which filter, mediate, moderate, or intervene between the transition and the process of transition.

The Transition

An event or nonevent resulting in change

Some authors use the term *crisis,* others *transformation,* still others *change.* In this framework, *transition* includes all these concepts and is defined broadly as any event or nonevent that results in change in relationships, routines, assumptions, and/or roles within the settings of self, work, family, health, and/or economics.

Transitions include not only obvious life changes (such as high school graduation, job entry, marriage, birth of the first child, bereavement) but also subtle changes (such as the loss of career aspirations and the nonoccurrence of anticipated events, such as an expected job promotion that never comes through). Thus a transition can be both an event and a nonevent—if it results in change. Beeson and Lowenthal (1975) enlarge on this point: "Stress reactions may result from (1) the general absence of change or new life events, (2) the failure of an expected event or change to occur, or (3) the mitigation of events or circumstances formerly considered stressful" (p. 173).

The definition of transition given here actually grows out of crisis theory, the foundations of which were laid by Lindemann's classic study (1965) of grief reactions among the relatives and friends of victims of the Coconut Grove fire. According to Moos and Tsu (1976):

> Crisis theory asserts that people generally operate in consistent patterns, in equilibrium with their environment, solving problems with minimal delay by habitual mechanisms and reactions. When the usual problem-solving mechanisms do not work, tension arises and feelings of discomfort or strain occur. The individual experiences anxiety, fear, guilt or shame, a feeling of helplessness, some disorganization of function, and possibly other symptoms. Thus a crisis is essentially a disturbance of the equilibrium, an "upset in a steady state" (p. 13).

Moos and Tsu elaborate on this last point, defining crisis as a "relatively short period of disequilibrium in which a person has to work out new ways of handling a problem" (p. 13). Other researchers have offered other definitions. For instance, according to Hill a crisis is "any sharp or decisive change for which old patterns are inadequate . . . and new ones are called for immediately" (1949, p. 51).

While retaining the emphasis of these definitions on the necessity for new patterns of behavior, we follow Parkes' lead (1971) for the framework here and reject the term *crisis* because of its negative connotations. We need to be concerned with the kinds of life events that often involve gains rather than (or as well as) losses. Moreover, *crisis* implies a dramatic event, and we need also to be concerned with less observable events and with nonevents.

In place of crisis, Parkes proposes the term *psychosocial transition,* which he defines as a change that necessitates "the abandonment of one set of assumptions and the development of a fresh set to enable the individual to cope with the new altered life space" (p. 103). The term *transition* is also preferred by other authorities. Levinson and his associates (1978) use *developmental transition* to mean "turning points between stable periods" (p. 49). Further, according to Spierer (1977), a transition is any change that has "important consequences for human behavior. . . . These transitions may be due to biological, sociological, environmental, historical, or other phenomena. They may have consequences that are evident now or are manifested at some future date (and thus have 'sleeper effects'). They may be evident to friends and to society (going bald, becoming rich, losing a job) or remain unnoticed, although still dramatic, such as losing one's career aspirations. They may be sudden or, more likely, cumulative, as is true, for example, of some diseases" (1977, p. 6).

A transition is not so much a matter of change as of the individual's own perception of the change. For the framework here, a transition is a transition only if it is so defined by the person experiencing it. If, for example, menopause does not have much impact on a particular woman, and does not change her set of assumptions or her relationships, then (in my view) it cannot be regarded as a transition. If, however, another woman experiences menopause as an event that marks her passage from youth to old age, from sexuality to nonsexuality, it does constitute a transition.

Transitions: Types

Anticipated, unanticipated, chronic "hassles," and nonevent

The first step in examining a transition is to look at what type of transition has happened or is happening: Was it anticipated or unanticipated? Is it a chronic "hassle"? Or is it a nonevent?

Anticipated transitions are those normative "gains and losses or major alterations of roles that predictably occur in the course of the unfolding life cycle" (Pearlin & Leiberman, 1979, p. 220). These expected events include marriage, a child leaving home, the birth of a first child, starting a first job, and retiring. Because these are events that have a "likelihood of occurrence for the individual" (Brim & Ryff, 1980, p. 374), individuals can anticipate and rehearse for them.

Unanticipated transitions are the "nonscheduled events" that are "not predictable." These usually "involve crises, eruptive circumstances, and other unexpected occurrences that are not the consequence of life-cycle transitions" (Pearlin, 1980, p. 179). "Events of this type in the occupational arena are being fired, laid off, or demoted; having to give up work because of illness . . . being promoted, and leaving one job for a better one. Divorce, separation . . . premature death of a spouse, . . . illness or death of a child represent such events in the parental arena" (p. 180).

Brim and Ryff make another useful distinction between events that have a high probability of occurrence in the life of the individual (getting married, starting work, having a child, retiring) and those which are improbable and happen to comparatively few people (inheriting a fortune, being convicted of a crime, having one's home destroyed by an earthquake or flood). Brim asserts that we need to "search for hidden unnamed events" because the more events we can identify, the better people can be prepared to deal with them through anticipatory socialization.

Chronic hassle transitions are characterized by their continuous and pervasive presence. Lazarus writes, "Some hassles may recur because of a permanent but not always harmonious relationship in marriage or at work, such as sexual incompatibility with a spouse or personality conflict with a coworker" (1981a, p. 60). Some persistent hassles identified as most frequent by a middle-aged sample population include concern with weight, health of family member, home maintenance, misplacing or losing things, crime, physical appearance (p. 61). These chronic hassles can erode self-confidence and lead to an inability to initiate necessary changes.

Nonevent transitions are those an individual had counted on but which did not occur, thereby altering his or her life, such as the marriage that never occurred, the promotion that never occurred, the child that was never born, the cancer that did not metastasize. For example, a couple who had planned for and counted on having children finally in their mid-forties face the fact that this will not occur. If the wife has not pursued a career because of her expected role as mother and homemaker, the realization that the expected transition did not and will never occur alters the way she sees herself and might well alter the way she behaves.

George and Siegler address this issue: "In some cases the non-occurrence of an anticipated and/or desired event may be more stressful—or at least perceived as more stressful—than its occurrence. This issue is logically ignored by investigators employing the traditional life events approach because stress is assumed to reflect degree of change—and nonoccurrence of an event presumably will also mean non-change" (1981, p. 34).

Deciding which type of transition it is can sometimes be complex, since each type is not totally discrete. An event or nonevent can be somewhat planned, somewhat unplanned. It may be more useful for us to think of these four types of transitions as being on a change–no-change continuum rather than as discrete entities.

Several other points about types of transitions need to be mentioned. One is that what is an anticipated change for one person—going to college—might be unanticipated for another. I interviewed a school janitor who had always wanted to go to college but was committed to educating his children. On the day the last child graduated from the state university, the family presented the father/janitor with an application blank to fill out for school. When I interviewed him, he had completed several years of college and was an emergency substitute teacher. A nonevent for one person—not getting married—can be a planned decision for another and not a transition at all. Another important conceptual point is that "major life events, in addition to their obvious or immediate impact, can create continuing hassles—a kind of 'ripple effect.' Divorce, for example, might force a man inexperienced at such tasks to make his own meals, do the laundry, or clean the house; it might force a woman to handle household finances or repair a leaky faucet for the first time" (Lazarus, 1981a, p. 60).

Because the same event has different meanings for different

individuals, George and Siegler interviewed 100 adults over age 50 asking them to identify the best and worst events of the past year, as well as of their whole lives (1981). For one person retirement was "the best," for another "the worst." For some it was planned; for others unexpected.

What would be a most interesting topic to research but probably too complex to undertake would be to find out how the same person copes with anticipated, unanticipated, chronic, and nonevent transitions. Another research topic—also probably too difficult to undertake—would be to find out how effective copers—whoever they might be and however they might be identified—cope with these four types of transitions. Are there preferred modes of coping with each? Do different groups tend to utilize different strategies?

George and Siegler write, "We thus hypothesize that imposed, unexpected, and negative events, as well as those that involve a high degree of change, will be more stressful and more likely to lead to negative outcomes than those that are chosen, expected, positive, and involve little behavioral disruption" (1981, p. 29).

Transitions: Context

Relationship of person to transition (personal, interpersonal, community); setting in which transition occurs (self, family, friends, work, health, economics)

The relationship of the individual to the event or nonevent resulting in change is central to our understanding of transitions. Does the primary event start with the individual (his or her illness) or with some other person (his or her boss's illness)? Is the transition personal (the individual has lost his or her job) or interpersonal (the individual has had a disagreement with his or her employer)? Or is the transition involved with the public or the community (the individual feels disgraced by having to go on unemployment)? Often if something is happening to an individual, he or she can mobilize resources and affect the transition process positively. But if something is happening to someone else—doom impending for an adult child—the individual often can only sit by, suffer, and offer support. We need to note that many feel the tragedies and excitements happening to their children as if they were happening to themselves.

What is the setting in which the transition occurs—within self, family, friends, work, health, or economics? Of course, what starts out as personal and economic—lack of income through job loss—can also affect family relationships and precipitate other transitions.

George and Seigler (1981), who stress classification of events according to whether they are personal, interpersonal, or community based, developed a two-dimensional matrix to help us understand the context of a transition from the point of view of the individual whose transition it is. The "scope of the life experience" is looked at "in terms of the people involved and the nature of those persons . . . personal, interpersonal, community" as well as in terms of the "life arena (or setting) in which the event is based . . . self, family, health, work, economics" (1981, pp. 102–104). What differentiates this from previous classification systems is what they call the "cross-classification of life experiences" by both setting and relationship to the person involved. Such cross-classification helps us to understand that divorce may be stressful to an individual either because it is his or her own divorce and/or because it is the divorce of another, such as a parent, child, or friend.

An examination of the 15 cells of the matrix indicates the usefulness of these distinctions for helpers. Illustrations of the types of life experiences are included for some. The cells are grouped here by relationship to the individual (personal, interpersonal, community).

Life Arena (Setting)	*Life Experience (Transition Event)*
Personal/Self	Identity crises, periods of unusual personal development, pursuit of solitary hobbies, loneliness, feelings of freedom.
Personal/Family	Decisions about whether to marry or have children, worries about performance as a spouse, guilt about treatment of a relative. An example is the empty nest, which can be described as a crisis, especially for women, or as a time of happiness, liberation, and renewed interest in sex.
Personal/Health	Personal illness or injury, adaptation to physical handicap, recovery from illness. Examples are heart attacks and mastectomies.

Personal/Work	Decisions about career choice, self-satisfaction gained through work, retirement. For example, career changes for professional athletes, displaced homemakers, plateaued midmanagers, and automobile workers are an inevitable part of life. Another example is the employee who feels boxed into the same slot for the rest of his or her working life.
Personal/Economics	Financial problems, gambling losses, inheritance.
Interpersonal/Self	Disagreements with friends, breakup of a love affair or friendship, pleasure gained from meeting new people.
Interpersonal/Family	Marriage, marital problems, problems or joys associated with parenting, close relationships with siblings. For example, new concerns, conflicts, and possible joys are faced by remarried adults who blend two families as well as by single parents and siblings facing the need to care for an aging parent.
Interpersonal/Health	Sickness or death of family member.
Interpersonal/Work	Relationships with boss and co-workers, concern about friend or family member's work.
Interpersonal/Economics	Financial problems of friend or family member.
Community/Self	Receipt of public award or recognition, public personal disgrace, arrest and/or conviction for a crime.
Community/Family	School and plant closings, changes in drinking laws.
Community/Health	Epidemics, contamination of water supply, an outbreak of Legionnaire's

disease, discovery of hazardous wastes as in the Love Canal incident, tampering with medicines, as with Tylenol capsules.

Community/Work — Public recognition gained through work, disgrace suffered as a result of business failure.

Community/Economics — Concern about economic policies, objections to tax policies, sense of disgrace suffered as a result of economic losses.

In examining a transition's context, we will often find that several cells of the matrix are involved. An individual's career change (personal/work) can equally affect his or her family (personal/family). For example, the increasing number of dual worker/career families creates new pressures on mother, father, and children, particularly in relation to geographic moves and promotions into top management jobs.

There are other ways to conceptualize the context in which transitions occur. Pearlin, working with others, writes: "The adult portion of the lifespan is peppered with problems and strains." The "problems of everyday life" are identified as the "persistent life strains that people encounter as they act as parents, jobholders, and breadwinners. By strains we mean those enduring problems that have the potential for arousing threat" (Pearlin & Schooler, 1978, p. 3). Through first interviewing 100 people in an unstructured manner and then developing a structured interview with 2,300 people between 18 and 65 living in the Chicago area, they identified key strains in occupation, marriage, and parent roles. Further, they showed the differential impact of life strains on different segments of the population (Pearlin & Leiberman, 1979). This useful way of viewing various arenas of life—occupation, marriage, parenthood—in terms of unexpected "nonnormative events" and expected normative and persistent problems can be extended to other arenas, such as economics, health, and education.

Table 2-1, which follows, illustrates this conceptualization of transition context. By emphasizing related role changes, it leads us into our examination of the impact of transitions.

Table 2–1
Types of Life Strains in Different Roles

Occupation
A. Nonnormative events
    1. Job movement, that is, changes from one job to another resulting from promotion or movement to another job
    2. Loss of job, that is, role loss resulting from elimination of job, being fired, being laid off, or illness
B. Normative role transitions
    1. Gain of role, that is, first job or reentry to labor market after giving birth or after following full-time homemaking or training
    2. Loss of role, that is, exit from occupational life and into retirement or homemaking
C. Persistent occupational problems
    1. Noxiousness of physical working environment
    2. Job pressures, role overloading
    3. Deprivation of rewards
    4. Depersonalizing work relations

Marriage
A. Nonnormative events
    1. Serious illness of spouse
    2. Loss of marriage and currently single as a result of divorce or separation
B. Normative role transitions
    1. Gain of marital role
    2. Loss of marriage and currently single as a result of death of spouse
C. Persistent role problems
    1. Lack of marital reciprocity
    2. Nonfulfillment of role expectations
    3. Nonacceptance of one's self by spouse

Parenthood
A. Nonnormative events
    1. Serious illness of child
B. Normative role transitions
    1. Gain of role by becoming parent for first time
    2. Progressive movement toward independence within role: entering school, becoming adolescent
    3. Loss of role resulting from last child leaving home or marrying
C. Persistent role problems
    1. Unacceptable general deportment
    2. Children's failure to act toward goals or values
    3. Children's failure to be attentive, considerate of parents

---

From L. I. Pearlin and M. A. Leiberman, "Social sources of emotional distress." In R. Simmons, ed., *Research in Community and Mental Health* (Vol. 1), p. 225. Greenwich, Conn.: JAI Press, 1979. Reprinted by permission.

Transitions: Impact

For an individual undergoing a transition, it is not the event or nonevent that is most important but its impact, that is, the degree to which the transition alters his or her daily life. Thus, when an event—a husband's promotion which involves a geographical move—creates problems for an individual, we need to look not only at the type and context but also at the impact of the event on the individual's relationships, routines, assumptions about self and the world, and roles. (Table 2-1 includes illustrations of role changes.) We may assume that the more the transition alters the individual's life, the more coping resources it requires, and the longer it will take for assimilation or adaptation. (More theoretical work must be done on events that happen to someone else but have impact on the individual we are trying to help. We need to distinguish between those who are living vicariously and those whose life patterns are changing because of others' transitions.)

One way of examining the impact of a transition is to assess the degree of difference between the pretransition and the posttransition environments. Leiberman (1975), studying four groups of old people who made radical changes in living arrangements, concluded that the intensity of stress experienced depended not upon the individual's subjective interpretation of the change in living arrangements (whether it was welcomed or feared, whether regarded as a change for the better or the worse) but rather "upon the degree to which an individual is required to make new adaptations associated with environmental change. . . . The greater the difference between the Time 1 life space and the Time 2 life space, the higher the degree of stress and consequent adaptive requirements" (p. 151). He found "a rough ordering between frequency of breakdown and amount of environmental discontinuity" (p. 153). That is, the individual's success or failure in adapting to the new environment was strongly correlated with the similarity or dissimilarity of the pretransition and posttransition environments, whatever the individual's attitude toward or definition of the change.

Another way of assessing pretransition and posttransition environments has been developed by Wapner through studies of transitions ranging from entering nursery school to entering a nursing home (1981). Each person lives in "multiple worlds" in the family, school, work, and community. Wapner's studies focus on the changes in the structure of these multiple worlds for each individual.

This research assesses the pretransition and posttransition environments and the degree to which individuals eventually become integrated by using a "psychological distance map" (1981, p. 225). Individuals in transition enter their interactions on these maps over time. Thus we can graphically compare the proportion of interactions in the old and new environments. By using such maps, we can look, for example, at families who move geographically and ascertain the degree to which they maintain prior contacts as well as the number of new contacts made. Thus we have a better idea as to the impact of the transition on relationships, routines, assumptions, and roles. A person who moves or enters a nursing home, who is able to maintain most of his or her former contacts, will experience the transition very differently from someone who loses all contacts.

Parkes (1971), however, believes that changes in the "life space" are important only insofar as they affect the individual's "assumptive world," which includes "everything we know or think we know. It includes our interpretation of the past and our expectations of the future, our plans and our prejudices. Any or all of these may need to change as a result of changes in the life space" (p. 103). The life space is changing constantly, but not all these changes call for a major restructuring of the assumptive world. I have adopted Parkes's view: The degree of difference between the pretransition and the posttransition environment is significant insofar as that difference affects the individual's assumptions about self and the world and, consequently, the individual's relationships in family, work, and community.

This conflicts with theorists like Holmes and Rahe (1967) who assign a numerical score to transitions. For them, the higher the score the greater the degree of change inherent in the transition. For example, moving is 20 and retirement 45. This difference in approach can be illustrated by the transition faced by a middle-aged couple whose first daughter is marrying. Can we score that transition? I would say not. Understanding the transition requires examining the impact on the middle-aged couple's life. If the daughter has lived across the country and will remain there, the marriage will not impact the daily or weekly life of the parents. Some changes will, of course, occur. If, however, the daughter who has lived away returns to the parents' city to marry, has one small stepchild and little money, comes home three times a week to do laundry, and asks the parents to babysit, then it is a transition of much greater impact. As Pearlin and Leiberman conclude,

"It is not the tearing away from old roles that matters to well-being, but what is discovered in the context of the new roles" (1979, p. 239).

Summary of Transitions

To understand the meaning a transition has for a particular individual, we need to examine the type of transition (antici-pated, unanticipated, nonevent or chronic hassle), the context of the transition (relationship of person to transition, setting in which the transition occurs), and the impact of the transition on the individual's life (on relationships, routines, assumptions, roles).

Type. Retirement when the plant closes may be unantici-pated, although for many retirement is anticipated. For those forced by economic necessity to continue working (and who are able to find work), retirement is a wished-for but never-occurring nonevent. Retirement may also be a chronic hassle, a worry which supersedes all other issues. Thus it is not the transition itself that determines its meaning for the individual; rather it is whether the transition is expected, unexpected, never occurring, or chronic. Clearly, one person may be thrilled at a nonevent (such as rediag-nosis of no cancer) but another may be very sad with the realiza-tion that a promotion is not ever likely.

Context. Our own retirement, our spouse's retirement, and the local mayor's retirement all produce different reactions. The primary setting for the retirement transition also affects our reac-tions. The transition may involve the self, friends, family, work, health, or economics. In the George and Siegler study, which pro-vides the 15-cell matrix of life arenas (1981), individuals chose their best and worst life experiences. Most of these experiences resided in the family setting, followed by self and work. Worst life events predominated in the health setting, followed by family and self. Retirement can be a "best" experience if it makes possible a long-desired trip, or it may be a "worst" experience if it is necessi-tated by ill health.

Impact. Assessment of a transition's impact on relationships, routines, assumptions, and roles is probably most important in understanding the situation. As we think of all the possible set-tings for a retirement transition (self, family, friends, health, work, economics), and assess the impact in each, we may find that retire-ment affects family more than self, health more than economics.

It never rains but it pours. This point needs to be further underscored: Often people in the midst of one transition experience other transitions, which makes coping especially difficult. One man who had to take early retirement explained that it was particularly difficult since that year his wife left him and his father had moved in because of a debilitating illness.

The Transition Process

Reactions over time for better or for worse

The term *adaptation* is used by many to indicate the result of a transition; but it often connotes a static, normative concept. Hopson's term *response to transition* (1981) is better; it asks how an individual responds over time to a particular life event.

Weiss (1976) uses the term *transition state* to mean a period marked by relational and personal changes, including attempts to deal with upset, tension, or fatigue and attempts to find new sources of support. For instance, if the spouse dies, the bereaved partner must not only deal with grief but must also alter his or her life and behavior, usually in very profound ways. The end of the transition state is usually marked by a stable new life organization and by a stable new identity. If these prove to be inadequate, the individual is said to be in a deficit situation. Thus, the widow or widower may not be able to accept the new role or to summon the support needed to replace the support previously provided by the spouse.

Weiss's view implies that a transition may be either for better or worse, and Moos and Tsu (1976) state clearly that a transition may provide both "an opportunity for psychological growth and a danger of psychological deterioration" (p. 13). Thus the transition process is not always positive, but neither is it always negative. For example, some of the elderly subjects who moved to nursing homes (Leiberman, 1975) "remained intact in the face of radical environmental change" (p. 156), "whereas about half suffered marked declines . . . behaviorally, physically (including death), socially, or psychologically" (p. 142).

That the transition process often has both positive and negative aspects for the same individual was confirmed by interviews with men whose jobs had been eliminated (Schlossberg & Leibowitz, 1980a) and with couples who had recently undertaken geographical moves (Schlossberg, 1981). Many tended to find both positive and negative elements in the transition event. In the job elimination study, one man saw his job loss as a "kick in the back" but at the same time recognized it as an opportunity to get out of both the job and his marriage. Another man reported feeling "a little shaky . . . but at the same time hopeful." In the geographical study, one woman talked about the miserable experience of moving: "I kept thinking, 'If only I were back home,' " but at the same time she described such positive results of the move as the opportunity it offered both her husband and herself to break away from their families, with whom they were "almost too close." This ambivalent nature of many transitions is dealt with more thoroughly in the section on the variables characterizing transitions in Chapter 3.

In the framework here, transitions are viewed as a process of continuing and changing reactions over time—for better or for worse—which are linked to the individual's continuous and changing appraisal of self-in-situation.

Phases of Assimilation

Pervasiveness, disruption, integration for better or worse

As an individual undergoes a transition, he or she passes through a series of phases (or stages) of assimilation, a process of moving from total preoccupation with the transition to integration of the transition into his or her life.

Lipman-Blumen (1976) describes this movement as being from "pervasive-ness" (an awareness of the transition permeates all of a person's attitudes and behaviors) to "boundedness" (the change is contained and integrated into the self). Thus, in the early stages, a person is totally conscious of being a new graduate, a new widow, a new mother. In the later stages, the person is aware of having graduated, having been widowed, having become a mother—but this awareness has become only one of the dimensions of living.

White (1976) comments on the time dimension of adaptation. He states that an individual's ability to adapt should not be judged on the basis of short-term observations: "Strategy is not created on the instant. It develops over time and is progressively modified in the course of time" (p. 29).

This dynamic view of adaptation contrasts with the static view, which is epitomized by such terms as *mental health, life*

satisfaction, homeostasis, and *effective role and social functioning.*
These terms involve assessment of the individual against some
rather arbitrary and vague standard, whereas the dynamic view
constitutes a more fluid approach to measuring adaptation.

Many researchers have identified a series of stages following
transitions. For example, Moos and Tsu (1976) identify two phases:
There is "an acute phase in which energy is directed at minimizing
the impact of the stress, and a reorganization phase in which the
new reality is faced and accepted. In the acute period feelings may
be denied while attention is directed to practical matters. . . . The
reorganization phase involves the gradual return to normal function" (pp. 14–15). Hill (1965) too, believes that reaction to crisis
takes a roller-coaster form: The crisis event occurs, the individual
dips down into a period of disorganization, then gradually rises up
again, and levels off into a period of reorganization.

There is also a wealth of literature dealing with human adaptation to specific types of transitions which specifies series of
phases. For example, based on her work with terminal cancer patients, Kübler-Ross (1969) identifies five stages experienced by
people who realize they are dying: (1) denial and isolation, (2)
anger and resentment, (3) bargaining, (4) preparatory depression
over impending loss, and (5) acceptance. Similarly, bereavement
over the loss of a loved one moves from "almost global denial or
'numbness,' . . . bitter pining and frustrated searching, . . . suc-
ceeded by depression and apathy . . . with a final phase of reorganization when new plans and assumptions about the world and the
self are built up" (Parkes, 1971, p. 106). Lindemann (1965), who
has done extensive research on grief, maintains that if the person
does not do the necessary "grief work"—passing through each of
the stages in its turn—trouble can erupt later on. This is also the
conclusion of Kaplan and Mason (1965), who found that the mother
of a premature infant has four tasks to perform: (1) preparation for
possible loss of the child (but hope for its survival), a stage that
resembles anticipatory grief; (2) acceptance of her failure to deliver
a normal child; (3) resumption of hope and of an active relationship
with the infant; and (4) recognition of the baby's special needs as a
premature baby, along with an awareness that these needs are
temporary. "Her task is to take satisfactory precautions without
depriving herself and the child of enjoyable interactions" (Kaplan
& Mason, 1965, p. 125). If the mother fails to perform these tasks
(for instance, if she reacts to the premature birth with apparent
cheerfulness and lack of anxiety), the depression will catch up with

her later. Indeed, failure to perform any one of the tasks in its proper order may interfere with the development of a warm and loving relationship with the child.

Levine (1976) found a sequential pattern of adaptation among draft dodgers and deserters: (1) disorganization, a stage characterized by "the sense of isolation, loneliness, and psychic pain," along with feelings of guilt and sometimes suicidal impulses; (2) acting out, a stage in which the individual becomes apathetic, antisocial, and manipulative of others; (3) searching, "in which the individual explores . . . relationships, looks for meaning in life, and pursues . . . interests" (p. 217); and (4) adaptation and integration, a period during which the individual becomes totally involved in a new lifestyle. Levine adds that few of the subjects he observed reached the final stage; most either returned to the United States before becoming fully integrated into life in Canada or simply joined enclaves of exiles and led insular lives.

Hopson and Adams developed a seven-stage transition process model which Brammer and Abrego have used and found applicable to most transitions (Brammer & Abrego, 1981, pp. 21–22; Hopson, 1981, p. 38; Adams, Hayes, & Hopson, 1976). According to this model, at first the individual experiences temporary *immobilization*—either with despair or elation. The intensity depends on the impact of the transition. Then follows a period of *denial or minimization* which serves a "stop-time function to provide the person some relief from suffering" (Brammer & Abrego, 1981, p. 21). The utility of denial as a coping strategy has been documented by Vaillant (1977). The next phase, *self-doubt,* can take many forms including depression, anxiety, anger, or sadness. Then comes a *letting go* when the person experiences the transition deeply.

Following this is the *testing-out* stage during which mood swings occur, accompanied by irritability and impatience. The next phase, *search for meaning,* is identified when the individual begins to ask, "What did I learn from this experience?" The final phase, internalization, is *integration*. Hopson writes, "Integration not only involves renewal but also incorporates an acceptance that the transition is now complete. This means that it has become part of one's history. . . . It will have an influence over future directions, but it is not imprisoning one in the past" (1981, p. 38). This outcome can take the form of acceptance, deterioration, or renewal. It is not possible to assess the final outcome until the person has experienced the range of phases or stages outlined. Thus, a helper interviewing a client in the self-doubt phase might consider that the person has opted for deterioration only to find six months later a new sense of hope.

An illustrative example comes from the pilot study of couples who moved (Schlossberg, 1981). One woman reported she had undergone a "year of turmoil" following the move. She felt angry at her husband, seeing him as her enemy because he had forced her into a move that had deprived her of the resources she had had in her old community: a good job, involvement in her church, close contact with friends and relatives. Gradually, however, she began to find new resources, made new friends, served as an advisor to college students in a religious organization, and otherwise became more involved in the new community. We cannot say that in the early stages she was "sick" and later "healthy"; we can only say that a better balance between resources and deficits was achieved over time. Our assessment of the woman's mental health depends on when we meet her. Thus, the skilled counselor must be able to distinguish between pathology and a normal reaction to a stressful transition.

A recent study of men whose jobs were eliminated (Schlossberg & Leibowitz, 1980a) confirmed the notion that a transition can be an opportunity for either growth or deterioration. Reactions changed over time; there seemed to be a definite pattern, a series of stages that most of the men moved through. We identified five phases—disbelief, sense of betrayal, confusion, anger, resolution—as marking the movement in a transition process from disequilibrium following the transition to a new state of equilibrium. Each of the phases can be described as follows.

Disbelief. When the reduction in force (RIF) was first announced, many of the affected men reported feeling a sense of numbness and disbelief: "Why me?" One man said that when he was called into his supervisor's office, he thought he was going to be commended for his work or would receive a challenging new assignment; the news of the RIF stunned him. Several of the men refused to accept and incorporate the loss. Instead, they felt an unrealistic hope: "Maybe it's not true."

Sense of betrayal. Almost coterminous with disbelief was the sense of betrayal. Most of the employees said they felt they had entered into a psychological contract with the organization, the terms of which were, "If I am loyal and competent, the orgnization will take care of me." The RIF represented a breach of that contract, a "slap in the face," a "kick in the back." One man who was within three months of being a career veteran was especially bitter about the betrayal: "If a RIF must be done, it should be based on a man's production."

Confusion. Once they had recovered from the initial shock and their immediate sense of having been dealt with unjustly, the men began to accept the reality of the situation. At this point, many began to panic: "What do I do now?" They tended to be immobilized, waiting for some "magical" solution to occur. Around this time, a special program of career assistance (described in more detail in Chapter 5) was started, giving rise to some ambivalence. On the one hand, the men were dismayed and angry at being fired; on the other hand, they were grateful to the organization for the help and support it offered. They wanted to be able to put the blame somewhere but could not find a suitable object. Their emotions fluctuated from anxiety and anger to excitement and anticipation. Some men contradicted themselves in a single statement. For instance, one man began by talking about the problems created by the reduction in his income—but then immediately after spoke with great excitement about his plans to move to Florida.

Anger. Among those employees who could not resolve their confusion, the natural progression was to anger, usually directed at themselves or at the organization. Often, the anger was expressed in inappropriate ways by "bad-mouthing" or "dumping on" the organization. In other cases, anger was directed elsewhere, for instance, at the veterans-preference provision in the Civil Service regulations or at the computer which had actually selected the men to be fired. Sometimes the anger took a very concrete form: 14 of the 53 employees affected by the RIF filed formal grievance complaints against the employer. One man articulated his anger by saying, "I'm going to appeal this case and become a thorn in somebody's side."

Resolution. By the time a questionnaire survey of the entire group of 53 men was done three months after the RIF, 19 had been reassigned to other jobs in the organization, nine had decided to retire, and the remaining 25 had found new jobs. In virtually all cases, they seemed to have positive feelings about their new situations.

One man, who said that he had been very depressed when the RIF was first announced, reported that now he felt "great." As it turned out, the day he was to leave a decision was made to keep him on in the same job. In the meantime, he had been interviewed for several other jobs and had made the discovery that he was "saleable" and had a lot more options than originally presumed. Another man who at first felt betrayed later felt "lucky"; with his new job, he "feels like a king." The following comments also reflect a resolution:

- Despite the computer, I found a job. I'm still at Goddard.
- I was lucky. I am better off as an early retiree. I would not have taken an early retirement without the RIF.
- I'm really satisfied with how things turned out. They may have done me a favor.
- This was really a marvelous opportunity to find something new.

Summary of phases of assimilation. Despite the fact that these many researchers have identified the actual stages following a death, a move, graduation, job loss, parenthood—and it is tempting to do so—such identification oversimplifies what really is usually a complex and individual matter. Conceptually it is more realistic to see the transition process as one with three major phases: the introduction, during which time the individual is pervaded by the transition; a middle period of disruption, in which the individual is a bit at sea as old norms and relationships are changing and new ones are in process; and a final period in which the individual integrates the transition. This integration can take several forms: renewal, acceptance, or deterioration. The degree to which the individual is pervaded and disrupted depends on the degree to which the transition has great consequences for the individual's life. If we look back at our examination of the transition's type, context, and impact, we can visualize our examination as a kind of Geiger counter: the greater the transition as measured by its impact or consequences, the more time it will take to assimilate it.

Appraisal

Of transition, resources, results, and of preoccupations
vs. life satisfaction

But how do we know when a transition is assimilated? How can we assess the transition process, particularly in view of the fact that much of adult life is a reworking of earlier transitions? For example, many adults never assimilate the death of their parents or their sibling rivalry. If we interview an adult at a period of time when all is quiescent in relation to his or her siblings, it appears that those earlier transitions have been integrated. If, however, the interview takes place just at the time that decisions are being made about the care of an ailing parent, then the sibling rivalries may have reappeared, indicating that assimilation is not yet finished, and the transition process is still going on (Cicirelli, 1980).

Thus the primary way we can assess where an individual is in the transition process is through the individual's own perceptions and appraisals. This means we need also to think about what perspective the individual brings to life—a perspective unique to the individual and formed by the variables which characterize the transition itself, the individual, and the environment which focus and filter the world differently and individually. (These variables, which filter and mediate between the transition event or nonevent and the transition process, will be discussed at length in Chapter 3.) It also means that the reality of the world is not the issue. Rather what is at issue is the perception of reality, the way each individual views his or her reality.

Lazarus and his associates write: "When confronted with a dangerous or demanding situation, a person copes, thus altering the stressful person-environment. . . . What is called for is a new assessment technology, namely, the measurement of process in contrast to most current practices of sampling traits or environmental conditions on a single occasion. . . . Even adaptational outcomes are changeable things, with morale, social functioning, and illness patterns differing from time to time (Lazarus, Cohen, Folkman, Kanner, & Schaefer, 1980, pp. 108–109).

Lazarus and his associates conclude, based on their extensive work on coping, that it is the individual's appraisal of self, transition, resources, and options that is central to the resolution of the transition. The importance of primary appraisal is emphasized, that is, the assessment of whether the transition is positive, stressful, or irrelevant. If stressful, further distinctions are made, primarily whether the stress is perceived as a challenge, a threat, or a loss (1980). For example, of ten women experiencing menopause, each will probably appraise it differently. To one woman it may signify the end of her femininity; to another it may indicate the release from pregnancy concerns; and to the other eight it may have no salience at all.

In addition to the primary appraisal of whether a transition is positive, stressful, or irrelevant, individuals make a secondary appraisal—an appraisal of their coping resources which include themselves, their supports, their options. This secondary appraisal further influences which coping strategies the individual will employ. There is a feedback loop to all of this. For example, a person might make a primary appraisal of early retirement as a great opportunity but, on secondary appraisal, feel anxious about taking advantage of it due to his or her assessment of skills, resources, and options. This might then force a reappraisal of early retirement, and a decision not to take it. Thus, people are always evaluating what is happening to them, what their resources are for coping with it, and lastly how they are dealing with it. People often express surprise at how well they are doing—or disappointment at how poorly they are doing.

Weinberg and Richardson base their study of the impact of the first child's birth on individual appraisals of the event. Couples who appraise the event as one which restricts their own lives over a long term will clearly react differently than those who perceive it differently. The researchers illustrated that sex and social class differences influence the appraisal process. Their major conclusion is "that the debate over the degree of crisis inherent in the parenthood transition should be superseded by a concern . . . with this life event . . . to individuals" (1981, p. 692).

Another similar way to assess the transition process is to look at the individual's time perspective. The transition process consists of reactions over a period of time; as reactions change they can shift an individual's perspective from a feeling of "this is forever" to one of "this too shall pass." It is useful for helpers to share this knowledge, as Caine (1974) points out in writing about widowhood: "I am convinced that if I had known the facts of grief before I had to experience them, it would not have made my grief less intense . . . [but it] would have allowed me to hope" (1974, pp. 91–92).

Thus the individual's own appraisal (and reappraisal) of the transition, of his or her resources for coping, and of the results of the transition is a crucial element in the transition framework. The appraisal can be conscious or unconscious; but helpers need to understand that the appraisal is central to understanding the individuality of the framework presented here.

Measurement of the transition process. Other ways we can assess an individual's place in the transition process are by measuring the individual's preoccupation with the event (or nonevent) and/or the individual's life satisfaction. As we noted in the initial description of the phases of assimilation, the process can be seen as movement from total preoccupation with the transition to integration or containment of it in one's life. While a person who has just begun a transition may be preoccupied with the event or nonevent, two years later the person will probably have incorporated the event into his or her life.

An assessment tool for an individual's preoccupation with the event is the Impact of Event Scale developed by Horowitz and Wilner (1980), which measures subjective distress of the individual. Based on work with clients, they found two responses to stressful life events: intrusion and avoidance (p. 366). Intrusion "was characterized by unbidden thoughts and images, troubled dreams, strong waves or pangs of feelings, and repetitive behaviors. Avoidance . . . included ideational constriction, denial, . . . blunted sensation, behavioral inhibition, and counterphobic activity, and awareness of emotional numbness" (p. 366). Both intrusion and avoidance—or preoccupation and denial—can be seen as effective coping responses to stressful life events; it is only when they persist for years that we need to be concerned, for the expectation is that individuals will change. The researchers compared scores measuring distress of persons who came to treatment right after the death of a parent with those whose "next of kin" died but did not start treatment. Those in the treated population were able to handle their distress more effectively; their scores on "intrusion items declined from a mean of 20 at entry to the clinic to a mean of 10 at the first followup . . . eight months later. . . . Avoidance scores also declined, from a mean of 17 at entry to a mean of 6 at the first followup" (p. 367).

An assessment method for an individual's life satisfaction is suggested by Campbell and associates, who write that "level of satisfaction can be precisely defined as the perceived discrepancy between aspiration and achievement, ranging from the perception of fulfillment to that of deprivation" (Campbell, Converse, & Rodgers, 1976, p. 7). This highly personal matter is one which has been measured by Cantril's self-anchoring striving scale that asks the individual in question to define his or her own satisfaction (Campbell, 1981, p. 32). Cantril presents a ladder to each person asking him or her to locate his or her estimate of the current, past, or future situation (Kilpatrick & Cantril, 1960). The scale has also been related to various arenas of an individual's life by asking the person where he or she is on the ladder in his or her work life, personal life, community life.

Life satisfaction needs to be assessed at different points in time, for, as we have already noted, an individual's appraisal changes; we often hear people express current pleasure about an event that earlier was painful. An example would be a happily attached person who had been previously jilted.

Summary of appraisal. The primary way we can assess where an individual is in the transition process, and how she or he is handling the transition, is through the individual's own appraisal, which often includes a time perspective. Other ways include measurement of preoccupation and life satisfaction; this enables us to ascertain the degree to which the individual has moved from being overwhelmed by the event or nonevent to achieving integration, and reinvesting in work, love, and play.

Summary

This chapter provides a way of organizing the adult development knowledge base which is based on the premises that

- Adults continuously experience transitions.
- Adults' reactions to transitions depend on the type of transition, the context in which it occurs, and its impact on their lives.
- Transitions have no end point; rather transitions are a process over time which include phases of assimilation and continuous appraisal.

In this framework for viewing adults in transition, we need first to examine the transition for type, context, and impact, then the transition process in terms of phases of assimilation and the individual's appraisal of the process.

We now need to turn to an examination of what creates an individual's appraisal or perspective. As we have already indicated, each individual's perspective is unique, which is why we as helpers must rely on each individual's appraisal in the transition process. The individual's coping resources, which determine his or her balance of assets and liabilities in undergoing the transition process, stem from variables which characterize the transition, the individual, and the environment. These variables filter, mediate, moderate, and intervene between the transition and the transition process of assimilation and appraisal.

Peck talks about "cathectic flexibility versus cathectic impoverishment" in reference to an individual's ability "to shift emotional investments from one person to another and from one activity to another" (Troll, 1982, p. 19). This, of course, is tied in to such variables as the individual's personality, ego strength, supports, options—all of which will be described in Chapter 3. But, for helpers, the final evaluation of a transition is based on the answers to such questions as these: Can the individual now invest and commit himself or herself to work, love, and play? Can the individual be helped to reinvest and renew now that internal or external events and nonevents have interrupted the persons or activities that had given meaning to his or her life? This is really what the transition process is all about—a curiosity, excitement, and hope about the future even when the present may be a time of sorrow. Helpers need to keep this firmly in mind if they are to help adults be kind to themselves—and hopeful.

3

A Framework for Helping:
The Individual in Transition

People faced with change in their personal situations, jobs, communities, or in other significant aspects of life often feel trapped, and as if time has run out. Some people feel despair at times of change, while others face change with hope that the future will offer more fulfillment.

It is important for helpers to discover what determines whether a person grows or deteriorates as the result of a transition. Why do some people adapt with relative ease, while others seem unable to do so and may even suffer severe strain? Why does job loss become for some a stimulus to develop new interests and take up new activities, while for others it is a dead end marked by inactivity, boredom, and feelings of worthlessness? As we have seen, we cannot assume that all people react similarly to a similar change, nor can we assume that one individual will react similarly over time.

The transition framework for the adult development knowledge base presented in Chapters 2 and 3 attempts to depict the extraordinarily complex reality that accompanies and defines the human capacity to cope with change in their lives. Using that framework, helpers can analyze transitions of all kinds—positive and negative, dramatic and ordinary—and formulate possible interventions to help people achieve, increase, or maintain their capacity to love, work, and play.

Three major sets of factors (see Figure 3-1) influence the individual in transition process; the variables characterizing the particular transition (a retirement is different than a first baby); the variables characterizing the particular individual (each individual

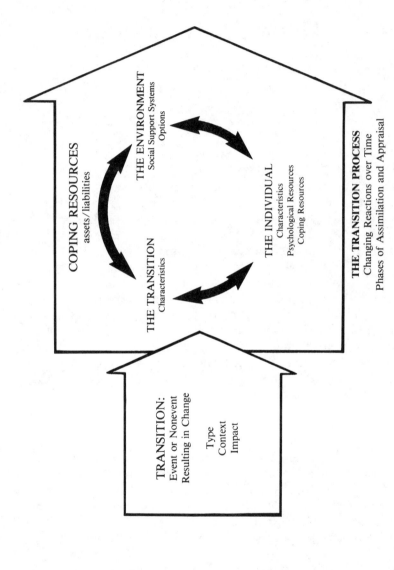

Figure 3–1. The Individual in Transition

is different in terms of life issues, coping strategies, personality); and the variables characterizing the particular environment (supports and available options vary for each individual).

It is never one variable by itself but the way many variables interrelate that makes the difference. These three sets of variables are seen as potential assets or liabilities, depending on the individual's appraisal of the transition, his or her own self, and his or her environment. We need to first look at the interrelationship or balance of these assets and liabilities and then discuss in detail the three major sets of variables concerning the transition, the individual, and the environment.

Balancing Assets and Liabilities

Coping effectiveness is best examined and explained by using a model that balances opposing forces: Every individual has both assets and liabilities—resources and deficits—within his or her psychic makeup. The balance between recent positive and negative affective experiences more effectively predicts the individual's subjective sense of well-being than either type of experience alone.

By identifying the psychological deficits and resources and scoring them, Chiriboga and Lowenthal (1975) were able to identify individuals high on both resources and deficits; those high on one, low on the other; and those low on both. They argue that a dual model—rather than the degree-of-impairment model—is more meaningful since people with one strong resource (such as a best friend) can offset many deficits. Further, "a resource at one life stage may not prove to be a resource at another stage" (p. 118).

An example may clarify this balance between resources and deficits, assets and liabilities. Two women suffer slipped spinal discs. For both, the experience is painful, incapacitating, and psychologically distressing because of the uncertainty about whether—or when—the condition can be corrected. One of the women has ample assets to balance this deficit in her physical well-being: a tenured position in a university, a highly supportive family as well as friends and colleagues who rally around her, and a coping personality. The other woman is low on assets at this particular point in her life: She has recently had a double mastectomy, which means her physical stamina and her self-esteem are low, and she has just gone through a divorce, which means part of her support system has crumbled. Moreover, this particular disability threatens her very economic survival by making it impossible for her to work at her low-income job as a potter; and besides, her ability to cope has always been no better than average. For her, the liabilities outweigh the assets, making assimilation especially difficult.

Thus, rather than assessing a person's assimilation in terms of health or sickness, 'this dual model assesses the ratio of assets to liabilities and allows for changes in the ratio as the individual's situation changes. This approach allows for at least a partial answer to the question of why the same person reacts differently to the same type of transition at different times in his or her life. The difference may be that the assets–liabilities balance has changed; assets may outweigh liabilities making assimilation relatively easy. Or, liabilities may now outweigh assets, so assimilation is correspondingly more difficult. It is important that psychologists and others in the helping professions delay diagnosis of someone as "ill" when, in fact, all that may be wrong is a temporary shift in the balance between assets and liabilities.

Figure 3-2 displays the variables that create the balance of assets and liabilities, and the coping resources that intermediate between the transition and the transition process. The clusters of variables are discussed in the following sections.

Variables Characterizing the Transition

The birth of a baby is clearly different from a geographical move, and both will have different effects at different times in an individual's life. Some of the discussion of what produces these different effects here overlaps with our earlier examination of transitions. Indeed it was tempting to look at all aspects of transitions together, and the division is somewhat arbitrary. In Chapter 2 the discussion centered on type, context, and impact. Here other characteristics which influence the coping process are identified:

- Trigger (What has triggered the transition?)
- Timing (Does the transition relate to the social clock?)
- Source (Where does control lie?)
- Role change (Does the transition involve role change?)
- Duration (Is it viewed as permanent or temporary?)

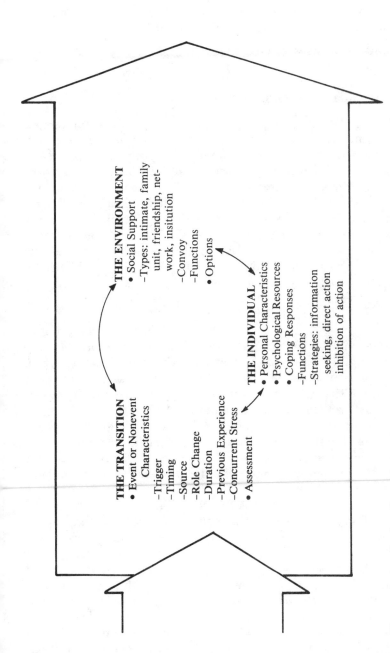

THE TRANSITION
- Event or Nonevent
  Characteristics

  -Trigger
  -Timing
  -Source
  -Role Change
  -Duration
  -Previous Experience
  -Concurrent Stress
- Assessment

THE ENVIRONMENT
- Social Support
  -Types: intimate, family
   unit, friendship, net-
   work, insitution
  -Convoy
  -Functions
- Options

THE INDIVIDUAL
- Personal Characteristics
- Psychological Resources
- Coping Responses
  -Functions
  -Strategies: information
   seeking, direct action
   inhibition of action

Figure 3–2. Coping Resources

- Previous experience with a similar transition (How has the individual met earlier similar transitions?)

- Concurrent stress (What and how great are the stresses—or are there any?)

Event or Nonevent Characteristics

Trigger. A transition, as we have defined it, is anticipated, unanticipated, a nonevent, or a chronic hassle. But there is always something specific that triggers a transition, something particular that happens which assumes special meaning and makes individuals look at themselves and their lives differently. For example, a change in the body—an illness such as a heart attack or cancer—can act as a trigger for a midlife transition. Job changes, especially job losses, are another common trigger. But what triggers a transition differs for each person, just as each person assimilates and appraises a transition in a different way. For one man, the trigger was being in bed for five months with a slipped disk, coupled with the death from cancer of one of his closest friends: "If I can get sick, if John can die, then life is not forever."

Further, events that at a particular time are culminating or marker events which push the individual to question the very foundation of his or her life may at other times have little effect. In a study of men whose jobs were eliminated, those who felt most threatened either were in midlife or were preretirees with not-yet-vested benefits (Schlossberg & Leibowitz, 1980a).

A transition can also be triggered by something that happens to someone close to the individual: A husband's heart attack may trigger a fear of aging in his wife; a wife's mastectomy may trigger similar fears in her husband. Yet other triggers are class reunions, movies, books.

Aslanian and Brickell (1980) differentiate transition from trigger as follows: A transition is a "change in status . . . that makes learning necessary. The adult needs to become competent at something that he or she could not do before in order to succeed in the new status" (pp. 38–39). A trigger, however, is the specific life event that precipitates "the decision to learn at that point in time" (p. 39). The trigger is not necessarily directly related to the transition—as in the example of an unemployed woman, suddenly widowed, who enrolls in a medical technology course in order to become qualified for a job. The transition is her change of status from nonworker to worker; the triggering event is her husband's death.

Timing. As we have already noted in our review of adult development theory, most adults still have built-in social clocks by which they judge whether they are "on time" or "off time" with respect to life events. To be off time, whether early or late, often carries social and psychological penalties. The individual may be branded as deviant and may feel himself or herself to be so. Such transitions as getting married, having children, going to college, taking a job, and retiring are usually linked in people's minds with a certain age. Although Neugarten (Hall, 1980) points out that the issue of timing has become somewhat confused as we move toward what she sees as an emerging "age-irrelevant" society in which more people of all ages engage in activities formerly reserved to one age group, helping professionals must nevertheless take into account the fact that most people probably still use age as a defining variable for themselves. Although the concept of age irrelevancy may be acknowledged by some, most individuals are still concerned with being on or off time.

In addition to being thought of as on or off time, transition events or nonevents are also experienced as happening at "good" and "bad" times. For example, for an adolescent in senior high school, a geographical move is usually experienced as happening at a bad time, but for a newlywed couple, a move away from parents and in-laws is experienced as happening at a good time. A major illness at a time of job loss would be both bad and off time, whereas if illness happens when an individual has a tenured faculty position, it would be a bad event but not necessarily off time. A RIF before pension rights are vested is worse than after; a major disability—always devastating—a month before marriage is clearly at a terrible time. Thus, events—both anticipated and unanticipated—can be at better or worse times, making it easier or more difficult for individuals to go through the transition process.

Source. The source of some transitions is internal, a deliberate decision on the part of the individual, whereas the source of others is completely external, and the transition is forced upon the individual by other people or by circumstances. It is hypothesized that the individual more easily assimilates transitions in which the source of the transition is internal. Thus the worker who retires because of ill health or a mandatory age limit probably finds retirement a more difficult and troubled period than does the worker who retires voluntarily. Similarly, wives often experience considerable negative stress in connection with residential moves when the move is forced upon them by the job requirements of their husbands (Seidenberg, 1973). The issue here is how an individual perceives control over his or her own life.

This issue of control was described in greater detail in the section on autonomy, as we discussed recurring themes in the life course in Chapter 1. But an important distinction—also made earlier—deserves emphasis. Even if the transition is beyond the individual's control, the response to it can be within the individual's control. The two sources of control—internal and external—interact: The degree to which the trigger or transition is in or out of the individual's control and the degree to which the individual can control his or her reactions to it are important in characterizing transitions. When we look at the variables characterizing the individual, we will discuss control further.

Role change. Many, but not all, transitions involve role change. We have already noted that role changes are an important aspect in determining the impact of a transition. Lowenthal, Thurnher, and Chiriboga (1975) distinguish between role gains (such as getting married, becoming a parent, taking a job, getting a job promotion) and role losses (such as getting divorced, retiring, being widowed). Similarly, in talking about transitions that the family as a unit may undergo, Dyer (1976) makes a distinction between accession (remarriage, birth) and dismemberment (divorce, death). Regardless of whether a transition involves a role gain or loss, some degree of stress accompanies it.

Some kinds of change—getting married, being promoted—generate feelings of pleasure. Other changes—losing a job, being divorced—are accompanied by painful feelings. For instance, LeMasters (1957) found that the period after the birth of the first child often constitutes a mental health crisis for the mother; along with her feelings of joy and satisfaction, she may be physically exhausted, anxious about her responsibilities, frustrated over her loss of freedom, resentful of her husband for not sharing more of the duties, and—on top of it all—guilty about her negative feelings. Similarly, though an individual may look forward with pleasurable anticipation, for instance, to retiring from employment or seeing the last child launched into the world, the actual event may carry with it feelings of pain. Again, any role change—whether primarily positive or negative in affect—involves some degree of stress.

Role is the "behavioral enacting of the patterned expectations attributed to a position" (Merton, 1957, p. 368). "Role theory in sociology centers on others' expectations as to the behavior of the individual who occupies a given position. These expectations . . . sustain order and consistency in human interaction. These expectations are essentially normative prescriptions for behavior" (Zaleznek & Jardim, 1967, p. 210). The individual who is betwixt and between roles often feels marginal. The more an individual engages in "anticipatory socialization"—that is, orientation toward the values and norms of the new role—the sooner the individual will be comfortable (Merton, 1957, p. 265). When there are no role models available for the new role, the individual remains marginal for a longer period, as did the first women executives.

Thus, role change can be more or less difficult (and have greater or lesser impact) depending on whether the new role is a loss or a gain, positive or negative, or has explicit norms and expectations for the new incumbent.

Duration. Another variable which affects the ease or difficulty of assimilating the transition is its expected duration. A change that is regarded as permanent will be perceived differently from one that is viewed as temporary. A wife may be willing to tolerate the inconvenience involved in moving to a new location so her husband can attend graduate school if she believes that the move is temporary and that they will return to their former home when he has received his degree. A transition that is painful and unpleasant may be more easily borne if the individual is assured that it is of limited duration, as when someone enters the hospital for surgery that he or she knows will be minor and will have no lasting effects. Conversely, if the change is desired, then the certainty that it represents a more or less permanent state may be reassuring.

Uncertainty, however, is connected with perhaps the greatest degree of stress and negative effect. Chodoff (1976), talking about the psychological stresses of being in a German concentration camp, says, "A healthy personality [can] defend itself against a peril, which though grave, is predictable and is at least potentially limited in time, but . . . the absolute uncertainty of [the concentration camp inmate's] condition was a barrier to the erection of adequate psychological measures" (pp. 337–338). To have an illness whose cause and prognosis is uncertain may be more stressful and unsettling for an individual than to know for sure that he or she has a terminal disease.

The salience of duration rests with the individual in transition.

Is it perceived as permanent, temporary, or unknown? Does the individual assess that as positive, negative, or mixed? In a recent study, 50 clerical workers were questioned about ways they coped with transitions. One woman selected remarriage as the transition of most recent impact. When asked whether she saw the remarriage as permanent or temporary, she thought a moment and said it was too hard to answer. She would like it to be permanent, but since she was on her fourth husband, she would probably have to say temporary (Schlossberg & Charner, 1982).

Previous experience with a similar transition. Experts agree that the individual who has successfully weathered a particular kind of transition in the past will probably be successful at assimilating another transition of a similar nature. As Danish and D'Augelli (1980, p. 114) state, "The past experience has provided both constructive attitudes about the event and behavioral competencies that were reinforced by the success experience." Conversely, the person who has been defeated by a situation may become more vulnerable and less able to cope in the future. Past experiences to some extent determine the person's mental set, and if that past experience was unfavorable, then the mental set may be something of a self-confirming prophecy. Of course, given possible changes in the balance of assets and liabilities (discussed earlier), the correlation between successful assimilation in the past and at a later point in time is by no means perfect.

Some types of loss seem to have long-lasting negative effects. For example, Lowenthal and Chiriboga (1975) found that of the one quarter of their sample who had suffered an early childhood loss through death or divorce, one-half belonged to the "overwhelmed" category; that is, though they had been relatively lightly stressed, they were preoccupied with stress. Undoubtedly, some experiences are so harrowing that many people are left permanently damaged.

Concurrent stress. Often transitions in one area stimulate other stresses and transitions. Holmes and Rahe originally showed the impact of multiple life events on physical health. To study this they developed a Social Readjustment Rating Scale (1967) which assigns numerical values to different kinds of life events, with "death of a spouse" ranking at the top of the scale and such items as "vacation," "Christmas," and "minor violations of the law" at the bottom. The Holmes-Rahe scale is useful not only in ascertaining the probable degree of stress connected with a given life event but also in indicating a person's general state of mental and physical health. By adding up the numerical values of the life events that the person has experienced during a given period of time (for example, a year), we can arrive at a total score which serves as an index of that person's general condition. The person who has gone through a number of changes in a relatively short period of time is more vulnerable to illness.

But as Dohrenwend and associates point out, the Holmes-Rahe scale must be used with reservation (Dohrenwend, Krasnoff, Askenasy, & Dohrenwend, 1978). In the first place, the numerical values represent empirically-derived averages and are subject to individual variation. Thus, the person who has suffered the loss of a loved one around Christmastime may for many years afterwards find the holiday season more stressful than other events given a higher value on the scale. In the second place, the stressfulness of a particular event depends not so much on the event itself as on the balance between a person's liabilities and assets at the time the event occurs. The construction of a new scale, the Peri Life Events Scale (Dohrenwend, et al., 1978, p. 205) expands the Holmes-Rahe Scale by including 102 items covering such categories as school, work, love and marriage, parenthood, family, residence, crime and legal matters, finances, social activities, and health; it also differentiates whether the event happened to the individual directly or to a significant other.

The important point is that the birth of a baby will have different meanings for the newly widowed or newly fired person than for a person in a relatively quiescent period.

Assessment

In Chapter 2, we described how Lazarus emphasizes the importance in the transitional process of what he calls primary appraisal—that is, the individual's assessment of the transition according to whether it is irrelevant, positive, or stressful. Such appraisal/assessment is central in the transition framework.

The individual's attributions about the transition affect how an individual appraises the transition (and himself or herself and the environment). Does he or she see the divorce as attributable to the other's deficiencies, to his or her deficiencies, to societal problems, or to idiosyncratic causes? The individual's attributions about self and situation provide a theoretical base for many studies explaining behavior. The studies which examine individuals' assessment of causation feed into "attribution theory" while those that examine the consequences of attributions are labeled "attributional research." "What these two types of research have in common is an interest in the causal explanations given for events by ordinary people" (Kelley & Michela, 1980, p. 548).

Variables Characterizing the Individual

The transition framework for connecting knowledge of adult development with the helping skills, as we have earlier emphasized, views the individual as the critical factor in understanding the transition process. It is the interaction of the variables characterizing the transition, the individual, and the environment that provides a multidimensional approach to understanding human development and mediates and moderates between any transitions and transition process.

Next we will look at the following variables that characterize individuals:

- Personal and demographic characteristics
  Socioeconomic status
  Sex role
  Age and stage of life
  State of health

- Psychological resources
  Ego development
  Personality
  Outlook
  Commitment and values

- Coping responses
  Functions: Controlling situation, meaning, stress
  Strategies: Information seeking, direct action, inhibition of action, intrapsychic behavior.

Personal and Demographic Characteristics

An individual's personal and demographic characteristics—socioeconomic status, sex role, age and stage of life, and state of health—bear directly on how he or she perceives and assesses life.

Socioeconomic status. The data on the relation between assimilating a transition and socioeconomic status are not always consistent, perhaps because of the different measures of socioeconomic status used (income, occupation, education, or some combination). Thus, Lowenthal and Chiriboga (1975) found that high status (as measured by education among men and by socioeconomic background among women) was related to greater exposure to stress, probably because high status is associated with a more varied life style (p. 149).

Pearlin and Leiberman (1979) examined the relative impact of different life strains on various segments of society. They concluded that many of the life strains that are "statistically significant at .05 or better are disproportionately concentrated among women," for example, being fired, being unemployed with health problems, demotion, homemaking, depersonalizing work relations, loss of spouse from death, nonfulfillment of expectations in marriage, lack of reciprocity and nonacceptance by spouse, death of a child, child's failure to act toward goals. In the occupational arena, the strains are felt more by those in lower socioeconomic groups. They conclude that, "in general, . . . women, the young, and—most clearly in occupation—those of low socioeconomic position are most vulnerable to the severest life strains" (p. 242).

The importance of socioeconomic status is further underlined in Rubin's study of the empty nest (1981). Women from advantaged situations can anticipate that their children will go away to college; therefore, children's departure from the home is expected, and those women engage in anticipatory socialization. Women from working-class homes, for whom money is sometimes a problem and children's attendance at an out-of-town college is uncertain, experience a more difficult transition in the event of their children's departure. Rubin stresses the fact that the empty nest is not a problem for most women. What makes it a problem is when it is unplanned, ambivalent, and not clear (1981).

The effects of the individual's racial and ethnic background on his or her ability to assimilate are probably mediated through other factors such as value orientation and cultural norms and should not be underestimated. However, as we have already noted, there is a problem with existing data because most studies of adults have focused on white middle-class males. It is to be hoped that the next decade will see an increase in studies of many populations so that insights will be gained into the differing adult experiences.

Sex role. The relationship between sex and the transition process is complex. Many observers have suggested that because in our culture men are socialized to hide emotion and deny problems (whereas women are given greater freedom to express their feelings), men present a more favorable picture with respect to mental health. Despite appearances, however, women's greater capacity for intimacy and mutuality may make it easier for them to assimilate certain transitions; the example of widowhood has already been cited. Moreover, evidence suggests that women "can apparently integrate many and diverse emotional experiences. Men seem more distressed by ups and downs of emotional life; they apparently thrive either on a preponderance of positive emotional experiences or a relative lack of any kind [of experience]" (Chiriboga, 1975, p. 97).

As we would expect, the sources of stress differ for the sexes, that is, men and women face somewhat different kinds of transitions. The transitions and stresses that a man experiences are more likely to be connected with work, whereas those a woman undergoes are more likely to be connected with family life. Moreover, Beeson and Lowenthal (1975) point out that the "person focus" differs for the sexes; men undergo stress as a result of events in their own lives, whereas women undergo stress as a result of events in the lives of their husbands and their children (or other family members). Thus, a decline in the husband's health may be as much a transition for the wife as a change in her own health, bringing about significant changes in her assumptive world. They conclude "that the sex of the individual rather than his or her stage in life accounts for most of the variation within our sample." This is corroborated in preliminary data from a study of clerical workers (Schlossberg & Charner, 1982) in which women report significantly more often than men that their transitions started with someone else.

A further illustration of sex differences is found in the data on friendships gathered by Lowenthal, Thurnher, and Chiriboga (1975): "Within each gender, the qualities attributed to close and to ideal friends are surprisingly constant across the four life stages, men tending to emphasize shared interests and activities, women commonly more concerned with affect and reciprocity. . . . Women at all stages also tended to provide more complex descriptions of friends than men did" (p. 227). Sex differences in self-concept and subjective sense of well-being were also in evidence.

In addition, their study documents the changing value commitments of men and women in midlife, when women begin to desire achievement in the outside world and men begin to value interpersonal, affiliative goals (p. 233). Other authors have suggested that the parental emergency works to keep men and women behaving in traditional ways; then, with the completion of the childrearing years, men and women can express that side of themselves that was dormant. Thus androgyny—the incorporation of masculine and feminine qualities in the same individual—becomes more possible. Levinson corroborates this view: "The difficulty in integrating the masculine and feminine in early adulthood has many sources . . . : cultural traditions . . . evolving life tasks. . . . Most men get to the late thirties with roughly the same balance of masculine and feminine they had in the early twenties. The midlife transition is the next major developmental opportunity to reintegrate the masculine/feminine polarity" (1978, pp. 235–236).

Many researchers have looked at sex differences and work. Some theories and studies of career development emphasize differences between the sexes on such variables as attitudes toward job and career, drive to achieve, and work-related behavior. Often such approaches involve analyzing these differences on the basis of early socialization patterns.

In our society, girls have traditionally been brought up to be passive, dependent, and nurturant, whereas boys are brought up to be active, independent, and aggressive. Thus, women come to be inculcated by the "vicarious achievement ethic" (Lipman-Blumen & Leavitt, 1976). They define their identities not through their own activities and accomplishments but through those of the dominant people (usually men) in their lives: at first their fathers, later their husbands, still later their children. As a corollary of this tendency, they perceive themselves primarily in such roles as wife, mother, and homemaker; even the woman who has a job outside the home tends not to value or emphasize her role as worker. Men, on the other hand, are governed by the direct achievement ethic and tend to base their identities on their career achievements. They are "success objects," whose value as human beings is measured by their ability to provide for their families.

One implication of these differences is that the man's work usually takes precedence over the woman's. For instance, in a marriage where both partners work, the family must make a residential move if the husband is transferred by his company to another location, but only in rare cases will the wife's occupational needs bring about drastic changes in the family's situation.

Some of these patterns are reflected in a study of women in middle management and top executive positions (Hennig & Jardim, 1977). Most of the women in the sample had made their career decision (defined as "a conscious commitment to advancement over the long term") ten years later than is generally true for men. For some of these women, that decision was in some sense a passive one, something that "just happened" when the woman suddenly realized that she was probably going to be working the rest of her life. These managerial women were inclined to attribute their success to luck or to the kindly intervention and encouragement of a superior. Nonetheless, most of them believed that further advancement would come about through their own efforts at self-improvement, their development of competence on the job. What these women lacked, according to Hennig and Jardim, is "a sense of the organizational environment—the informal system of relationships and information sharing, ties of loyalty and of dependence, of favors granted and owed, of mutual benefit, of protection—which men unfailingly and invariably take into account. . . . " (p. 12).

This difference is attributed in part to men having learned early in their lives to play games such as football that involve teamwork, the long-range goal of winning, and the use of short-term strategies with a view to reaching that goal. Women have little exposure to such sports, concentrating instead on such activities as swimming, tennis, and gymnastics that focus more on the display of competence and do not involve working with team members. Their failure to recognize the team-sport aspects of the managerial career leads women to behave in certain ways that decrease their chances of success in the organization.

Hennig and Jardim specify the following behavioral differences between men and women in management. First, the sexes interpret "risk" differently: women see only the immediate negative aspects (the danger of failure) and men see not only negative but also long-range positive aspects (the opportunity for success and advancement). Second, in deciding on what style to use in playing the role of subordinate—helper, follower, junior colleague, equal, friend—men are more aware of the expectations of others, especially the boss, and choose a style that will satisfy those expectations, whereas women are inclined to adopt a take-me-as-I-am attitude. They are less skilled at dissembling than men are, again because they lose sight of the long-range goal of winning the (career) game. Finally, men take a more instrumental view of human relationships in the corporation and are thus more willing to work with people whom they may not like personally. On the other hand, women often view human relationships as an end in themselves; they cannot accommodate themselves so easily to the demands of such situations and thus lay themselves open to the charge of "overemotionalism" on the job.

As we have already noted, Gilligan makes the point that though sex differences are identified and discussed, they are not incorporated in most models of human development. We must recognize that sex and gender differences are critical in understanding the transition process.

A slightly different approach is taken by Kanter (1977), who looks at how the large corporation evolved historically to its present form, with men dominating the managerial ranks and women the clerical ranks. Kanter's analysis is based on two premises: (1) jobs create people rather than vice versa; that is, an organization's structure influences people's options, and (2) expectations about working women in general are derived from expectations about secretaries. One chapter of Kanter's book is devoted to the subculture of secretaries, whose relationship with their bosses constitutes an example of "patrimony," the traditional feudal system of lord and vassal.

Kanter's point is that the behavior of women as workers in large organizations is determined not by their sex but by their position of relative powerlessness in the structure. Unfortunately, the behavior patterns they are forced to develop as secretaries may carry over when they are promoted to managerial positions, where such patterns are no longer appropriate. In addition, these behavior patterns affect the expectations and stereotypes of other people about the behavior of all women workers.

Thus, currently, because of different socialization, the thinking and behavior of men and women differ. Nevertheless, change on many fronts makes it necessary for helpers to explore with each individual his or her orientation to his or her gender and sex role.

Age and life stage. Again, the wealth of data about the relation between age and ability to assimilate precludes all but a cursory discussion here. One point that makes analysis difficult (which we discussed in Chapter 1) is that most experts agree that chronological age is relatively unimportant compared to psychological age ("the capacity to respond to societal pressures and the tasks required of an individual"), social age ("the extent to which an individual participates in roles assigned by society"), and functional age ("the ability to function or perform as expected of people in one's age brackets, which in turn, depends on social, biological, and personality considerations") (Spierer, 1977, p. 10).

Another complication is that the process of aging itself constitutes a series of events that requires adaptation on the part of the individual. That is, the biological and physiological changes that occur over the lifespan may themselves be regarded as transitions.

An example of how an individual's age may affect his or her reaction to a crisis comes from a study of men aged 37 to 67 who were hospitalized following heart attacks (Rosen & Bibring, 1968). Whereas the younger men were generally cheerful and the 60-year-olds fatherly and easy going, the 50-year-olds were hostile, withdrawn, depressed, and difficult as patients. The authors interpret these age differences as follows: Those under 50 simply denied the seriousness of their condition; those in their sixties accepted it as an on-time event; but those in their fifties experienced "open conflict from the active orientation of youth" (p. 207). "A heart attack theoretically accentuates the very issues with which the [middle-aged man] has been actively struggling" (p. 207), that is, with his anxiety about aging and his reluctance about shifting from an active to a passive role.

Life stage may be a more useful concept than chronological age in examining transitions. Chiriboga and Gigy (1975) identified numerous stage differences with respect to the sources and nature of stress, the number of significant life events, and the ratio of positive to negative experiences. The younger subjects (high school seniors and newlyweds) reported two-and-one-half times as many "stressor events" during the last ten years of their lives than older subjects (middle-aged and preretirement couples), which gives support to the notion that the "density" of time—its fullness and eventfulness—seems to lessen with age: "The self-reports of older people . . . suggest a more restricted perception of things happening in their lives and also less involvement in the circumstances that do occur" (Chiriboga & Gigy, 1975, p. 127). As was pointed out previously, in the later stages of life more subtle factors cause changes in self-perception and satisfaction, that is, the realization that one has not achieved as much as one had planned, the shift in time perspective so that one thinks in terms of years left to live rather than years since birth.

According to Lowenthal and Chiriboga (1975), "the young may thrive better on stress than on the lack of it" (p. 160). Middle age (more specifically, the period immediately preceding the empty nest), is a period of high risk for both sexes, in that they are more likely to experience negative rather than positive stresses and to be overwhelmed by them. The preretirement couples in the San Francisco study were generally in better psychological shape than the middle-aged parents, though Chiriboga points out that "among older people a greater breadth of activities actually weighs against life satisfaction. . . . Getting rid of unwanted duties and obligations and settling for ease and contentment . . . as a way of life may represent one of the major adaptive tasks for older people" (Chiriboga, 1975, p. 98).

Leiberman (1975) suggests that "the processes for adequate coping . . . may be life-stage specific" (p. 155) and that "characteristics or processes [that] predict adaptation at other life stages appear to be irrelevant in predicting adaptation in old age" (p. 154), when adequate cognitive and physical resources are essential— though not necessarily sufficient—to assure successful adaptation. The importance of physical resources is discussed more thoroughly in the next section.

State of health. As with age and aging, the individual's state of health not only affects his or her ability to assimilate a transition but also may itself be a source of stress: That is, ill health in itself constitutes a transition. In some cases, a person may recover quickly from an acute but minor illness and be left relatively unaffected, with little change in self-perception. In other cases, an illness—though brief—may remind the person of his or her own mortality and thus have lasting psychological effects. In still other cases, the illness may be chronic, leading to a gradual decline in physical resources and energy level and thus profoundly affecting the individual's coping ability. As was mentioned before, Leiberman believes that "physical capacity . . . may be the most important and perhaps the only salient predictor of adaptive failure, at least among the elderly" (1975, p. 145).

Health has a subjective as well as an objective aspect. For instance, Shanas and her associates, comparing self-ratings of health with degree of actual incapacity, classified people as health pessimists, health optimists, and health realists. They found that among people over age 80, women were more likely to fall into the first category than were men, although men were less optimistic about their health immediately after retirement than either earlier or later (Shamas, Townsend, Wedderburn, Friis, Milhoj, & Stehouwer, 1968, p. 218).

The San Francisco study found some relation between self-reported health status and psychological adaptation, with the direction of the correlation differing by sex. Women who said they had few health problems were less likely to have psychological deficits than women who saw themselves as having many or major health problems; whereas men who reported themselves as healthy were more likely to suffer psychological deficits than men who reported themselves to have health problems (Chiriboga & Lowenthal, 1975, p. 114). One explanation for this difference comes from the additional finding that among older men the "challenged" (those high in exposure to stress but low in preoccupation with stress) were more likely to be physically impaired than were the "overwhelmed" (those high on both dimensions). This suggests that the former are basically noncomplainers who repress and deny their problems and that this repression exacts a physical toll (pp. 161–162).

Thus, demographics and personal characteristics are important as filters and mediate whether or not an individual's life will be altered in ways basic to the particular person. Since an individual's social class, sex, age, life stage, and health all bear on his or her options—perceived and real—these variables need to be explored.

Psychological Resources

Psychological resources are the "personality characteristics that people draw upon to help them withstand threats" (Pearlin & Schooler, 1978, p. 5). The next section discusses ego development, personality, outlook, and commitments and values.

Ego development.   People exposed to the same situation or material will approach it from a different frame of reference. This frame of reference differentiates the way people react to the world, whatever their age or stage. For example, if there were 100 45-year-old women enrolled in the same educational program, they would react according to their frame of reference, their level of maturity. As noted in Chapter 1, Loevinger uses the term *ego development* to describe this process (1976). The conformist, at a lower level of maturity, will think in stereotypes, conform to the rules, and follow the course outlines without question. At a midpoint, according to Loevinger's schema, some adults, classified as conscientious, will see the world as complex and incorporate their own standards into the material. The autonomous, at a higher level, undergo a major shift and become more critical, acknowledge conflicting and sometimes irresolvable information, and tolerate ambiguity. Some evidence exists showing that while· traditional 18- to 24-year-old students fall in the first four stages (impulsive, self-protective, conformist, conscientious-conformist), older adults will both span those four and the remaining four (conscientious, individualistic, autonomous, integrated) (Weathersby, 1981, p. 58). In this schema, a self-protective person is motivated to learn to satisfy immediate needs; a conformist is motivated to impress significant others and gain social acceptance; a conscientious person is motivated to achieve skills and competence; and an autonomous person is there to deepen understanding of himself or herself and others (p. 62) as well as to develop increasing capacity to tolerate ambiguity, uncertainty, and be responsible for his or her own destiny.

Thus we see that this construct of ego development involves two aspects: (1) the developmental sequence which ranges from impulsive and self-protective through conformist, conscientious, individualistic, and autonomous to integrated, and (2) the description of individual differences in any age or stage cohort which also ranges from impulsive to integrated. Ego development is a "pervasive self-reinforcing frame of reference for experiencing . . . in which learning of any kind is embedded" (p. 52).

Personality. In pointing to the difficulty of writing about personality development, Troll calls personality an "ambiguous, controversial, and conglomerate construct" (1982, p. 227). Everyone uses the term but often in different ways.

Some theorists have used personality types for explaining the different ways individuals react to the world. For example, Beeson and Lowenthal (1975) identify four personality types by analyzing their different reactions to various intensities and frequencies of stress: Those who encounter frequent and/or severe stress are characterized as either "overwhelmed" or "challenged": those who encounter infrequent and/or mild stress are seen as either "self-defeating" or "lucky." The challenged and the lucky types are much less preoccupied with stress than the overwhelmed or the self-defeating.

Others talk of temperament, affect, characteristics, conventionalism, morality, achievement, sex behavior, values, and interests.

Troll offers a simple way to think of a person: "the feeling of being oneself—the *I*—and the way one describes oneself or is described by others—the *me*" (1982, p. 250).

Outlook. The role complexity of men and women for four groups at different points in the life course—high school seniors, newlyweds, middle-aged parents, and preretirees—has been identified by Spence and Lurie (1975, pp. 13–15). They obtained role involvement scores based on a number of roles, and involvement ranging from complex roles (many and varied) to simple (few and limited), and from diffuse (few and varied) to focused (many but narrow range). This conceptualization helps us examine the way adults handle transitions. The degree to which an individual's life is complex, simplistic, focused, or diffuse influences what he or she seeks, what he or she is able to tolerate, and how he or she filters the transition. For example, women handle returning to school differently depending on whether they are full-time students with major family responsibilities; full-time students with minor family responsibilities; full-time workers, part-time students with minor family responsibilities; or full-time workers, part-time students with major family responsibilities. The degree of role complexity not only determines who goes to school, but also whether the school experience will be positive and salient (Campbell, Wilson, & Hanson, 1980, pp. 59–60). Obviously, for some, school will be a necessary hassle; for others it can be a leisurely pursuit of knowledge. As roles change over the lifespan, so will the importance and utility of education.

Another way to examine outlook is to examine an individual's overall style of coping. According to one study, women coping with breast cancer can be categorized as fighting spirits, stoics, deniers, helpless, and magical thinkers. The fighting spirits and deniers had less recurrence in a followup study (Schain, 1981). Fighting spirits have "the will to fight, struggle, resist"; stoics subscribe "to the philosophy that people should be free from passion and submit without complaint to unavoidable life circumstances"; deniers refused "to recognize the reality of a situation"; helpless persons are "unable to help themselves without help of others"; magical thinkers feel "that results will come through mysterious and unexplained powers."

Pearlin and Schooler have identified self-esteem and mastery as two major psychological resources, and thus part of an individual's outlook. Self-esteem refers to an individual's positive attitude about self, in contrast to self-denigration. Mastery, like locus of control, refers to an individual's ability to be in charge of his or her life (1978, p. 5).

Perhaps this discussion can be simplified by saying that some people approach life and see it as half full, while others see it as half empty. Thus, an individual's outlook, itself a result of the complex interplay of many factors, colors the way change is viewed.

Commitments and values.   As we discussed in Chapter 1, Fiske studied men and women's changing commitments over the lifespan (1980). An individual's major commitment—whether it is his or her relationships (interpersonal), working for others (altruism), self-improvement (competence/mastery), or survival (self-protective) determines his or her vulnerability. The father of a 26-year-old boy who committed suicide explained how differently he and his wife reacted. He said it was easier for him because he could bury himself in work—commitment to mastery—whereas his wife, whose lifelong commitment had been to relationships, especially in the family, was unable even after two years to reinvest in life. Clearly the reaction to and assimilation of transitions is greatly influenced by commitments—which, of course, change, thereby changing an individual's areas of vulnerability.

An individual's basic values and beliefs are also a factor in his or her ability to assimilate transitions. On the basis of subjects' responses to the question, "What is the main purpose in life?" Thurnher (1975) developed a seven-category value typology: (1) instrumental-material (economic or occupational productivity or achievement, social status, household chores), (2) interpersonal-expressive (intimacy, friendship, sociability), (3) philosophical-religious (including concern with the meaning of existence and adherence to an ethical code), (4) social service (helping others, community service), (5) ease and contentment (simple comforts, security, relaxation), (6) hedonism (sensual pleasure, enjoying life to the fullest), and (7) personal growth (self-actualization). Values may be valuable or dysfunctional, "dependent on the ease with which they can be translated into goals and behavior and successfully pursued" (p. 184). Moreover, a value system that contributes to assimilation at one life stage may be dysfunctional at another; thus, people at different stages tend to emphasize different values.

Religious beliefs are an obvious example of value orientation that is often said to sustain people through the trials of life. For instance, grief over the death of a loved one may be eased by the belief that the death is "God's will." Among preretirement women, however, high philosophical-religious values were related to low satisfaction, suggesting that "if the intensification of religious beliefs and practices arose from the search for solace, the comfort derived would seem only partial and not such as to result in full acceptance of one's self or one's life course" (p. 188). On the other hand, "among people of both sexes in the later stages . . . there was evidence that involvement in religion, either through feelings of religiosity or through greater participation, allows for more direct handling of the prospect of personal death" (Chiriboga & Gigy, 1975, p. 143).

The specific content of an individual's religious beliefs, and the cultural norms associated with particular religions, need also to be considered. For example, a woman from a Catholic background facing divorce may find her distress exacerbated by the church's strictures against divorce. A man from a Protestant background who has grown up with a strong commitment to the work ethic may find forced unemployment especially hard to take, quite apart from the financial strain it entails.

Beyond the comforts of religion, strong commitment to an ideology or cause may be a necessity in some situations. Thus, those draft dodgers who moved to Canada not to escape from some difficult personal situation or to seek adventure but for ideological reasons—because they believed the Vietnam War to be immoral or regarded themselves as political refugees from an oppressive system—were more likely to adapt to the new situation (Levine, 1976). Concentration camp victims who saw themselves as surviving for some greater purpose were able to mobilize their coping resources more effectively (Dimsdale, 1976).

Thus, people face transitions, problems, and joys with characteristic psychological patterns and resources. These vary according to ego development, personality, outlook, and commitments and values. Psychological resources "represent some of the things people are . . . ; coping responses [to be discussed in the next section] . . . represent some of the things people do . . . to deal with . . . life strains" (p. 5).

Coping Responses

Our lives are filled with unexpected and anticipated life strains. They cannot be eliminated. An important goal is to help people cope more effectively with these strains, to help them develop effective coping responses to assist the transition process.

Here we are going to look at the functions of coping responses which help the individual control the situation, the meaning, and the stress, and at the strategies involved in coping responses: information seeking, direct action, inhibition of action, and intrapsychic behavior. The work of Pearlin and Lazarus, two independent and major researchers on coping, is central to our discussion of these areas.

Some definitions set the stage for examining coping responses: "By coping we refer to the things people do to avoid being harmed by life strains" (Pearlin & Schooler, 1978, p. 1). "We will define coping as the overt and covert behaviors individuals use to prevent, alleviate, or respond to stressful situations. . . . Coping can occur before, during, or after a stressful or challenging situation" (George & Siegler, 1981, p. 37). "In my view, stress itself as a concept pales in significance . . . compared with coping. . . . Stress is ubiquitous, an inevitable feature of normal living. . . . What makes the difference in adaptational outcome is coping" (Lazarus, 1980, p. 52).

On the basis of interviews with 2,300 people between 18 and 65 living in the Chicago area, Pearlin and associates identify major life strains and the coping strategies people use to deal with these strains—in other words, what troubles people and how they deal with their troubles. Coping "represents . . . concrete efforts to deal with the life strains they encounter in their different roles," that is, those things an individual does in his or her own behalf (Pearlin & Schooler, 1978, p. 5). They distinguish three types of coping: (1) "responses that modify the situation" (such as negotiation in marriage, discipline in parenting, optimistic action in occupation, and seeking advice in marriage and parenting), (2) "responses that . . . control the meaning of the problem" (such as responses that neutralize, positive comparisons, selective ignoring, substitution of rewards), and (3) responses that help to manage stress after it has occurred (such as "denial, passive acceptance, withdrawal, magical thinking, hopefulness, avoidance of worry, relaxation"). Specific mechanisms include "emotional discharge versus controlled reflectiveness, . . . passive forebearance versus self-assertion, . . . potency versus helpless resignation, . . . optimistic faith" (1978, pp. 6–7).

Families of the unemployed provide many examples of coping responses. In one family, in which the husband had been unemployed for 18 months, the wife reported three major coping mechanisms. First, they kept trying to modify the situation by continuous, systematic job hunting. In fact, their phone bills averaged $400 a month, indicating that the husband was working on networking and contacts. Second, they tried to control the meaning of the problem. They joined a support group, made up of others with the same problem, which focused on the economic aspects of structural unemployment as well as job-searching strategies. The family also identified the positive aspects of the situation; for example, the father was now able to be involved with the children on a more regular basis. In this way, they took the blame away from themselves personally. Third, they utilized responses that helped to manage stress by keeping busy with a rental property, running, and gardening.

Pearlin also points out that people's coping strategies are related to their "psychological resources of self-esteem and mastery" (p. 5). With chronic unemployment, damage to the ego can limit the individual's flexibility in selecting coping strategies. In discussing such a situation of chronic unemployment, a physician commented on her unemployed husband's shattered ego. Despite the fact that they tried to manage the stress, redefine the situation, and change the situation, there were some lasting and damaging effects on their marriage. Another family—the wife a nurse, the husband an unemployed air traffic controller—reported feeling at the end of their rope. They did not know how to change the situation, redefine the problem, or manage their stress. Counseling could help them develop strategies in one or all of these areas.

Of course, the question crops up as to which coping strategies are best in different situations. Pearlin reports there are many options for people to use in every area of their lives, and that certain strategies do reduce stress in certain role areas, but he also reports that individual coping has the greatest chance of being efficacious with interpersonal problems rather than work-related problems. He further cautions that if helpers tell people their individual coping efforts will work in all settings, frustrations are sure to build up. The need is rather to see coping in a broader context. In some cases, collective coping, that is, helping people share in a problem they cannot undo individually, is essential (1982). The structural unemployment of the 1980s is just such a case, for it needs to be addressed collectively and politically. However, clearly some individuals are going to cope more effectively than others, and the person with a repertoire of responses—at least five or six—for each role area will be able to more effectively handle the strains of life.

The coping strategies identified in the Pearlin study "constitute but a portion of the full range of responses people undoubtedly call upon in dealing with life-exigencies" (Pearlin & Schooler, 1978, p. 5); nevertheless they indicate a systematic way to think about strategies. The following outline is adapted from the study. Questions or descriptors illustrate each strategy or coping response.[1]

1. Responses that modify the situation and are "aimed at altering the source of strain" (p. 20)
   • *Negotiation.* "How often do you try to find a fair compromise, . . . sit down and talk things out?"

[1]The items for the responses are taken from Appendix 4 in "The Structure of Coping" by L. I. Pearlin and C. Schooler, *Journal of Health and Social Behavior,* 1978, *19,* 20. Reprinted by permission.

- *Optimistic action.* "When you have difficulties in your work situation, how often do you take some action to get rid of them, or to find a solution?"
- *Self-reliance vs. advice seeking.* "In the past year . . . have you asked for the advice of friends . . . relative . . . doctor . . . or other professional?"
- *Exercise of potency vs. helpless resignation.* "How often do you decide there's really nothing you can do to change things?"

2. Responses that control the meaning of the problem in order cognitively to neutralize the threat (p. 6).
   - *Positive comparisons.* "A device . . . [to enable] a temporal frame of reference, . . . captured in such idioms as count your blessings."
   - *Selective ignoring.* A "positive attribute . . . within a troublesome situation. When you have difficulties in your work situation, how often do you tell yourself that they are unimportant, [and] try to pay attention only to your duties and overlook them?"
   - *Substitution of rewards.* "Hierarchical ordering of life priorities . . . to keep the most strainful experiences within the least valued areas of life. If I have troubles at work, I value other areas of life more and downplay the importance of work."

3. Responses that help the individual manage stress after it has occurred to help "accommodate to existing stress without being overwhelmed by it" (p. 7).[2]
   - *Emotional discharge.* "Expressive ventilation of feelings: How often do you yell or shout to let off steam?"
   - *Self-assertion.* "When you have differences with your spouse, how often do you fight it out?"
   - *Passive forbearance.* "When you have differences with your spouse, how often do you keep out of his or her way?"

Pearlin relates the selection of coping strategies to the individual's psychological resources (which we discussed in the preceding section):

---

[2]In this group, self-assertion and passive forbearance are separated since each is a useful strategy. The study speaks of self-assertion vs. forbearance.

Coping, in sum, is certainly not a unidimensional behavior. It functions at a number of levels and is attained by a plethora of behaviors,
cognitions, and perceptions. It is useful . . . that coping responses be
distinguished from what we have identified as psychological resources
for coping, those personality characteristics that minimize threat to
self . . . we cannot completely understand coping without looking beyond the personality attributes of individuals to the specific responses
to problems in different social roles (pp. 7–8).

Pearlin and his associates identify a number of coping strategies. None contains magic; rather, effective coping means flexible
utilization of a range of strategies as each situation demands.

Like Pearlin, Lazarus has made many studies in the field. He
has looked at stressors and, most recently, contrasted those aspects
of life that "hassle" and "uplift" people (1981a).

Like Pearlin, Lazarus also sees the coping strategies a person employs as more relevant than the event, hassle, or strain,
and the person's appraisal of the situation as more central than
the event. As we described in Chapter 2's discussion of ways to
assess how adults cope with transitions, the key is the way the
person sees the strain, stressor, event—whether it is perceived as
harmful, benign, or challenging. Individuals are constantly appraising the event and their resources to deal with the event.
For example, a person might see winning a bike trip as a great
opportunity, yet feel anxious about taking advantage of it due to
his or her assessment of skills, resources, and coping abilities in
strange settings.

Concurrent with appraising and reappraising events, resources, and results, an individual engages in coping behavior.
Lazarus classifies coping in two major ways: instrumental behavior
that intends to change the situation and palliative behavior that
intends to help minimize individual distress.

Whether the individual wants to change the situation or reduce
his or her distress, he or she can choose from among four coping
modes: information seeking, direct action, inhibition of action, and
intrapsychic behavior. The first three seem self-explanatory; the
last one (intrapsychic) refers to the thoughts an individual employs
to resolve the issue he or she faces. These thoughts, which include
denial, wishful thinking, and distortion, enable the individual to
carry on.

George and Siegler base their work on this formulation, since
most theorists see direct action as the preferred mode of coping.
Lazarus, however, finds that "effective copers use both direct ac-

tions and palliative coping modes" (1980, p. 54). Similarly, Pearlin identifies "selective ignoring" as an adaptive strategy.

Lazarus emphasizes the fact that selection of a coping strategy depends on personal dispositions, situations, and available responses. Norman Cousins provides a superb example of coping with what appeared to be a terminal illness. He took direct action with massive doses of vitamin C and funny movies. His intrapsychic processes included denial that the illness was terminal and reappraisal of self and situation. Clearly, not everyone responds this way.

Lazarus argues for the kind of research George and Siegler did, studying individuals intensively as they cope with good and bad times. They interviewed, in depth, 100 older persons who had been part of the Duke University Center on Aging's longitudinal study and asked them to define the events they considered "best" and "worst." Lazarus's model provided the framework for coding the way these people coped with these best and worst events. For example, was their coping instrumental—an attempt to change the situation—or palliative—an attempt to minimize the individual's distress? What mode was utilized—information seeking, direct action, inhibition of action, or intrapsychic?

It is interesting to compare different coping responses for best and worst events. George and Siegler point out that coping responses described in the context of the best in a whole life are more likely to be instrumental in orientation than those described as the worst: "compared to 'worst' contexts, coping responses in the Best Whole Life are . . . more likely to be direct action . . . Greater proportions . . . in 'worst' are intrapsychic . . . [which] reflects . . . less need for tension management in dealing with experiences perceived as positive" (1981, pp. 239–240).

An important point for helpers to remember is that effective copers are flexible and utilize a number of methods. Ability to cope is not a trait, but a dynamic process constantly in flux throughout the continuing process of appraisal. A series of studies on postoperative recovery illustrates this complexity. For example, Cohen looked at ways people coped with surgery. She reviewed studies based on a theoretical framework which suggested that people's appraisal of a situation would determine subsequent emotion and behavior (1980, p. 376). She studied 59 hernia, gall bladder, and thyroid patients the night before surgery and rated them on a continuum from avoidance (avoid information and knowledge about surgery and outcome) to vigilance (seek out information about surgery). Then she measured recovery on a number of dimensions. Contrary to expectations, neither age nor life change score was a factor in recovery, but the coping strategy of denial was. Those who knew the most had more "complications and a longer hospital stay" (p. 377). In this kind of situation, dependency, passivity, and lack of knowledge seem to be the best coping mechanisms; too much knowledge can lead to panic. Furthermore, trying to be in charge in a situation the individual is unable to control can lead to frustration. Although in general most of us will work to help people take control, in some situations this strategy is counterproductive.

Summary of coping responses. The preceding section has described the way several researchers have conceptualized and studied coping. According to Pearlin, most individuals—when faced with a transition—try to control the situation (for example, by publishing a great deal to insure promotion), control the meaning of the situation (by seeing promotion as irrelevant), or control the stress (by jogging to release tension caused by promotion worries). Lazarus identifies two major coping orientations—changing the situation (instrumental) or relaxing oneself (palliative) and suggests four possible modes of coping: direct action, inhibition of action, information seeking, and intrapsychic.

Since there is such overlap in these models, I suggest that they be integrated by categorizing coping responses in two ways: as functions and as strategies.

1. Functions
     Controlling the situation
     Controlling the meaning
     Controlling the stress

2. Strategies
     Information seeking
          Seeking advice vs. self-reliance
          Searching for resources
          Reading/TV
     Direct action
          Negotiation
          Discipline
          Emotional discharge
          Self-assertion
          Stress management

Optimistic action
Potency vs. helpless resignation
Inhibition of action
Selective ignoring
Controlled reflection
Passive forbearance
Denial
Positive comparisons
Substitution of rewards

Variables Characterizing the Environment

Environment here refers to those conditions that surround the individual. It encompasses a wide range of physical and psychological influences, but before we analyze the two major aspects of an individual's environment—social support and options—we need to set the stage by establishing the ecological perspective on human development on which the analysis is based.

The Ecological Perspective

Ecology, a term borrowed from biology, deals with the interaction of the organism and its environment. An individual or plant flourishes in one setting and fails in another. Thus, to understand human development, we must be aware that although behavior is determined in part by the chance of the individual's birth, certain evidence exists to illustrate that when the environment is altered, behavior and performance will also alter. To talk about "normal" growth and development is all very well, but for those whose development does not follow the normal sequence, such questions arise as, "What's wrong with me?" or, "What's wrong with the environment?" Ecological questions would instead ask, "Why does one person fail in one seting but achieve in another?" "Why does one social class have differing degrees and kinds of mental illness?" The essence of the ecological perspective is that the onus cannot be placed on either the individual or the environment; rather human behavior is a continuous interaction of individual and environment.

Maccoby distinguishes behavior that results from intrapsychic problems and from dehumanizing work settings. Since pathological family and work settings can produce mental illness, a change in these systems can facilitate mental health; and since most people work in organizations, it is important for us to examine the relationship of health and work. Symptoms can be the result of psychopathology, but they can also result from an unhealthy work environment. Maccoby states that the essential question is whether such symptoms as destructive behavior, fear, and inability to act are rational reactions to threatening situations or whether they would persist even in benign situations (1980).

Maccoby also refers to Kornhouser's studies of automobile workers who suffer "from routine and repetitive jobs" which lead to "feelings of hostility and anxiety" (Maccoby, 1980, p. 4). According to Maccoby, doctors often administer medication to treat symptoms of workers that only social change would cure.

In examining worker behavior, Maccoby engaged in a major study of the various character types in organizations (1976). Though there is room for a variety of character subtypes in organizations, opportunities differ and their context is differently interpreted. For example, a technical craftsman feels secure in a very structured environment, but a risk taker will be frustrated in an environment which demands that every action be accounted for. Maccoby points out that we can show our concern with human development in the workplace by changing negative environments as well as helping individuals obtain recognition, security, equity, fairness, and power to influence at work (1980).

Individuals are viewed as both initiators and responders in their environment. Thus, when we discuss an individual's resources, we must examine not only the role of the individual and the available and potential options, but also the transaction between them. For, after all, individuals have an impact on environments—some more actively than others—and they can also set up or eliminate barriers, some more actively than others.

Environment, therefore, is both cause and result of individuals' behavior. Lazarus highlights this issue:

> This important Freudian discovery of unconscious, intrapsychic processes and their impact on thought, feeling, and action also got clinicians frozen into the study of internal processes exclusively, but we now cycle back toward a recognition of the important role played by environmental influences in adaptation and maladaptation (1980, pp. 66–67).

Two variables which characterize an environment reflect on the environmental condition and both are central to an individual's ability to function: his or her social support and options. We need to ask what types of social support and options exist for the individual. At the same time, we also need to look at how the individual develops a social network system and utilizes and creates options.

Social Support

The importance of social support is often said to be the key to handling stress. However, support needs to be defined operationally, for it comes in many sizes and shapes and can be for better or for worse. To clarify this term *social support*, we will discuss it in three parts: by types (intimate relationships, family units, networks of friends, institutions and/or communities), by functions (affect, affirmation, aid, feedback), and by measurement (identifying the convoy).

Types of support. People receive support from four major sources: their intimate relationships, their family units, their networks of friends, and the institutions or communities of which they are a part.

With respect to the first of these four types, Lowenthal and Weiss (1976) maintain that "*intimate relationships*—involving trust, support, understanding and the sharing of confidences" (p. 12)—are an important resource during stressful transitions. Moreover, "in the absence of overwhelming external challenge, most individuals find the motivation to live autonomous and satisfying lives only through one or more mutually intimate dyadic relationships" (p. 19). For instance, research indicates that the death of a spouse may be more traumatic for men than for women.

Men's inability to form close ties with other people may also contribute to their shorter life expectancy. As further indication of the power of intimate relationships, Lowenthal and Weiss suggest that "former intimate relationships, disrupted by death, distance, or interpersonal conflict, may continue to be a resource in terms of crisis, chronic and acute, throughout the life course. . . . Knowing through past experience that one is capable of having an intimate relationship, romantic or otherwise, may prove nearly as important a resource in difficult life situations as actually having an intimate at the time of crisis: a former relationship is reinforcing, and at the same time sustains hope for a future one" (1976, p. 147).

The *family unit* has long been a subject for study by sociologists and others, many of whom have attempted to define those qualities of the family that contribute to its ability to adapt to a crisis or to ease the process of adaptation for one of its members.

Thus, Angell focused on family integration, "the bonds of coherence and unity running through family life, of which common interests, affection, and a sense of economic interdependence are perhaps the most prominent" (Hill, 1965, p. 41) and on family adaptability (Hill, 1949).

Evidence of the importance of the family unit as a support system in times of transition comes from the San Francisco study. Lowenthal and Chiriboga (1975) found that of their four "stress" personality types, the challenged had the highest ratings on family mutuality, and the overwhelmed had the lowest. In addition, the challenged—those who were heavily stressed but not preoccupied with stress—had warmer and more positive feelings toward members of their families. A study of draft dodgers and deserters who fled to Canada during the Vietnam era (Levine, 1976) indicates that those who received parental support for their move adapted better to the new situation than did those whose parents disapproved of their action; the latter were more likely to seek professional help for their difficulties, and lack of parental support "remained a crucial factor until the young people joined a group that made them feel welcome and worthwhile" (p. 219).

The individual's *network of friends* is also an important social support system. One of the most stressful side effects of divorce for the woman is that often she loses many of the family friends that were available to her as part of a couple; such a loss is particularly likely if the marriage was a traditional one, in which family friendships were based on the common occupations of the husbands. Loss of the network of friends may also result from a residential move or from the death of a spouse, thus exacerbating the difficulties of those transitions. Conversely, the presence of friends can cushion sudden shock.

Kahn (1975) suggests that "the adequacy and stability of social support is a determinant of objective and subjective well-being, of performance in the major social roles, and of success in managing changes in those roles" (p. 3). As partial evidence for this proposition, he cites the findings of several investigations. For instance, in a 12-year study that compared the predominantly Italian-American residents of Roseto, Pennsylvania, with residents of four surrounding communities, death from myocardial infarction was found to be much less frequent among the Roseto citizens despite their bad dietary habits; this difference was attributed to their closely-knit families, mutually supportive and gregarious behavior, respect for the elderly, and use of family conclaves for the resolution of problems (Kahn, 1975, p. 4). A study of white-collar workers found that those who received high support from supervisors, peers, and subordinates were relatively unlikely to suffer from stress-related health disabilities. Similarly, a study of factory workers who had been laid off from their jobs found that stress-related physiological changes (elevation of cholesterol and serum uric acid levels) were more likely to occur among those workers who received little support from their family, friends, and neighbors.

What follows is an extreme example: Dimsdale (1976), discussing the coping strategies of people in Nazi concentration camps, cites group affiliation as one necessary type of behavior: "If an inmate was unsuccessful in affiliating with a group within the first few days of internment, his chances of survival were very limited" (p. 357). He adds that the group provided the individual with information, advice, protection, and—just as important—reinforcement of his or her sense of worth. Spaulding and Ford (1976) assert that one reason the Pueblo crew (imprisoned by North Korea in 1968) held up better than American prisoners of war during the Korean conflict was that the former were kept together rather than isolated, "thus reducing the stress upon the more dependent and vulnerable members of the crew" (p. 319). That there were no deaths during the imprisonment of the Pueblo crew is attributed to "the organization of the crew and group support [which] offered protection against the 'give-up-itis' previously described [i.e., with respect to Korean war prisoners] as a frequent cause of death" (p. 319).

Another category of support is found in *institutions:* religious institutions, political groups, work settings, social welfare, or community support groups, as well as various other more-or-less formal outside agencies are places to which an individual can turn for help. The need for such agencies has become more widely recognized: there has been a proliferation of counseling programs— which may take the form of seminars, lectures, workshops, or simply discussion groups—aimed at people experiencing particular transitions: midcareer change, divorce, retirement, a return to school.

Different people seek different kinds of institutional support. For instance, one study (Chiriboga, Coho, Stein, & Roberts, 1979) found that young women tend to seek support from a variety of sources, including clergy, counselors, and lawyers, whereas men and older women seek support from a more limited number of sources. Weiss (1973) reports that low-income, single-parent women seem to need a "temporary alliance with an authoritative figure" (p. 321) from whom they seek help of two kinds: the provision of concrete services and the provision of support and guidance. All too often, however, they have difficulty gaining access to such people. Moreover, even when they do succeed in making contact with professional helpers, those helpers—while able to offer specific services—generally cannot provide the needed support and guidance.

Counselors may also be a part of institutional and community support, through career development programs and the like. (Strategies that counselors may use to be part of individuals' social support systems are discussed in later chapters.)

Functions of support. According to Caplan, support systems function mainly to help "the individual mobilize . . . psychological resources and master . . . emotional burdens; they share . . . tasks; . . . they provide . . . extra supplies of money, materials, tools, skills, and cognitive guidance to improve . . . handling of . . . situations" (1976, pp. 5–6). Developing this even further, Kahn and Antonucci (1980) identify the functions of social support as an incorporation of one or more of the following key elements: affect, affirmation, and aid. *Affect* refers to expressions of liking, admiration, respect, or love; *affirmation* refers to expressions of agreement or acknowledgement of the appropriateness or rightness of some act or statement of another person; *aid* (or assistance) includes the exchange of things, money, information, time, and entitlements (pp. 267–268).

In addition to functions of affect, affirmation, and aid, I have included another: honest feedback. This refers to reactions offered which might be negative as well as positive. For example, if a parent is complaining about a teenager's behavior and telling how the teenager is going to be punished, a friend might suggest the coping strategy of selective ignoring; or if the parents always selectively ignore, a friend might suggest providing more structure. When friends are close, they can risk giving honest feedback.

Measurement of social support. Robert Kahn (1975) introduced the concept of the convoy of social support, "the idea that each person moves through the life cycle surrounded by a set of significant others related to him [or her either] by the giving or receiving of social support" (p. 1). Two notable features of this concept are, first, that it implies movement and change, and, second, that it emphasizes "the giving as well as the receiving of social support."

Kahn has used several methods to measure social support,

based on some operational definitions. "Convoy is a person-centered network; each convoy is a personal network of social support, defined around a focal person whose activities and well-being we wish to understand. . . . The network stops with that set of other persons with whom the focal person has direct relationship of support—receiving or giving. . . . The convoy structure is the delivery system" for social support (p. 278). An individual's convoy includes those who are stable over time and not role dependent, those somewhat role-related and likely to change over time, and those "tied directly to role relationships, and most vulnerable to role changes" (p. 273). Figure 3-3 illustrates a convoy with the focal person (P) in the center. The first circle around the person represents his or her stable supports, irrespective of roles; the second circle represents the group that is somewhat role dependent; the outside circle represents those supports most likely to change.

One way Kahn recommends as a measure of support is a procedure, based on the convoy model, in which the adult in transition is first asked to identify people close to him or her and place them in such categories as family, coworkers, other organizational members, neighbors, professionals, friends; and then asked to rate each person listed in terms of the social support offered. Three measures are thus obtained: one for affect, one for affirmation, one for aid (pp. 279–280).

Another way Kahn measures a person's convoy is by presenting him or her with an unlabeled diagram like the one in Figure 3-3, with the P for the focal person in the center but with no other labels. Kahn then asks the interviewee to enter in the pertinent circle the initials of "people who are important in your life right now. This you enter in the circle closest to P. Then fill in the next circle with the initials and category of persons next closest; then fill in the initials and category of persons who are part of your life but most likely to change if you changed jobs, moved, or changed roles" (p. 280).

This method of visualizing support in concentric circles enables us to see the degree to which a transition interrupts or increases an individual's support system. For example, geographical moves can interrupt the relationshp of husband and wife. Those wives who do not want to move—but who agree to it for the sake of the family—have deep resentment and anger. Thus, pre-move family members were close; but post-move they become "intimate enemies." If a retired couple moves away from many supports to a place with no supports, the transition can be very difficult. If, how-

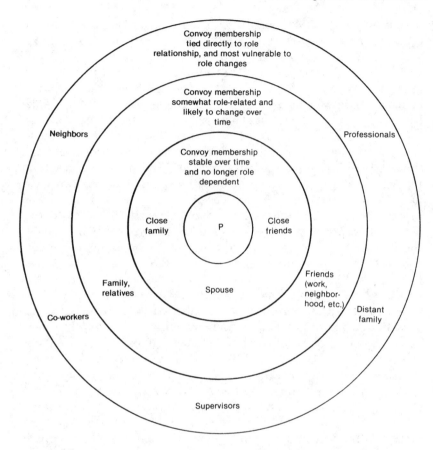

Figure 3–3. Hypothetical Example of a Convoy (From R. L. Kahn and T. C. Antonucci, "Convoys over the life course: Attachment, roles, and social support." In P. B. Baltes and O. G. Brim, Jr., eds., *Life-Span Development and Behavior,* Vol. 3, p. 273. New York: Academic Press, 1980. Reprinted by permission.)

ever, an individual moves to an area with more support than in the one left, obviously the transition will be much easier. Thus, it is not the particular transition but what it does to the individual's convoy. A recent widow was discussing the fluidity of her convoy. First, her greatest support, her husband, died prematurely. Next, some of her/their closest friends began to put up a psychological wall as she began to reinvest in life through a romantic involvement. She was perplexed and asked, "Aren't friendships that are close forever?"

Options

As we have already noted, individuals assess their transitions (primary appraisal) constantly. If the transition is appraised as significant, the individual begins the coping process that "requires a set of complex cognitive appraisal processes devoted to coping decisions" (Lazarus, 1980, p. 51). These secondary appraisals are related to the evaluation of the individual's resources for coping.

These resources, according to Sussman (1972), include the individual's options which may be actual, perceived, utilized, or created. Sussman, who discusses "an options-maintenance model" of retirement, sees that the central variable in determining whether a person is and feels successful when coping with retirement resides in the number of options that person can exercise. He further contends that options are directly related to self-esteem. Chronic job loss, feeling forced to stay in a low-level job or an unsatisfactory marriage erodes an individual's confidence and self-esteem (Pearlin, 1982).

Sussman discusses two levels of options: structural and psychological. Structural options are related to the availability of options. When unemployment is structural, more people are affected and the individual alone can do less about it. Opening up the opportunity structure requires political action, such as Claude Pepper's efforts in legislating changes in the retirement age, thus changing the options for older people. Psychological options are related to the individual's skill in *perceiving* and *utilizing* alternatives (Sussman, 1972, pp. 28–73).

A recent discussion with three 60-year-old widows in which each was assessing her options for intimacy serves as an illustration. One said, "I don't care about men. It's finding a man or woman with whom I can be close. I figure I have more chances with women." The other two disagreed, saying they cared about men. One said, "The demographics are against me. I'm miserable because I know I won't ever have another close relationship again." The other said, "I know I'll meet men—even if I have to run an ad in the *Washingtonian*." Clearly, assessment of actual options as well as perceiving and utilizing them is a very individual matter.

Another category of options emerges here: that of *created* options. The history of oppressed groups in this country—blacks, women, the old, other ethnic minorities—reflects a shift from a time when each accepted that there were no options for their group to a time when the group fights en masse to change the opportunity structure. The ability to create new options is not restricted to political activists. Career development experts run workshops designed specifically to help people take control of their lives, break out of their boxes, identify what they want, and create their own jobs and options.

The story of a 36-year-old man who became a paraplegic as the result of an automobile accident illustrates this point. After the initial physical battle to survive, he became preoccupied with how to live. Not surprisingly, at first he saw no options. Before the accident he had been a construction worker. Clearly he would be unable to continue that activity. His first attempt to build a new life was aborted when his application to law school was rejected. After exploration it became clear that this application had been a response to his mother's influence, who was a lawyer. A year after the accident, and before he clarified his vocational goals, he wrote his mother, "I want to share with you the perspective I now have on my future. Because of your love and support I am facing the future with courage, hope, and curiosity." The word *curiosity* showed that on a deep level he was going to make it, that he was going to create options, that he was going to be in control. And, in fact, soon afterwards he applied and was accepted in a school of architecture, thereby combining his interest in building with his disability. He created an option.

In a study of 50 clerical workers at the University of Maryland (Schlossberg & Charner, 1982), who were asked to identify a significant transition, the workers' identified transitions fell mostly in the family category, followed by geographical moving and work. When presented with a list of possible coping strategies (taken from Pearlin's 1978 study), they reported using most of them. When asked, "Generally, in change situations how do you perceive options?" 94 percent saw more than one. However, when asked, "For this transition how many options did you perceive?" over 34 percent saw only one. This indicates that individuals in transition usually see options, but under stress or when in the midst of a transition which has significantly altered their lives, they often "freeze" and can see only one option—which seriously affects their assimilation of the transition.

Possibly the most important task for helpers is to help individuals see options. People in transition often freeze and see few if any options; remembering that may be the key to helping some people cope more effectively. Providing the support and safety necessary for adults in transition to see alternatives is essential. A useful technique for doing this is group brainstorming, as illustrated by a gerontologist who uses this method to help adult children consider options for elderly parents. She feels brainstorming groups are particularly effective because participants help each other develop many more options than they otherwise would.

The concept of options also explains the difference between those who have a midlife crisis and those who experience a midlife transition. Everyone has a midlife transition, that is, a time when he or she begins to feel closer to death, faces physical and health issues, and reassesses the gap between aspiration and reality (Brim, 1976). But only a few run off, as did Gauguin or one president of a Maryland community college. Those having a "crisis" probably see no options.

Thus, the options can be both objective (at one time there were few professional jobs for blacks) and subjective (because I am black I will not apply to medical school). A fine line exists between actual options and the perception of actual options. Further, political action groups may assist in the creation of options for some groups, for example, women wanting to be astronauts. Thus, any discussion of options is highly complex, and involves the interaction of the actual world with the individual's perceptions and actions on the world.

Assets and Liabilities: Another Look

The discussion at the beginning of this chapter emphasized that an individual's ability to cope with transitions depends on the changing interaction and balance of his or her assets and liabilities. Thus, to study or understand an individual's balance, we need to ask such questions as these: What are the variables characterizing the particular transition in terms of timing, assessment, duration? What are the personal and demographic characteristics of the individual at the time of the transition? Is he or she sick or well? What is the individual's level of ego development, personality, and outlook? What coping strategies does he or she use? What types of support does the individual have? What are his or her actual and perceived options? These variables could also be scored as to whether the individual sees them as assets or liabilities.

In an initial transition instrument, which has already been administered to 50 clerical workers at the University of Maryland (Schlossberg & Charner, 1982), each individual rated each of the variables characterizing the transition, the individual, and the en-

THE TRANSITION event or nonevent resulting in change	COPING RESOURCES Balance of assets and liabilities			THE TRANSITION PROCESS Reactions over time for better or for worse
	VARIABLES CHARACTER-IZING THE TRANSITION	**VARIABLES CHARACTER-IZING THE INDIVIDUAL**	**VARIABLES CHARACTER-IZING THE ENVIRONMENT**	
TYPE	• *Event or nonevent characteristics*	• Personal and demographic characteristics	• Social support	**PHASES OF ASSIMILATION**
• Anticipated			–Types: intimate, family unit, friendship network, institution	• Pervasiveness
• Unanticipated	–Trigger	–Socioeconomic status	–Functions: affect, affirmation, aid, feedback	• Disruptions
• Nonevent	–Timing	–Sex role	–Measurement: convoy	• Integration, for better or for worse
• Chronic hassle	–Source	–Age and stage of life		**APPRAISAL**
	–Role change	–State of health	• Options	• Of transition, resources, results
CONTEXT	–Duration			• Of preoccupation *vs.* life satisfaction
• Relationship of person to transition	–Previous experience with a similar transition	• Psychological resources	–Actual	
	–Concurrent stress		–Perceived	
• Setting in which transition occurs		–Ego development	–Utilized	
	• *Assessment*	–Personality	–Created	
IMPACT		–Outlook		
• Relationships		–Commitments and values		
• Routines				
• Assumptions		• Coping responses		
• Roles				
		–Functions: Controlling situation, meaning, or stress		
		–Strategies: Information seeking, direct action, inhibition of action, intrapsychic behavior		

Figure 3–4. The Individual in Transition: A Detailed Look

108

vironment as plus, minus, or mixed. From these ratings, a balance score can be derived which indicates whether or not the individual has many or few resources at the time the instrument is administered. Further, the individual can determine where his or her liabilities lie. This instrument, though still in the preliminary stages of development, is discussed as a counseling tool in Chapter 4. All aspects of the framework, which conceptualizes the way an individual copes with transitions, are now in place. Figure 3-4 illustrates the central importance of assets and liabilities in the framework. The balance of those liabilities and assets not only determines how individuals cope with transitions but also indicates to helpers the areas in which they can be most effective in providing motivation, support, and resources in order to help adults who are having problems in their love, work, and play lives.

4

A Model for Helping Adults in Transition

The preceding chapters have explicated the adult experience by looking at many theorists who study adult development and presenting a transition framework for synthesizing the growing body of knowledge on the adult experience.

Now for the hard question: How can this transition framework assist professionals to help their clients gain a better understanding of their problems, which will lead to more effective working, loving, playing, living?

Very often, adults who experience difficulties coping with transitions are doubly disadvantaged because they feel that, as adults, they should be "mature," "competent," and able to make whatever adjustments are required of them. The transition framework can give assurance that such difficulties are, if not universal, at least widespread; that the problem is susceptible to analysis; that many transitions have similar patterns. For instance, it may be helpful for a client and counselor to realize that most changes have negative as well as positive aspects, and that the passage of time is an important dimension to all transitions.

But the question of how the effective helper can integrate appropriate helping skills and strategies with the transition framework still remains. I propose integrating two models: a content model—the transition framework—with a process model—a modification of Egan's helping model (1975). Indeed, the essence of this chapter—and of this book—is that *helping depends on integrating knowledge of adult development with the process skills of helping.*

110

Egan's Helping Model

Egan's developmental model of helping and interpersonal relating incorporates a simple three-pronged approach: *Explore* the client's situation, *understand* it more fully, and then help the client *cope* more effectively by taking appropriate action (or inaction). For each phase of helping, there are goals for the client and goals for the helper. The client goals are exploring, understanding, and acting; the helper's goals are responding appropriately, providing integrative understanding, and facilitating action.

Egan's model has a prehelping phase and three stages as follows[1]:

- Prehelping or precommunication phase: Attending
  Helper's goal: Attending. To attend to the other, both physically and psychologically; to give himself or herself entirely to "being with" the other; to work with the other.

- Stage I: Responding/self-exploration
  Helper's goal: Responding. To respond to the client and what he or she has to say with respect and empathy; to establish rapport and an effective collaborative working relationship with the client; to facilitate the client's self-exploration.
  Client's goal: Self-exploration. To explore his or her experiences, behavior, and feelings relevant to the problem in his or her life; to explore the ways in which he or she is living ineffectively.

- Stage II: Integrative understanding/dynamic self-understanding
  Helper's goal: Integrative understanding. The helper begins to piece together the data produced by the client in the self-exploration phase. The helper sees and helps the other identify behavioral themes or patterns and see the "larger picture." The helper teaches the client the skill of going about this integrative process himself or herself.
  Client's goal: Dynamic self-understanding. Developing self-understanding that sees the need for change, for action; learning from the helper the skill of putting together the larger picture for himself or herself; identifying resources, especially unused resources.

[1]From *The Skilled Helper,* 2nd Ed., by G. Egan. Copyright © 1975, 1982, by Wadsworth, Inc. Reprinted by permission of the publisher, Brooks/Cole Publishing Company, Monterey, California.

- Stage III: Facilitating action/acting

  Helper's goal: Facilitating action. Collaborating with the client in working out specific action programs; helping the client to act on his or her new understanding of himself or herself; exploring with the client a wide variety of means for engaging in constructive behavioral change; giving support and direction to action programs.

  Client's goal: Acting. Living more effectively; learning the skills needed to live more effectively and handle the social-emotional dimensions of life; changing self-destructive and other-destructive patterns of living; developing new resources.

In the first phase—responding/self-exploration—the helper responds by listening, with respect and empathy. This enables the client to describe the situation more fully. In the second stage of the model—integrative understanding—the helper begins to piece together the total picture from the data produced by the client in the first phase. Themes and patterns which underlie the initially stated problem are identified and shared with the client so that he or she can gain a fuller understanding of what the issue really is. The third phase—facilitating action—involves collaboration between helper and client to develop an action plan based on the new understanding of self.

A dimension of collaborating to implement the action agreed on has recently been added to the third or action stage by Egan (1982, p. 51). (He now terms his model the "problem-management helping model.") Egan's model, which is clear and easy to understand, has provided a basis for training beginning counselors and paraprofessionals. It is applicable to most situations where one person seeks the help of another. The model can be used with success if one moves through the stages sequentially and does not rush into problem-solving or integration before a full exploration of the situation.

A Helping Model Integrating Content and Process

Figure 4-1 illustrates how Egan's model of skillful use of appropriate helping strategies can be most effectively integrated into the transition framework, with the knowledge base of adult develop-

	EXPLORE	UNDERSTAND	COPE
GOALS OF HELPING			
KNOWLEDGE BASE	THE TRANSITION event or nonevent resulting in change Type Content Impact	COPING RESOURCES balance of assets and liabilities 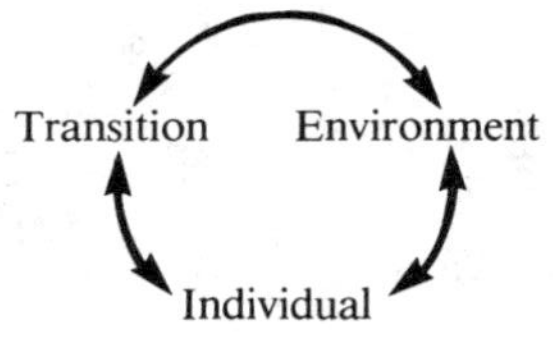 Transition — Environment — Individual	THE TRANSITION PROCESS changing reactions over time Phases of Assimilation Appraisal
HELPING SKILLS	PROVIDE NONBIASED RELATIONSHIPS Listen/ Respond Attend/ Focus	PROVIDE A NEW PERSPECTIVE Interpret Identify Themes Confront Present Information: Internal and External	INFLUENCE ACTION OR INACTION Problem Solving Teaching Coping Skills Structuring Support Counseling: Individual and Group

Figure 4–1. Helping Adults in Transition: A Content Process Model

113

ment. The content/process model has three major components: the goals of helping (exploration, understanding, and coping), the knowledge base (focus on the transitions, the coping resources or balance of assets and liabilities, and the transition process), and the helping skills (necessary for facilitation of exploration, understanding, and coping). These helping skills include provision of a safe nonbiased relationship and atmosphere, provision of a new and clarifying perspective, and influencing action or inaction through utilization of various strategies.

The goals of helping in the content/process model come from Egan's three phases. The final stage, which he refers to as facilitating action, I call *coping*. The use of this term stems from the definitions provided earlier. Both Lazarus and Pearlin identify inhibition of action as a coping strategy; and according to the dictionary, action means performing, whereas coping means to "struggle or contend . . . with some degree of success." Thus, the end result of helping in this integrated model is to help people deal, struggle, contend with life. It may or may not involve an action plan.

Counselors utilize a number of intervention strategies to help clients, as individuals or in groups, cope more effectively; these strategies need to be built on knowledge of adult development. As discussed earlier, Pearlin states that people cope in one of three ways: They act to change the situation, to control the meaning of the experience, or to control their own stress reaction (Pearlin & Schooler, 1978, p. 6). These three categories of coping provide the framework for helper intervention; that is, helpers can help clients change the situation, change the meaning of the situation, or control their own reactions. It is clear from examining adult development theorists on coping that stress, change, and transitions cannot be eliminated, but reactions can be modified. Thus, the three major sets of variables which are posited to intermediate between the transition and its resolution—the variables characterizing the particular transition, the individual, and the environment—need to be the target for helpers. (See again Figure 3-3), in which these variables are listed and placed so as to indicate how they moderate between the transition and the transition process.)

Of course, it is clearly impossible to mechanically link an intervention to a problem. Rather, helpers need to maintain a flexible approach to intervention. Helpers need to know the wide variety of strategies available to redress the balance of resources to deficits, and the helper and client need to collaborate on the appropriate stance to take, depending on the problem. For example, a woman whose frantic life included three small children, a three-fourths time job, and study to receive her certificate in gerontology faced problems which stemmed from her major commitments to work and to family. The helper helped change the meaning of the situation by helping her feel that both commitments were legitimate and that she did not have to prioritize. Further, when it became clear that the woman's intimate support—her husband—did not really approve of multiple roles and therefore had not assumed any new home responsibilities, the helper assisted her to change the situation by suggesting a way to negotiate new ground rules with her husband.

Clearly, the value orientation of the helper will determine what happens in counseling. A helper who is a believer that women must choose between family and work will engage in problem solving and prioritizing; a helper who believes that, for women, family must take precedence over career will help the client put her work and career on the back burner. It is important to remember that helpers have values which influence their interpretation of the situation and their eventual selection of strategies.

In another situation, a young woman in her twenties who supervised women in their sixties complained about her lack of control over the women in the work situation and about her feelings of incompetency. The focus of helping needed to be on developing an understanding of age bias, discovering ways that different generations can work together, and learning to control reactions to stress, all of which promote feelings of adequacy.

Sometimes psychotherapy or counseling can be the best vehicle for change. The individual may need help in changing perspective; for example, maybe a job loss can now be seen as an opportunity to regroup and rethink his or her career. The individual's coping repertoire may need to be increased, participation in a coping skills workshop may be indicated. The individual may need to relax and take up physical exercise.

In some situations the environment is the problem. An angry wife who moved because of her husband's job might feel cut off from her support system and see no options for regaining her community status. Here the counselor can focus on helping the client find a new supportive network.

In many career counseling cases, people catastrophize by saying, "I have no options. I can't . . . I can't." Helpers must focus often both on changing the individual's identity and creating new options.

By using the content/process model, the helper and client can look at the particular case and decide if the deficit is in the transition, the individual, the environment, or whether it is a combination—and whether the individual needs help in changing the situation, changing its meaning, or controlling stressful reactions. Thus the model can give assurance that many problems are susceptible to analysis.

Often, however, another perspective is most helpful. For example, a wider look at the process may help people experiencing a transition. A helper might provide a time perspective on the movement from pervasiveness to boundedness and remind the client that assimilation takes time and has a course to follow; that, for example, it is normal to mourn for a loss or to focus on a joyful addition to one's life. Often, people who lose a child—probably the most painful loss of all—complain that after a brief time their friends become impatient with their continued need to focus on the loss. Our model is meant to inspire a generosity toward oneself and others by showing that "normalcy" is not denial and rapid adjustment.

In addition to providing a perspective about transitions that have occurred, counselors can also stimulate adults facing transitions to begin anticipatory work by planning and preparing for such anticipated events or nonevents as retirement, parenthood, grandparenthood. As Parkes writes, "Adequate advance planning and preparatory training can transform what is potentially a major change in the assumptive world into a quite minor transition" (1971, p. 113). Levine points out that the single most effective strategy for coping with crisis is "seeking and utilizing information about a threatening situation" (1976, p. 26). Preretirement planning programs are based on this notion of advance planning.

But whatever the particular problem, the solution takes time. The more knowledgeable the counselor, the better he or she will be able to transmit information to the client so that people can deal with the psychic pain and turmoil that often accompany life's transitions. The content/process model provides a way for us to understand the nature and probabilities of change and personal assimilation of change—with an underlying set of assumptions about fluidity. The balance of an individual's assets and liabilities across all the variables is everchanging, and we cannot assume a static view of coping. The best coper armed with the best coping strategies can, in fact, fall apart. What we really need is a perspective on ourselves and on dealing with adult transitions and with life—a perspective that, in the last analysis, helps us to be a little kinder toward ourselves. By describing the transition and the variables which mediate it, helpers can offer a clarifying view of how transitions are assimilated—whether they are geographic moves, major surgery, job promotions, retirements, or other changes.

How the Content/Process Model Works

As we have indicated, the goals of helping rest not only on a knowledge base, but also on the process skills that facilitate exploring, understanding, and coping. Thus a helper working with an adult who is deciding to return to school, initiate a divorce, or have a child late in life, needs to explore that transition for that individual—what triggered it, what impact it will have. To enable full exploration of the transition, helpers need to establish nonbiased relationships. The process of helping includes the skills of listening, responding, attending, and focusing with empathy, genuineness, respect, and concreteness. To help an adult understand more fully the implications of returning to school or initiating a divorce, the helper needs to know what the individual man or woman brings to the situation, what assets or liabilities he or she has. The process of helping includes clarifying by interpreting, identifying themes, confronting, and presenting information related to both the internal and external experience. To help individuals cope and decide what action to take, helpers need to know how adults assimilate change. The process of helping includes solving problems, teaching coping skills, structuring support, and counseling.

The following look at how a helper might assist a midlife woman confronted with an ailing mother-in-law indicates the way this three-component model integrating content and process works.

- *Exploration.* Woman: "If my mother-in-law moves in, I have to give up my life dream of becoming an art dealer. I've been on hold raising my children—now it's my turn."

  Adult development knowledge (content): The helper needs to know that this is a health transition for the mother-in-law which has the potential for changing the daughter-in-law's routines, relationships, assumptions, and roles, and that it has the potential for being a major transition.

  Helper's attending response (process): Open question: "Can you explain a little more what this would mean in terms of your life?" Reflection: "So really, you're feeling caught in between your own needs and your mother-in-law's needs."

- *Understanding.* Woman: "First I was a wife, then a mother, now a daughter-in-law. How can I be responsible to others and attend to myself?"

  Adult development knowledge (content): The helper needs to know about the coping resources for the mother-in-law, daughter-in-law, and whole family. What is the balance of assets and liabilities? What are the supports? What are the options? What are the coping responses?

  Helper's clarifying response (process): "You seem to feel out of control—that you will be submerged. Let's talk about your fear of losing control over your life." *Focusing:* Helper stays with daughter-in-law.

- *Coping:* Woman: I realize now that the issue is not my mother-in-law but my inability to stand up for my rights and not feel guilty."

  Adult development knowledge (content): The helper needs to know the range of coping strategies, and ways to link the woman to parent care support groups. The helper also needs to know that the assumption that this is a no-win situation must be challenged.

  Helper's influencing response (process): "It seems that we have separated two aspects of the situation. You cannot control your mother-in-law's needing care, but we can explore how you can control your role in the situation. Let's brainstorm about that."

It seems complex for helpers to integrate a knowledge and skill base and then behave spontaneously with a client. However, when helpers have grounded themselves in adult development theory, this knowledge supplies them with the base upon which to reflect, to identify themes, and to initiate appropriate action. It is the knowledge base which makes the skills more meaningful. To illustrate the utility of the model integrating content and process, each phase will be discussed in greater detail.

Helping Skills that Encourage Exploration

This section focuses on the first stage of helping—exploring the transition. From the point of view of the adult in transition, the task is to articulate an area or issue—either positive or negative—

that needs elaboration. Often what a helper initially discusses is only the tip of the iceberg. Egan defines the client's goal as exploration of "experiences, behavior, and feelings relevant to the problematic in his or her life; to explore ways in which he or she is living ineffectively" (1975, p. 30); and I would add, to explore ways to work, love, and play more fully.

Counselors can help others to honestly and openly explore, or they can cut off exploration by a comment which distracts, criticizes, or puts the client down. The effective helper of adults needs both content and process knowledge. The content includes knowledge of the transition context out of which most adult problems and possibilities arise; the process includes communication skills which enable the process of exploration to take place.

Many of us have told someone an innermost thought or feeling only to feel rebuffed and stupid as a result of a well-meaning but inappropriate response from the listener. We have also probably experienced just the opposite—a feeling of being accepted and understood which leads to free exploration of the issue. Although there are many excellent texts on counseling, a brief review of some basic skills will refresh the experienced counselor and hopefully stimulate the new helper to dig further and learn more.

Providing Nonbiased Relationships

"The heart of the therapeutic process is the relationship established between counselor and client" (Brammer & Shostrom, 1977, p. 149). Adults repeatedly state that support and understanding are the crucial ingredients that they seek in a helping relationship. The first few minutes of such a relationship often serve to demonstrate to them whether these elements are present. Most adults are apprehensive about seeking help; many have never done it before. Many fear rejection; many fear that their age will be seen as *the* relevant variable. Most adults are caught up in the notion that they should be able to manage their own lives without help. They are all vulnerable at this point.

What helpers can do when adults seeking help enter their doors is to show that they are unbiased. Helpers can demonstrate their support and understanding by listening and trying to formulate accurate responses. Helpers can listen to the uncertainties and concerns of their clients and let them know by their responses that they are truly trying to understand. Helpers can reinforce clients for the often difficult task of talking to someone about their dreams, hopes, and aspirations.

Listening/responding skills. Important skills which underlie a nonbiased helping relationship are those of effective listening and responding. Listening and responding skills have repeatedly been lauded as the cornerstone of good counseling. They open up communication and help build rapport; they also help keep the helper's biases in check. When a helper truly listens to someone, he or she is tuned into the other's perspective, trying to make sense out of what the client is saying about his or her world. If helpers impose their values—giving advice or sharing their own experiences with clients—at that moment they are probably not listening to what is being said.

Empathy is central to the success of the beginning phase of helping. Almost every textbook on counseling deals with that issue. Egan lists "primary-level accurate empathy" as a key to facilitating exploration. He writes, "The goal of . . . empathy is to communicate to the client that the helper understands his [or her] world from the client's perspective" (1975, p. 73). Bramer and Shostrom suggest that empathy means to perceive the client's "internal frame of reference" (1977, p. 168).

One technique for helping helpers empathize is as follows:

1. Have a client state something either positive or negative, for example, "I'm thrilled that our daughter had a baby girl. It will be fun to take care of the baby."

2. The helper listens carefully and says verbatim what the client has said: "I'm thrilled that our daughter had a baby girl. It will be fun to take care of the baby."

3. Having said it, the helper begins to feel it. The helper then goes one step further saying, "I feel excited to be in a new role."

This process enables the helper to feel how the client feels. It can be done nonverbally, so the helper can be empathic by reflecting back the feelings and content of what the client said.

Helpers should *not* try to reinforce clients' feelings that what they have to say is unimportant, that what they are thinking is silly, that they are too old to want to change their life or career, that they should be able to work out their concerns without help.

For many, listening and support may be all that is necessary.

Others may need help in sorting out the decisions that they are facing and in establishing new directions. If the helper has listened carefully and demonstrated support, he or she will be able to work cooperatively in considering these possible options. If, on the other hand, the adult across from the helper perceives that the helper is judging him or her by some myth or bias, the helper will probably never get to that point.

An effective way to implement the goal of establishing a nonbiased relationship is through a process of self-verbalization. What did the helper think about or verbalize internally before finally making a response to someone else? The whole process of self-verbalization is an important focus, particularly for controlling biases in working with adults.

Although it may seem like a split-second process, we all go through a sort of self-monologue before we respond. We probably do more of this when we are beginning an initial interaction with someone, for we are trying harder to understand and to say the right thing.

One way to use this self-monologue to help us formulate more effective responses is to make it more explicit. Several researchers have explored and investigated a cognitive self-instructional modeling approach to learning empathy and communications skills (Meichenbaum, 1973; Ochiltree, Brekke, & Yager, 1975).

An adaptation of their work contains the following self-verbalization list of questions (Schlossberg, Troll, & Leibowitz, 1978, p. 118):

1. What is the adult/client expressing verbally/nonverbally?

2. How do I really feel about what a person his or her age should do?

3. How would I feel if I were in his or her place?

4. What would I really like to say? What's wrong with it?

5. What will I say? What would be the least biased or most effective response I could make?

By answering these questions, at first verbally and then nonverbally to themselves, helpers can begin to focus on some of the self-verbalization process that precedes their actual response. This might start with whispering the answers and go on to covertly answering them.

The main caution is to beware every time we find ourselves thinking, "He or she is too young or too old to do such-and-such." The issue of nonbias is central to effective counseling.

Attending/focusing skills. The skills designated as attending are central to this first exploratory phase and typically focus on the client and his or her needs and wishes, thoughts, and feelings. Ivey and Simek-Downing (1980) point out that beginning helpers often rush into the problem-solving phase before really listening and exploring the issue. These authors identify the key attending skills as open questions, paraphrases, reflections of feeling, and summarizations. Each of these stimulates and encourages the person being helped to discuss, disclose, open up, explore.

Open questions "usually begin with 'what,' 'how,' 'why,' 'could' . . . [they] facilitate . . . self-exploration . . . [and] discussion" (p. 74). For example, someone says, "I've just had a baby." Instead of responding, "Isn't that wonderful, what's her name?" the helper might say, "How has this changed your life?" or, "Could you share a bit of how you are experiencing this?" or even, "I'd really like to hear about it." Open questions let the client discuss and explore the transition.

Paraphrases are useful when a client has been discussing a transition for some time and it is necessary to "check on [the] clarity of counselor understanding." To do that, the counselor paraphrases, or repeats "back to [the] client the essence of a few past verbalizations and thoughts." A fine line exists between repeating verbatim and paraphrasing—but the line does exist. The dictionary definition states that a paraphrase is "a restatement . . . giving the meaning in another form . . . rewording." A paraphrase is a breather which can clarify and keep the discussion focused.

Reflections of feeling require the helper to be able to identify the feeling or emotion being discussed, label it, and reflect it back. "You sound thrilled about this change in your life." "I hear your anger." "You sound both thrilled and frightened." Listening for the emotional overtone and reflecting it back reassures the client that he or she has been heard.

Summarizations recapitulate the interview or parts of the interview. They often form the bridge between the three phases of helping, as when the counselor says, "We have been talking at some length on how your wife's disability has changed your lives. The main change you mentioned is your having to take over roles you had felt were inappropriate for a man." The interviewer's summary reflects selection—and therefore bias—of what the main points are. An interviewer with knowledge of the degree to which transitions have impact on an individual's life will focus on impact and change. If an interviewer is committed to an age/stage theory of adult development, the interviewer will relate the disability to stage in life. If the interviewer is committed to the notion of variabilty and is anti-age/stage theory, the focus may be on the alteration of the client's life. Again; the focusing—open questioning, reflecting, and summarizing—is grounded in the helper's implicit or explicit views of aging and human behavior.

Discussions between two people can follow many possible avenues. Focus can be on the problem, the person in need of help, the helper, or the environment. Ivey and Simek-Downing (1980) give examples of different ways to focus:

1. Client focus: "Donna, you're not sure what you should do . . ."
2. Others' focus: "Donna's been giving you a bad time lately . . ."
3. Topic focus: "Abortion . . . you're thinking of an abortion . . ."
4. Counselor focus: "I could share a similar experience. I, too, got pregnant . . ."
5. Mutual focus: "Right now I have several reactions to you . . ."
6. Cultural-environmental focus: "Sounds like a problem many women face in a sexist culture . . ." (pp. 72–73).

How a helper focuses at the beginning of an interaction will greatly affect its direction. A helper who is a nurse may want to think whether it would be most helpful to respond to a presurgical patient by focusing on the surgery, the patient's feelings, the nurses' experiences, other patients' experiences, or on environmental pollution which causes many illnesses. Sometimes, of course, it is important to focus on several dimensions. One of the important aspects of helping adults is flexibly incorporating several focusing dimensions. First and foremost, the focus is always on the person. But, secondarily, focus is on adult development—including the context discussed earlier and the knowledge base described in previous chapters.

As a person speaks of his or her concerns, the helper may digress by asking about the others in the client's situation, but the focus should remain on the person. For example, in the case of a middle-aged woman with an ailing mother-in-law who needs care, the focus belongs on the woman caught in between, not on the mother-in-law or the husband, and on the general problem of women's roles including assuming responsibility for aging parents. If the helper is working with the older parent in poor health, the focus will, of course, be on that person. Further, helpers also decide whether to focus on the person's feelings or the person's problems.

In addition to Ivey and Simek-Downing's and Egan's descriptions of attending/focusing skills, Brammer (1979) also provides a typology, which identifies these skills as listening skills (attending, paraphrasing, clarifying, perception checking), leading skills (indirect, direct, focusing, questioning), reflecting skills (feeling, content, experience), and summarizing skills (feeling, content, process).

Summary of Exploring Skills

Exploration is facilitated by content skills—which enable a helper to find out what the person is experiencing—and process skills—which enable the helper to attend to and focus on the client.

The following short interaction illustrates the usefulness of combined content and process skills.

In passing a secretary in the hall, the following exchange occurred:

SUPERVISOR: How are things going? (*Open question*)

SECRETARY: Good and bad.

SUPERVISOR: Good and bad? Do you feel like sharing any of the good and bad? (*Open question*)

SECRETARY: Well, Jim and I broke up.

SUPERVISOR: You're feeling upset. (*Reflection of feeling*)

SECRETARY: I didn't want it. Jim did it.

SUPERVISOR: A broken marriage is painful especially when it was unexpected. (*Knowledge of transition*)

SECRETARY: I don't known why Jim's feeling he needed freedom—why he suddenly left. I'm unhappy.

SUPERVISOR: You feel out of control of what's going on. (*Knowledge of transition process; reflection of feeling based on transition knowledge*)

To restate: The first goal of helping is exploration. Usually someone is discussing a transition that occurred, is occurring, or will occur. The knowledge base about transitions provides content to the helper so he or she can help effectively. Transitions can be classified as to type (anticipated, unanticipated, nonevent, or chronic hassle), context (relationship of person to transition, setting in which transition occurs), and impact (relationships, routines, assumptions, roles).

Helpers need to put aside their opinions, biases, and assumptions so that they can create a nonbiased setting in which full exploration of the transition can occur. The skills to provide this are listening and responding as well as attending and focusing—and include open questioning, reflecting, paraphrasing, and summarizing. When helpers utilize these skills, full exploration is possible. Janis demonstrates the utility of counselors beginning relationships with unconditional regard in which positive, nonbiased, accepting comments are made (1982). This acceptance helps clients overcome initial resistance and begins to build the trust that leads logically to the next step—understanding.

Helping Skills to Facilitate Understanding

Full exploration is occasionally all someone needs. More frequently, however, a person needs also to understand what is underlying the particular issue.

According to Egan, the goal of Stage II in his model is to "help the client achieve . . . understanding" of self, problems, and world which would lead to effective action (1975, p. 137). Egan points to some evidence which suggests that "acquisition of a new conceptual scheme for understanding one's behavior can mediate behavioral change" (p. 128).

Egan points to the basic shift in the helper's role from Stage I to Stage II:

> In order to help the client reach dynamic self-understanding, the helper shifts the perspective of the counseling process in Stage II. In Stage I the helper concentrates on the client's frame of reference. He or she tries to see the world from the client's perspective rather than his or her own. Primary-level accurate empathy is the principal tool used in this process. The helper tries to get a feeling for the experience of the client and then communicates this understanding to him or her. Generally, throughout the self-exploration process, the helper tries to understand the client's feelings, experiences, and behavior from the client's point of view.
> In Stage II, however, there is a shift. The counselor now helps the

client see the world from a more objective point of view. If the counselor sees the world only as the client does, he or she will have little to offer him or her. The client's implicit interpretation of the world is in some ways distorted and unproductive, at least in the areas of life in which he or she is having problems. The helper assumes, however, that the client has the resources eventually to see the world, especially the world of his or her own behavior, in an undistorted way. He or she needs a specific set of skills to help the client come to this kind of understanding. He or she does not ignore the client's feelings, experiences, and behaviors. Indeed, the helper uses these to help the client see the world more objectively. This change in perspective is necessary if Stage II is to be a bridge between the data of Stage I and the action programs of Stage III (pp. 131–132).

In order to shift from Stage I to Stage II, the helper needs to be rooted in adult development theory so he or she can listen with a "third ear." This is where the knowledge base of adult development becomes the cornerstone for effective helping of adults. This knowledge provides the basis for seeing the bigger picture (p. 133). Egan describes the heart of this as "mutuality," that is, as "each person moving out toward the other in understanding, self-sharing, caring" (p. 133) and as direct feedback. After a nurse in the hospital has listened empathically to the patient who is frightened of surgery, the nurse begins to listen differently and help the patient understand the issue as loss of control. But more than that, the nurse who knows about sex roles and the midlife crisis might then understand the particular salience of "loss of control." If the patient is a top male executive, and the operation is due to a serious illness, the patient may be frightened of two kinds of control loss: (1) the control loss that any surgery represents and (2) the control or power loss that accompanies the fear of getting older (and dying) and the fear that he or she has not realized his or her goals. In short, the surgery may be triggering the soul searching that often accompanies an individual's sense of being middle-aged. Thus, an exchange with a nurse who can respond and "go beyond the expressed to the implied" (p. 135) might be like this:

PATIENT: I'm afraid to be so at the mercy of the doctors—I'm afraid because I'm used to being so in charge of everything. It feels peculiar to not have charge of when, what, how, and why.

NURSE: The operation represents a new role for you, one that is scary? Maybe we can talk a little more about that.

PATIENT: It makes me realize my power might not be forever.

This exchange took less than one minute but reflected the nurse's awareness of adult development issues and skill in helping.

Providing New Perspectives

There are many skills helpers can employ to further understanding but all must aim at providing new perspectives by clarifying, for it is only through clarification that understanding is possible. If the helper and client are fuzzy in their discussions, if in fact the discussions mask the real issues, then clarification—and new perspectives—will not be possible. The skills which lead to clarification include interpretation, identification of themes, confrontation, and presentation of information for both the internal and external experience.

Interpretation. Interpretation is the cornerstone of this phase of the helping process. "Interpreting is an active helper process of explaining the meaning of events to helpees so that they are able to see their problems in new ways" (Brammer, 1979, p. 91). "An interpretation is used to integrate cognitive and affective states" (Ivey & Simek-Downing, 1980, p. 81). Interpretations are no better than the helper. Clearly the more we know about adult behavior, the more we can listen to the specific messages in the particular exchange and relate them to larger issues.

The content part of the integrated model—the transition framework—can provide a backdrop for interpretation. The helper can listen specifically to the balance of assets and liabilities the individual expresses. What are the characteristics of the particular transition? What about its timing, duration, source? What are the individual's personal strengths and weaknesses? How does the individual's environment appear in terms of support and options? The helper can lead the client to explore his or her assets and liabilities. This discussion can form the basis for interpretation.

The integrated content/process model offers a way to analyze the missing link(s) between transition and assimilation. Since the model identifies three clusters of variables—those characterizing the particular transition, individual, and environment—it is possible to examine each set to find the crux of the problem. Is the individual's problem related to the nature of the particular transition? To his or her support systems? To his or her maturity and coping skills? To options? For example, a person will react differently depending on whether the transition is permanent, on time, a role increment or deficit. A woman who becomes a grandparent at 40 when her daughter is 16 and unmarried will obviously react to the transition of grandparenthood differently than the woman of 65 whose daughter has her first child at 40. Again, what is significant is not the specific transition—retirement, grandparenthood—but the individual's relationship to the transition. For example, if counselor and client realize the particular difficulty is with the timing of the event, they will plan intervention accordingly.

The individual's difficulty might, however, be connected with the pre- and post-transition environment, especially in regard to support systems. Two women widowed "on time" may react very differently because of the difference in their social support systems if, for example, one lives in a community with a great deal of interaction and connection between neighbors and the other lives in an environment with friends not geographically available. The social support system for the first is much more inclusive and helps greatly ease the loss.

Institutional support in the individual's environment should not be underestimated. An example is the case of an energetic entrepreneur who became ill with melanoma. He was turned down for a major grant when the foundation learned of his illness. Fortunately, his oncologist wrote a convincing letter about the man's ability to carry out his work. Reactions by institutional personnel can provide needed support to an individual or foster devastating consequences. Concerned counselors can negotiate for humane support.

Assimilation of any transition is further mediated by the individual's characteristics, or what we might call "psychosocial competence." Some people are more "together"; some are in better health; some are members of a social class with available options; some are socialized to be independent. What the individual brings to a transition cannot, in any way, be ignored. To assume, however, that everyone who is depressed during a transition is neurotic is often a result of bias or lack of information or understanding. While it might be uncomfortable, a state of depression or anxiety during periods of transition—particularly those characterized by multiple changes—is a rather normal response to stress-producing situations. How the individual copes with this stress is the important factor.

In summary, the counselor can help in the understanding and redefinition of the transition; the counselor can assist the client to develop insight into the problem. Is there a need for new institutional and personal support systems? New coping skills? In actual practice, of course, understanding the problem and solution are not always so clear-cut.

Identification of themes. Closely related to interpretation is what Egan refers to as identifying themes (1975, p. 143). The ability to identify underlying themes depends on the skill of "advanced accurate empathy" and the knowledge of recurring themes adults express throughout the life course. "Advanced accurate empathy gets at the feelings and meanings that are somehow buried, hidden, or beyond the immediate reach of the client" (p. 135). The recurring themes identified in Chapter 1 provide a conceptual framework and knowledge base for the helper, for underneath most discussions are underlying questions about identity, intimacy, generativity, competency, autonomy, and belonging. For example, a woman interviewed about transitions reported that her husband, parents, and siblings were all dead. As she talked, the interviewer reflected, "You're feeling scared. Will you ever have an intimate relationship again?"

This skill—identifying issues and themes—shows very directly the interplay between adult development knowledge and helping skills.

The following exchange between a helper and an adult woman reflects this integration of skill and knowledge:

HELPER: What I hear you saying is that you're feeling caught in between children, parents, self, husband. The struggle to figure out a balance between your needs, wishes, future, and your responses to others' needs is sometimes overwhelming and confusing.

CLIENT: I'm really angry that everyone feels it is my job to care for my mother-in-law—yet I do feel caught. I'm especially furious with Jim who has no appreciation of me.

HELPER: So no one is really on your team. You're all alone in this struggle—all alone except for your guilt and anger.

CLIENT: God, I do feel alone, and I also know that whatever I do, I'll lose. If I take her in and give up my new training program, I'll be furious; if I say no, she goes to a nursing home. Jim will be furious; I'll feel guilty. Why is this happening to me?

HELPER: You keep coming back to this aloneness you feel—no one to help you, no one to consider you first, really no allies, just family enemies about to undo the progress you have made.

CLIENT: What I really feel like doing is splitting. No one loves me, and right now I hate everyone.

In this case the client saw the situation as negative, off time. She felt she had no support and saw no options. Her balance was heavy on the liability side. The issue of aloneness was central.

Confrontation.   Confronting necessitates that the helper point out what seems to be going on, especially in regard to discrepancies. For example, a helper might say, "On the one hand, you say you want to change careers; on the other hand, you keep pointing out you have no options." Or, "You say you really want to write a book, yet you schedule yourself so tightly you have no time."

Confrontation is not a strategy to use in the exploration phase. At the beginning, the client wants to be listened to; it is after the relationship is safe that the client can face what he or she is doing that sabotages his or her stated plan.

Another point about confrontation: It does not have to be—nor should it be—damaging. Brammer's discussion presents confrontation as a very supportive strategy (1979). Egan also underscores the need for care. Confrontation needs to be "a responsible unmasking of the discrepancies, distortions, games, and smokescreens the client uses to hide both from self-understanding and from constructive behavioral change" (1975, p. 158). Confrontation is also used as a challenge to the client to be more than he or she is currently. "Confrontation is an invitation by the helper to the client to explore his or her defenses" (p. 158).

Egan further points out the importance of style when confronting. It can feel like an attack when done improperly; it can feel like caring when done with empathy (pp. 165–168).

Presentation of information: internal/external.   People are reassured to learn that it is normal to be upset when they lose control over their destiny. Understanding of self and others widens with the knowledge that it is easier to deal with a transition which occurs when expected. So often counseling training stresses the value of developing active listening and reflecting skills and overlooks the value of providing such appropriate, timely information which, in many instances, is among the most therapeutic of interventions. Take the case of a man at age 55 who is laid off because his plant relocated, and is unable to move because of his wife's job and his children's senior high school status. He needs not only information for his outer experience, and the external world (what are the job possibilities; where and how to find counseling), but also information for his inner experience, his internal world (how usual it is for people in his situation to feel depressed and worthless).

Weiss (1975) calls this providing a cognitive framework so that adults can better understand their internal and external situations. He organized a program to help people weather the transition of marital separation and divorce, called Seminars for the Separated, which presented information on both the inner and outer experience. A major component featured was a series of lectures on such topics as the emotional impact of separation, issues likely to create conflict between separated spouses (property division, support, custody, visitation), and the problems of building a new life organization and a new identity. Such information extends participants' understanding and capacity to grasp what they are experiencing.

Information on the inner experience is especially appropriate in counseling the midlife woman, who often believes that her problems are unique and that her reactions to the problems are eccentric, deviant, or even "crazy." By making her aware that other women commonly experience the same emotions—whether dismay and resentment at having to make a residential move to accommodate the demands of her husband's job, fear and anxiety over returning to school, or boredom and frustration at the tedium of daily life—the counselor can do much to alleviate the woman's distress.

The counselor can also communicate to both midlife women and men helpful information about adult development. For instance, women may find relief in knowing that adults in the middle years commonly experience a sense of powerlessness and sadness, of loss of control over their own destinies, of missed opportunities; that transitions that are on schedule are easier to deal with than those that occur off time (for instance, retirement at age 65 rather than 45, widowhood at age 70 rather than age 35); that the first reaction to a transition is often emotional numbness; that the emotional "yo-yo syndrome" is common following divorce. People may find relief in knowing that some of their feelings of regret and sadness are occasioned by the reemergence of the dreams of their younger years and by the discrepancy between their earlier aspirations and their actual achievement. As they face retirement, both men and women can be helped by knowing that part of their anxiety may be based on a perceived loss of role and of status.

The helper's ability to provide the cognitive framework that can, in fact, extend the individual's understanding depends on knowledge of adult development. The more a helper studies, the more that helper can be effective. To illustrate, Lowenthal and Pierce found that "the sense of inner control was clearly the most important of the pretransitional cognitions, being strongly associated with a positive attitude toward the transition, as well as with planning for it" (1975, p. 209). Thus, the counselor who knows what kinds of transitions adults are likely to go through, and what feelings are likely to accompany such transitions, can help clients understand and plan for the transition, thus enabling them to develop an inner locus of control.

The integrated content/process model provides the link between intervention and theory, enabling the helper to provide the appropriate cognitive material for both individuals and groups. Examining the transition framework (as in Figure 3-3) in their discussions can be of particular value to retirement groups, returning women, and the newly disabled because it helps group members identify which variables are giving them trouble. Thus the knowledge base provides a cognitive framework about transitions, which enables people to get a better understanding of why they react differently to different life events and to feel reassured by knowing more about their own feelings and the origins and roots of those reactions.

Helping Skills to Promote Coping

Egan emphasizes that the goal of helping is action; however, the end goal of helping may be better seen as integration—or beginning to integrate—through the determination of an action or inaction. (An illustration of an inaction is sitting tight and not selling the house right after the spouse's death.)

It is in this phase of helping that the helper becomes more active. In fact, Ivey and Simek-Downing refer to influencing behavior as the "involvement of the therapist in effecting client growth or change. Attending behavior is critical for client growth, but if used as the sole vehicle for change, client growth can be slow and arduous . . . . All theories of counseling in some way incorporate the idea of the counselor as an agent of change and growth. By their very presence, counselors influence clients" (1980, p. 55). Brammer corroborates this view by describing "helping skills for positive action" (1979, p. 126).

Just as listening and attending skills help the client explore and understand, influencing skills help the client make changes and cope more effectively. It is important to note that these skills are usually delayed until the counselor understands the nature of the situation and has established mutual trust and respect—and the client wants to take action or to cope more effectively. It is at this point that the helper begins to influence the client to formulate a plan for integration or resolution of the issue. Although Ivey refers to this as influencing, I see it also as collaboration between client and helper on ways to cope more effectively.

That counselors have a role in influencing the outcome or stimulating new self-discovery which, in turn, can lead to new behavior, action, and integration is agreed to by most writers on this subject. Interestingly, Greenberg and Kahn suggest expanding Egan's three-stage model to include "stimulation." This emphasizes that counselors need to stimulate their clients to discover new understandings, and thus more effective coping. "Stimulation methods activate a reorganization of clients' views of themselves and the world by uncovering and bringing into awareness new information . . . Stimulation   skills . . . help   promote   perceptual change" (1979, p. 140). The authors review a number of methods intended to prompt awareness. These include "focusing, structured exercises, . . . Gestalt experiments, . . . evocative reflection, . . . fantasy, . . . encounter" (p. 141).

As we discuss helping skills to promote coping, it is important to keep in mind that, according to transition theory, there is no final outcome; rather, integration is part of a process over time. This means that strategies utilized at different points in the transition process will differ. This is illustrated in a retrospective study of parents' preferences for counseling strategies during the period of time following the death of a child. At the beginning, when parents feel numb, they are helped mostly by a "compassionate listener" (Alexy, 1982, p. 505). Later, when parents yearn for their lost child, the need is for a counselor who deals with ideas. Thus, during the phase of pervasiveness, attending to feelings in a supportive way is most useful. During the period of integration, attention to ideas and action take over (p. 506). Thus, our strategies for helping a client cope with a transition are not static or once and for all; rather they are differential and change as time goes on.

Among the strategies counselors can use to stimulate action (or inaction) and help people cope more effectively are problem solving, teaching coping skills, structuring support, and counseling. Each of these is discussed in the following sections.

Problem Solving

After helping the client with exploration and understanding, how can the helper best promote coping? In order to deal constructively with the issue at hand, for some, psychotherapy is the answer; for others, skill training in assertiveness, negotiation skills, coping, or stress management is called for; for still others, gaining perspective on transitions in general is sufficient. There is no one solution for everyone, no one-to-one match of problem and solution. Thus, problem solving is one of the most important skills for promoting coping.

Egan states, "The purpose of a problem-solving program is to help the client act." Basically, problem solving is a "way of ordering one's thoughts and resources systematically in searching out viable courses of action" (1975, p. 199). Although differences exist in the exact ordering of steps, most problem-solving scenarios include identifying the problem, setting a goal, exploring alternatives, selecting a course of action, planning the course of action, and taking the first step of the action plan. Clearly, problem solving skills connect to decision-making skills.

Problem identification and goal setting. Successful problem solving goals *must* be concrete. For example, a problem vaguely identified as incompetency needs to be turned into a goal, such as the ability to conduct a successful supervisory session. The more specific the problem and goal, the easier to plan a course of action.

Exploring alternatives. Because exploring alternatives is also part of decision-making, the model for decision-making presented by Tiedeman and O'Hara (1963) that has proved useful in counseling is just as useful here. In this schema, all decisions have two stages: anticipation and implementation. Both of these stages have two substages.

In the anticipation stage, the first substage is *exploration,* which has two aspects: self-exploration, including clarification of values, assessment of interests, and identification of skills; and exploration of the area in which the decision is to be made, including development of alternatives, gathering of information on these alternatives, and assessment of the probable outcomes of various alternatives. Gradually, the individual enters into the second substage, *crystallization,* in which patterns emerge, some possibilities are discarded, and the options are narrowed down. Finally, a choice is made, and then the individual organizes to implement that choice.

In implementation, the second major stage, the individual first moves into the new situation (*induction*). At this point, the orientation is primarily receptive—a willingness to accommodate to the perceived expectations of others. As the individual gains confidence in the new situation or role and comes to be accepted by others, he or she becomes more assertive and gradually enters into the final substage of *integration*.

Exploration, the first substage of the entire process, is crucial for it determines everything that follows, as it does in the integrated content/process model. If an individual is too timid during the exploration phase, whole areas of possibilities are cut off, and the future becomes unnecessarily restricted. For example, until recently, very few women have become outstanding physical scientists or top business executives. One of the reasons is that at no point in their lives were they encouraged to explore or even consider these possibilities. If an entire group limits its fantasies to getting married, having children, and keeping house—or to going into one of a very limited number of occupations such as nursing, teaching, or office work—then that is where most of the group will end up. What is true for women is equally true for other subgroups within the larger population, especially racial/ethnic minorities. Indeed, the occupational clustering of any subgroup can be examined in terms of the dreams that these subgroups allow themselves to have or are encouraged to have.

Helpers, then, should encourage clients to explore widely and even wildly during the anticipatory stage of problem solving; they should stimulate clients' fantasizing and dreaming; they should suggest possibilities the clients may never have considered. Only after such freewheeling exploration has taken place should they go on to the next stage. Eventually, clients will narrow down the choices in accordance with their own capabilities and values, but the crystallization will be very different for the adult who has fantasized about a variety of options than for the adult who, from the beginning, has viewed his or her future as given. The more options individuals entertain, the more likely it is that the final choice will be closer to their true desires.

Selecting a course of action. After encouraging exploration, counselors can help clients to obtain information about various options and to evaluate them. For instance, in the area of career decisions, counselors can guide clients to sources of information on various occupations and their requirements and rewards.

A force-field analysis can be very helpful in selecting a course of action once the client has explored widely and wildly and has focused on an alternative that appears reasonable. Both Egan and Brammer suggest this method, which is based on Lewin's force-field theory. The client is asked to list all the facilitating or helping forces in one column and all the restraining roadblocks in another. "This skill utilizes physics concepts of fields of force and polarized valences, and is a method comparing personal and social forces that are, at the same time, propelling and distracting helpers from their goals" (Brammer, 1979, p. 136).

Taking the first step of the action plan. Once a course of action is selected, the implementation can begin. The helper assists the client to take the first step by, for example, helping the client find a support group of newlyweds who were RIF'd the same week; helping the abused spouse find an assertiveness training workshop; helping the frustrated writer select a reasonable career that incorporates his or her love of writing.

Teaching Coping Skills

Another way to promote coping is by teaching coping skills individually and in training workshops. Two sets of researchers have identified coping skills that are useful in a broad range of transitions which can be taught to people in these ways.

Danish and D'Augelli (1980) have undertaken a comprehensive approach by developing three "packages" to teach coping skills for preventing crisis and stress. One of these packages teaches life development skills for dealing with expected transitions because anticipatory coping is helpful in moderating impact. Another package teaches life crisis skills for dealing with unplanned events, focusing on how to mobilize support when a tragedy occurs. The third package teaches basic helping and communications skills. The packages are based on the assumption that the skills, risks, and attitudes people need to cope with events overlap even though the content of events differs; and if people can be taught "to be planful in confronting life events" (p. 119), they have learned a basic coping skill that can be transferred. Danish argues that such different events as marriage, birth of a child, job promotion, being fired, divorce, and geographical moving can all be categorized in terms of role increase versus role decrease and expected versus unexpected. Further, "If crises can result in either negative or positive outcomes, the goal of intervention is not to prevent crisis, but rather to enhance or enrich individuals' abilities to deal constructively with these events" (p. 109). Because people generally need to overcome lack of knowledge, lack of skill, or inability to assess risks, the goals of the training packages are to enhance through teaching goal assessment, decision making, risk assessment, self-development, and goal attainment.

By tying together adult development knowledge, especially lifespan development with community psychology, and counseling psychology, Danish makes a clear contribution. He writes, "Implementing intervention always involves an understanding of developmental conceptions. Without a clear relationship to development, we are left asking the questions: Interventions: Why, how, and for what purpose?" (1981, p. 41).

Brammer and Abrego's approach to teaching coping skills uses Lazarus's definition of coping as "problem-solving efforts made by an individual when the demands he or she faces are highly relevant to his or her welfare . . . and when these demands tax his or her adaptive resources" (1981, p. 19). They have developed a taxonomy of coping skills based on the work of Pearlin and Schooler, who, as we discussed earlier, categorize coping skills into (1) those that change the situation, (2) those that change the meaning of the situation, and (3) those that control stress. For the purpose of teaching coping skills, the taxonomy combines this categorization with Lazarus's use of primary and secondary appraisal, that is, with how different people assess the condition, threat, and event differently, and how they differentially assess their resources and coping styles.

The Brammer and Abrego taxonomy is included here in Table 4-1. The first set of coping skills relates to perceiving and responding to transitions; the second to assessing, developing, and utilizing external support systems; the third to assessing, developing, and utilizing internal support; the fourth to reducing emotional distress, the fifth to planning/implementing. In other words, in order to cope, people may need help in viewing their situations, in mobilizing (if necessary) external and internal supports, in reducing their emotional distress, and in planning. Through using the taxonomy, people can be taught to cope with bad news by first assessing it realistically without denial or total hysteria and by mobilizing external supports which can include developing a temporary network of therapists and others in the same situation. Then, after learning how to relax and protect themselves from too much information, they are enabled to make plans, consider alternatives, and move ahead.

For example, when Rose K. learned she had cancer and needed immediate surgery, her own inner ability helped her to perceive the situation in a new way. She made the assumptions that maybe the doctor did not have all the answers, that she had some time to explore, that she did not have to act impulsively. She was able to

Table 4-1
LEVEL 1 Basic Coping Skills for Managing Transitions

1. **Skills in perceiving and responding to transitions.**
   1.1 The person mobilizes a personal style of responding to change. He or she—
   1.11 Accepts the proposition that problematic situations constitute a normal part of life and that it is possible to cope with most of these situations effectively. (Perceived control over one's life)
   1.12 Recognizes the importance of describing problematic situations accurately. (Problem definition)
   1.13 Recoginizes the values and limitations of feelings as cues to evaluate a change event. (Feelings description)
   1.14 Inhibits the tendency either to act impulsively or to do nothing when confronted with a problematic situation. (Self-control)
   1.2 The person identifies his or her current coping style. (Style of responding to change)

2. **Skills for assessing, developing, and utilizing external symptoms.**
   2.1 The person can assess an external support system. He or she can—
   2.11 Identify his or her emotional needs during times of transition.
   2.12 Identify people in his or her life who provide for personal needs.
   2.13 Describe a personal support network in terms of physical and emotional proximity.
   2.2 The person can develop a personal network based on data from 2.1. He or she can—
   2.21 Seek sources (groups, organizations, locales) of potential support persons.
   2.22 Apply social skills to cultivate persons to meet identified needs.
   2.3 The person can utilize an established support network. He or she can—
   2.31 Develop strategies for spending time with persons considered most helpful.
   2.32 Apply skills for utilizing persons in his or her network when a transition is anticipated or arrives.

3. **Skills for assessing, developing, and utilizing internal support systems.**
   3.1 The person can assess the nature and strength of positive and negative self-regarding attitudes. He or she can—
   3.11 Identify personal strengths.
   3.12 Identify negative self-descriptive statements as well as the assumptions and contextual cues which arouse such statements.
   3.2 The person can develop positive self-regard attitudes. He or she can—

3.21 Affirm personal strengths.

3.22 Convert negative self-descriptions into positive descriptive statements when the data and criteria so warrant.

3.3 The person can utilize his or her internal support system in a transition. He or she can—

3.31 Construe life transitions as personal growth opportunities.

3.32 Identify tendencies to attribute personal deficiencies as causative factors in distressful transitions.

4. **Skills for reducing emotional and physiological distress.** He or she is able to—

4.1 Practice self-relaxation responses.

4.2 Apply strategies to control over-stimulation/under-stimulation.

4.3 Express verbally feelings associated with his or her experience of transition.

5. **Skills for planning and implementing change.**

5.1 The person can analyze discrepancies between existing and desired conditions.

5.2 The person exercises positive planning for new options. To the best of his or her abilities, the person—

5.21 Throughly canvasses a wide range of alternative courses of action.

5.22 Surveys the full range of objectives to be fulfilled and the values implied by the choice

5.23 Carefully weighs whatever he or she knows about the cost and risk of negative consequences that could flow from each alternative.

5.24 Searches intensely for information relevant to further evaluation of the alternatives.

5.25 Utilizes feedback to reassess his or her preferred course of action.

5.26 Reexamines the positive and negative consequences of all known alternatives.

5.27 Makes detailed provisions for implementing or executing the chosen course of action including contingency plans.

5.3 The person is able to implement successfully his or her plans. He or she can—

5.31 Identify stressful situations related to implementing goals.

5.32 Identify negative self-statements which interfere with implementing plans.

5.33 Utilize self-relaxation routines while anticipating the stressful implementation of plans.

5.34 Utilize self-rewards in goal attainment.

5.35 Identify additional skills needed to implement goals (e.g., anxiety management, training in assertiveness, overcoming shyness).

From "Intervention Strategies for Coping with Transitions" by L. M. Brammer and P. J. Abrego, *The Counseling Psychologist*, 1981, *9*, 27. Reprinted by permission.

rely on her inner strength, thoroughly explore, and chart new territory for herself and others. What she did—relooking at a situation and acting more rationally—is what Brammer and Abrego contend are coping skills that can be taught to those experiencing such transitions as job loss, death, divorce. Such teaching is important because, as Brammer and Abrego write, "If persons believe they are powerless to respond effectively to change, they are not likely to attempt a proactive response. . . . They will adopt a fatalistic 'what's the use?' stance" (1981, p. 27).

Brammer and Abrego also teach professionals how to "design transition groups for specific client populations (e.g., women reentering college, first-time parent classes, groups for the disabled leaving the hospital)" (p. 30).

Although their coping taxonomy itself is related to the theoretical work of Pearlin and Lazarus, the actual teaching of these skills relates to several other models for skills training. The first is Meichenbaum's model of "stress inoculation" which involves three phases: (1) educating toward a conceptual framework for understanding the nature of the stress reactions and the rationale for later skills training, (2) training in behavioral and cognitive coping skills, and (3) practicing the skills under stressful conditions (1973). The teaching begins with presenting a conceptual framework to the participants about the meaning of coping skills. Next, participants are taught a method of self-management which includes a cognitive component. Finally, the participants practice their new skill. The workshops are designed so that, as participants learn, they can model and practice their new coping behaviors.

Structuring Support

The data are overwhelming and convincing that survival depends on human contact and support (Lynch, 1977). Social support is regarded as one of the keys to successful coping with transitions; it undergirds everything helpers do. Support is one of the most valuable resources available for helpers to offer their clients, and their ability to offer it is one of helpers' most valuable and essential skills. Adults of both sexes often feel alone with and confused by their problems. Because they have too readily accepted the fiction that adulthood is a period of stability and certainty, unmarked by the turmoil and change that characterize the earlier years of life, it is essential for helpers to give their clients the needed assurance that other adults have the same concerns and uncertainties as they do. As a counselor at one midwestern university center indicates, the first step in helping clients is to let them know that they are not alone in their pain. Her clients have repeatedly emphasized to her how important it has been for them to learn "that I'm not crazy. I'm not alone . . . and many other women feel this way, too."

When a recently widowed woman with four children who was returning to school was asked how she was coping she replied, "Barely." What was saving her sanity was a biweekly women's support group which provided the relief, support, and affirmation which she needed as well as a base for her to explore and develop a new identity, a new sense of purpose, a sense of hope.

The overriding and challenging question for helpers is how to help people develop the social support systems and networks necessary to their well-being and for effective coping. Often the need for support occurs at times of great vulnerability, as for a newly fired or widowed person who may be too sensitive, unable to reach out, fearful of rejection. It is easy for us to say, "Be preventive, get your social support system set up when all is going well," but with a large percentage of our population moving each year, people may find themselves in new communities where networks are not readily available. Further, people often rigidify their responses in crises, and are afraid to try a new way of responding or behaving. The support from peers in the same situation, as well as from helpers (professional or paraprofessional) who can teach new skills, attitudes, and cognition can be enormously helpful.

Caplan identifies mutual help and support as keys to mental health and competence. In *Support Systems and Mutual Help* he attempts to provide a "coherent framework" of theory and practice around the importance of support (Caplan & Killilea, 1976). Chapters deal with support through families, self-help groups, and the clergy. Caplan defines support systems as "continuing social aggregates (namely, continuing interactions with another individual, a network, a group, or an organization) that provide individuals with opportunities for feedback about themselves and for validation of their expectations about others." These are "health-promoting and ego-fortifying effects" which act as buffers against stress and disease. Support consists of three elements: significant others (1) helping the individual mobilize resources and master his or her emotional burdens, (2) sharing his or her tasks, and (3) providing extra supplies of money, materials, tools, skills, and cognitive guidance to improve his or her handling of situations. He points to the need to develop or stimulate nonprofessional support systems to augment capacities of individuals to master environments especially when in transition, crisis, or chronic privations (pp. 19–20).

Caplan's thesis is that professionals need to "appreciate the fortifying potential of the natural person-to-person supports in the population" (p. 20). A number of activities can be involved in making this happen: networking, linking, brokering, advocacy, and referent power.

Networking. The title of a recent book, *The Challenge of the Resource Exchange Network,* reflects the importance of this topic (Sarason & Lorentz, 1979). Its authors point to the "attractiveness" and extensiveness of the network concept both informal and formal: "The informal network is perceived as being based on some sort of mutual, voluntary exchange of resources, information, and shared values—a kind of 'willing giving and getting' . . ." The formal network (such as most people are part of in their work setting) is perceived as being not voluntary and suffused with competitiveness (p. 38). This point was made clear at a recent session at the Aspen Institute—a gathering of people from industry, unions, corporations, and academia who work and live together for two weeks—when one executive said, "This is the first time I've been in a group where I can say whatever I want. At work, every relationship is fraught with power and competitiveness."

Different types of support are potentially available to everyone and range from professionally-run and agency-based to self-help. All kinds of support are important and ameliorative, although Sarason and Lorentz particularly extol the virtues of self-help. The main point is that "an individual has varying degrees of connectedness . . . [and] through these connections the individual's scope can be potentially increased" (1979, p. 159). The authors point out, however, that individuals tend to "underestimate the scope" of their own networks and resources (p. 160).

One example of systematizing networking or mutual support to prompt adults to help themselves by creating new settings, new communities, new supports is a program in the Office of Women in Higher Education at the American Council on Education which aims to move women into leadership positions in education. To formalize this networking, the office has established state coordinators to connect panels of men and women with those talented women not yet in the system (Touchton & Shavlik, 1978, p. 103). Since the program began, women have made substantial gains as chief executive officers of state universities and as presidents of four-year institutions. Although their success stems from many sources, the impact of networking is clear (Touchton, 1982).

Brokering. As Heffernan points out, there is "no single best way to provide information and guidance to adults" (1981, p. 11); however, adults do need assistance to enable them to fight the bureaucracies. Brokering is a new approach for providing support to adults which includes such functions as "information, assessment, referral, counseling, outreach, and advocacy" (p. 1). In short, what the client needs, the client gets. The broker is part of an agency not tied to any work or educational institution.

Basically, the key to brokering is "putting individuals in touch with learning resources best suited to their needs" (p. 28) and bringing "together in a single service . . . six key educational support functions traditionally offered in isolation from one another: . . . outreach, . . . information, . . . assessment, . . . counseling, . . . referrals, . . . [and] advocacy" (Barton, 1982, p. 60).

The concept, originated by Bailey and first implemented in Syracuse, New York, is now gaining national attention through the National Center for Educational Brokering. Heffernan reports that in 1973 only 50 agencies approximated the brokering concept with 25,000 adults receiving such services. In 1979, according to surveys conducted by the center, 465 agencies were operating "serving nearly one million clients" (1981, p. 37) and are located in a variety of settings including libraries, Y's, community agencies, and colleges (Barton, 1982, pp. 61–62).

Linking. Similar to support through networking is the concept of linking people to resources. How does an adult woman or man find the scattered brokering agencies or community agencies designed to help? The primary way is through counseling centers.

According to the Women's Bureau of the Department of Labor, in 1963 there were about 20 counseling centers for adult women in the United States; by 1966, the number had increased to 100; and by 1971, to 376. In 1974, 752 such programs were identified, housed in five types of parent institutions: four-year colleges and universities, community and junior colleges, private agencies (such as the YWCA and B'nai B'rith), public adult schools usually attached to high school districts, and governmental agencies. Today, it is almost impossible to keep track of the number of counseling centers which provide services for adult women.

Both personal experience and a review of the literature reveal a wide variety of counseling programs, ranging from leaderless consciousness-raising groups to psychotherapy, from classes in self-defense to courses in career planning. Most centers link people to resources by offering some combination of the following: individual counseling; personal growth groups; career and life planning; special-interest workshops on such topics as coping with widowhood, divorce, or aging parents; information on available occupational and educational resources; and skill courses such as assertiveness training, financial planning, and job seeking. Some programs are conducted by professional counselors or teachers, others by peers. Such diversity is both positive and negative: positive, in that no single way has been found to connect people with each other at stressful and vulnerable times; negative, in that the existing programs are not widely known, and funding is problematic.

The discussion so far may give the impression that counseling services linking adults to resources are abundant, comprehensive, and readily available to anyone who wants them. Unfortunately, this is not the case. Such programs are unevenly distributed across the nation, with rural areas in particular likely to lack such facilities. Moreover, some groups of people—the poor, the unemployed, the less educated—may simply not be aware of such services even where they do exist. Displaced homemakers as well may simply lack information about the resources that are available to them. A recent survey by the American Institute for Research, carried out to determine what support services were available to adults (especially women and minority group members), found that though there is no dearth of programs for women, "not all groups of women are assisted in equal proportion. There are many more programs for middle-class educated women who have never worked or who have been out of the labor market for a considerable time than there are for low-income women and female heads of households. . . ." (Harrison & Entine, 1976).

Providing accurate information is another way to effectively link people and resources. People need information that will promote their cognitive understanding of a particular problem or situation and point out available options. One counselor explained that, in talking to adult women who want to return to school, she often links the provision of information with support: "I give strong doses of encouragement, based on the records of other women who have returned to formal education."

The use or nonuse adults make of tuition aid—money provided by employers for education related to work—highlights the importance of providing information (Barton, 1982, p. 162). Barton points out the paradox: Tuition aid provided by companies for workers is readily available but not used, mainly because both workers and educational institutions do not know of its availability. As of 1977, "9 out of 10 United States companies with 500 or more employees offered tuition-aid benefits." However, only "about 4 or 5 percent of workers avail themselves of this opportunity to go back to school. For hourly wage, blue-collar, and pink-collar workers, the participation rates are halved" (p. 164).

The National Institute of Work and Learning (NIWL) conducted a survey identifying the following as barriers which interfered with the utilization of tuition aid: "Insufficient management encouragement (56 percent), lack of counseling (51 percent), and lack of information about the tuition-aid plan (44 percent)" (Barton, 1982, pp. 164–165).

NIWL is conducting three experiments to test out what variables, in fact, do make a difference. One project is based on "information delivery." Every employee in the target group is being personally informed of the availability of tuition aid. The second experiment combines "information delivery and educational advisement," and the third experiment adds improved delivery of actual educational opportunities at the work site (p. 174). Although the data are not yet in, the information component is crucial to support as well as action.

The underlying point is clear: Linking people with the available options is facilitated, as Barton writes, by outlining opportunities (p. 13), by providing accurate information on, for example, appropriate medical, social, and educational resources.

Advocacy. Sarason, a student of individuals in bureaucracies, states the obvious: Many individuals are treated unfairly and are unable to obtain the services and respect due them. "In the absence of someone who becomes their advocate, they remain unheard, neglected, and robbed of their rights." With the ever "increasing size and complexity of organizations in the public sector . . ." there needs to be an "impartial person" (1979, p. 249)—an ombudsperson—to structure support for people in such cases. The Swedish word and concept *ombudsman* (which I will call ombudsperson), literally translated, means one who represents someone. He or she is a guardian of the people's rights, a public investigator, a person who "fights city hall." During the 1970s, many universities experimented with this concept. The need for such an office stems from the difficulty students and people have in fighting red tape and bureaucrats.

If the ombudsperson is seen as one way to give the individual—whether staff, faculty, or student—support and a voice when he or she is mishandled, then we begin to see a possible breakthrough in the asymmetry of individual to bureaucracy. The office of ombudsperson—if it becomes part of all bureaucracies—can become the vehicle for individuals to be heard and the catalyst for changing the system peacefully.

We see repeatedly that the individual is in a powerless position on every campus, and in most organizations. What is needed is systemic change, that is, a new agent in the bureaucracy to give power and weight to the individual, to redress the asymmetrical balance between person and institution.

The ombudsperson is, in a certain sense, an attempt to bureaucratize innovation, to give "an intellectual" the right and power to recommend and implement changes in the bureaucratic handling of situations. His or her actual power rests on his or her ability to negotiate, persuade, and inquire. However, unless this "bureaucratic intellectual" is of such stature and conforms to the successful Swedish model, he or she runs the risk of becoming an agent of the institution.

This strategy of advocacy is one that belongs in the repertoire of helpers. The helper must often adopt an activist stance in order to provide support and help for adults hindered by various structural and institutional barriers, including bureaucratic red tape. Many adults are both out of work and out of school; they need someone to lobby on their behalf, and the counselor may be highly suited to this role.

In recent years, a movement has developed to base guidance counselors in the community rather than in educational institutions. The rationale for this movement is that all too often institution-based counselors are more interested in maintaining and protecting the system rather than in helping their clients. If counselors are independent professionals rather than the employees of institutions, they will be in a better position and may be more inclined to bring moral and legal pressure to bear on institutions. They will then be more likely to rethink outmoded policies and to modify or eliminate antiquated and irrelevant rules.

Several years ago, some members of the College Entrance Examination Board's Commission on Tests urged that the board establish regional guidance centers to act as advocative, protective, and supportive agencies outside the established structures. Such agencies should be based on the legal conception of the ombudsperson—one who helps and even protects an individual citizen in encounters with agents of government. At that time, this proposal was branded "totally unrealistic." More recently, however, educational brokering services have turned this allegedly pie-in-the-sky proposal into a reality. The fact that advocacy is seen as a crucial element of these new services, which provide support for adults, attests to the importance of this strategy. Its many applications to the problems of women at midlife are obvious. For instance, employers and educational institutions often have been unwilling to give women credit for experience gained in managing the home. Through lobbying efforts, advocates can help to bring about changes in attitudes and regulations related to this issue.

Referent power. Social support, as already noted, is seen as one of the valuable resources available for counselors to offer clients. Janis (1982) is working to transform "the art of counseling into a science" by operationalizing when, under what circumstances, and how counselors can use their support in an effective manner. He suggests 12 variables (see Table 4-2) which determine the degree to which counselors are able to influence clients to adhere to hard decisions in such areas as losing weight, giving up smoking, and career planning. He refers to this ability as "referent power" (1982).

Janis writes, "There are three critical phases in almost every helping relationship." (p. 27). The first phase involves the counselor building up trust so that the counselor becomes an influence agent in the process of client change—which Janis describes as "building up referent power." It is during this exploration period that the client asks, "Does the counselor think well of me?" This is a very critical time. Often clients come to counselors when feeling vulnerable, and when they are extremely sensitive to the appraisal of others. Thus the key is how the counselor responds, especially to negative self-disclosures such as, "I can't stay on a diet."

In the next phase, the counselor uses this referent power by establishing some norms, some directions for a specific course of action. The problem here is how the counselor can move from unconditional acceptance to the "judicious use of selective" acceptance without losing the client (p. 33). Although Janis writes that this requires "considerable sensitivity and artistry," he outlines what the counselor can do: Criticize actions of the client which are going counter to the client's goals, and praise those behaviors which are

Table 4–2
Critical Phases and Twelve Key Variables That Determine
the Degree of Referent Power of Counselors as Change Agents

Phase 1: Building up referent power	1. Encouraging clients to make self-disclosures *versus* not doing so
	2. Giving positive feedback (acceptance and understanding) *versus* giving neutral or negative feedback in response to self-disclosure
	3. Using self-disclosure to give insight and cognitive restructuring *versus* giving little insight or cognitive restructuring
Phase 2: Using referent power	4. Making directive statements or endorsing specific recommendations regarding actions the client should carry out *versus* abstaining from any directive statements or endorsements
	5. Eliciting commitment to the recommended course of action *versus* not elicting commitment
	6. Attributing the norms being endorsed to a respected secondary group *versus* not doing so
	7. Giving selective positive feedback *versus* giving noncontingent acceptance or predominantly neutral or negative feedback*
	8. Giving communications and training procedures that build up a sense of personal responsibility *versus* giving no such communications or training
Phase 3: Retaining referent power after contact ends and promoting internalization	9. Giving reassurances that the counselor will continue to maintain an attitude of positive regard *versus* giving no such reassurances
	10. Making arrangements for phone calls, exchange of letters, or other forms of communciation that foster hope for future contact, real or symbolic, at the time of

terminating face-to-face meetings *versus* making no such arrangements
11. Giving reminders that continue to foster a sense of personal responsibility *versus* giving no such reminders
12. Building up the client's self-confidence about succeeding without the aid of the counselor *versus* not doing so

---

*By selective feedback is meant a combination of (a) negative feedback in response to any of the client's comments about being reluctant, unwilling, or failing to act in accordance with the recommendations and (b) positive feedback in response to all other comments, whether relevant to the decision or not.

From I. L. Janis, ed., *Counseling on Personal Decisions: Theory and Research on Short-Term Helping Relationships.* New Haven, Conn.: Yale University Press, 1982. Reprinted by permission.

enhancing clients' goals. In the final phase, the counselor helps the client begin to internalize what has gone on so the client can assume responsibility.

Janis has also reported on some interesting experiments which show that when people in the same situation pair up without the support of a counselor, they do not adhere to their commitment.

Counseling

Many books and courses deal with individual counseling and group counseling. Rather than reviewing them here, an illustrative counseling interview will be presented. This interview reflects the integration of adult development and helping skills which can be applied in individual or group counseling sessions.

The interview is part of a one-time session in which a counselor attempts to influence the client to seek therapy. The interview goes through the three important phases of exploration (providing a nonbiased relationship), understanding (providing a new perspective), and coping (influencing action). Further, the interview illustrates not only how the counselor goes about influencing but also many other helping skills and techniques. Amplifying comments are provided for each phase.

Exploration Phase

COUNSELOR: Paul, you are very nice to agree to videotape this session. When you called for an appointment you said you would like to talk a little bit about your career. Can you tell me about why you wanted to come in and talk?

CLIENT: I have recently moved here and have had trouble locating a position in my field. I've answered ads for quite some time, and I answered one a couple of weeks ago that stated, "Personnel reentering job market, enjoy people, work independently, etc." I talked to this person, and I thought I wanted to reenter the job market. I enjoy people and thought perhaps I could at least find out how to prepare for this position. After talking with her, she assured me that my experience was too limited for what she had in mind and asked me if I would sign up. If I were willing to pay her, she might be able to get a job for me. I thought this was unfair. My experience and background is architecture and city planning. I've hired people, I've trained people.

COUNSELOR: You're really experiencing some discouragement, some disappointment.

CLIENT: Yes. I have been geared to the idea that once you find your field, it will continue to open up and up and up . . . and I had no trouble as long as I was willing to move anywhere in the country but right now I feel frozen to this area. I can't move so I have to explore what I can do here and get paid for it.

COUNSELOR: From what I can gather, you're feeling boxed in a little bit.

CLIENT: Oh yeah, I have with me here a whole file folder of letters that I have sent out. I'd say out of the letters I've sent out, I got returns from 25 to 30 percent at the most. I've gotten down to the three people, and they've all said they don't really need anybody with my skills. They would much rather take somebody with less because they feel he will stay with them longer. Yet when I apply for a job that is about my level, I find there are apparently 50 others that have applied and out of those there are probably 12 that are equal to me and usually there are 11 that are better than me.

COUNSELOR: So it is really confusing, isn't it, to know why you aren't getting these jobs? Is it you? Is it them? You must be having a lot of questions.

CLIENT: Right. I am interested in photography. I would be willing to study photography, and the first thing the man said was, "Well, if you expect to make money in it, don't waste your money because this is a glamour profession and there are already hundreds of people that are already trying to make a living at it." So every place I've said I am willing to pay for additional education but tell me what education I need.

COUNSELOR: There are a lot of different things you're talking about, and there are two ways we might go. One is to talk about what you've done and what the options are out there, but another possibility is for us to talk about your internal career—what's going on with you right now and how you are trying to make sense out of all this.

CLIENT: Yes.

COUNSELOR: Maybe this would be a good time to ask what you hoped to get from our discussion when you called.

CLIENT: Well, I hope to get some ideas .... Here I'm thinking that I have a lot of knowledge, but I am being shut out, and I think that I don't know that anybody could have told me what to do 20 years ago that would save me now. But nobody knows where they are going to be 20 years later. But I think there are opportunities; there are things that you could do and again, I am not even necessarily focusing on a single career job. I would be willing to work two or three things instead of one. I am very flexible, I'll work day or night or weekends.

COUNSELOR: Let me see if we're togethc. What I hear you saying is that you are going up all these alleys; you are flexible, you are willing to do a lot of things, and somehow nobody is giving you an opportunity. You seem to be asking for some help in trying to figure out how you can get yourself together with the options that are available.

CLIENT: The whole thing of career counseling is very interesting to me. Everybody writes books on figuring out what you are to do. If you like to fly kites, then send enough letters to kite manufacturers and talk yourself into getting a job where they'll pay you to do what you want to do. Well, this is nice in theory but you have to be more or less a promoter. I feel if you are not a promoter, this theory does not work.

COUNSELOR: A lot of glib answers, a lot of glib books, and yet they don't really address the struggle you are feeling.

CLIENT: I went to a career counselor who told me to write a resume a new way to promote yourself. I've tried that and that hasn't helped me at all.

COUNSELOR: It is like a maze. You go up this way and get stopped, and then you try this and you try that. And then people shift you from person to person or place to place or read this book or go there.

CLIENT: And yet I was in a number two position in planning, and I would get letters from people in planning school saying, "You know I am interested in this; I am going to be in Cleveland, would you talk to me?" And I would always spend time—I would spend time and say, "We can't afford to hire you here," but I would try to give them three or four names where they could try. It is amazing how I tried to help others get in, and I would suspect some of these people that I helped get jobs are above me now.

COUNSELOR: So, that is kind of painful too, seeing people pass you by and also being on the outside not able to get on the inside. This going down blind alleys kind of creates some self doubts, too. On one hand you feel you have a lot of flexibility and a lot of talent; on the other hand, nobody is recognizing it.

CLIENT: Right. This also brings in a family conflict because my wife and I are both professionals. She is a writer, and we both wanted to leave Cleveland. We decided that it was almost impossible for two people to get a job at the same institution because this is pretty rare. So we agreed that whoever would get the first job would spring the family, and hopefully, in a reasonable amount of time, say six weeks to no more than six months, the other one could get a job. Well, when she took the job, she commuted between here and Cleveland for a year until we felt prepared to make the jump. The person that employed me was in housing, and he knew people down here; and when I left, he said, "If you need any help, I know some people there that could probably help you." I thought I wouldn't have any trouble. So I moved here, and probably four or five months later I sent him a letter and said, "O.K. I need help, give me some of those names." He did and those all struck out.

COUNSELOR: So you've done all the responsible things; you and your wife worked something out; you've done the things you were supposed to do in terms of contacts, you've followed the procedures that you thought would work out, and it is still not working out.

Content/process comments: Exploration. The counselor's first goal is to establish a nonbiased relationship and enable the client to explore his situation. The transition framework (Figure 3-4) provides the knowledge base for the counselor. For example, in this case the transition is both an event and a nonevent. He has recently moved (the event) and cannot find employment (the nonevent). The transition was anticipated and initiated by the client and his wife, motivated by a desire to move. The impact of the transition appears to be very high: His role has altered from worker to nonworker, his physical environment has changed, his daily routines have clearly been affected. His initial discussion further indicated an erosion of self-confidence.

The counselor uses all the helping skills, but especially important are open questioning, reflecting, paraphrasing, and focusing. Indeed, the major task is keeping the focus on the client and his struggles and feelings and not on the job search. The counselor could have been more effective if she had reflected on the impact of the transition by saying, "You're really saying that every part of your life has been changed—your physical location, your daily life."

Understanding Phase

CLIENT: This presents other problems because, frankly, I'm willing to take jobs under my professional level, and she has not accepted this fact, so there is a psychological barrier. When I suggest taking a volunteer job, she resists this.

COUNSELOR: You're sensing her disappointment in you and that increases your own sense of disappointment.

CLIENT: Right, and I constantly hear we have to have more money. She puts pressure on me and in turn puts pressure on herself and that creates psychological difficulty.

COUNSELOR: That just increases your sense of panic about what you are going to do.

CLIENT: Yes—that is probably why I called you. I think you ought to be aware of these problems that don't seem to get through to job counselors.

COUNSELOR: It never is so simple as just getting a job because there are family pressures, self-doubts.

CLIENT: In addition, one of our children is hyperactive which means that there are other psychological problems. Now I am afraid they would say, "Gee, you've got a family problem, we can't afford to pay you while you pick up the kid all the time," or they would say, "Keep your family problems out of your job, you are not producing." After you're established in your job, then they will allow some of this. But in a new position, you are being tested, and you can't afford to do this. So I felt from a family viewpoint, this has been good because I have been available for my son when the school has called me. About three weeks ago, for instance, the principal called me; we solved the problem. She said, "It was lucky you could get here so fast"; because if I hadn't been able to, it might involve putting our kid into some other school. So there are advantages to not working, but these don't pay money, they don't buy bread, they don't keep you fed, they don't buy gas for the car.

COUNSELOR: One of the reasons you called is to share all of this with someone and maybe gain some understanding and mobilize in some new ways. You called me and you called other people indicating your desire to break through the cycle and see if there is a way out. So really, one of the things you are looking for is some way to figure out what it is that you really want to do with the rest of your life, to make sense out of the pressures that are on you.

CLIENT: I think those will be reduced as long as I get back in the job market. My wife thinks sometimes that I am getting used to not working, but believe me, doing housework gets pretty boring too.

COUNSELOR: I don't understand what you mean.

CLIENT: My wife kind of feels that I am not trying as hard as I should. I can't make her believe that what I am doing is pretty boring. And I'd give anything to have any kind of income, to broaden what I can do during the day.

COUNSELOR: So that adds another piece to the puzzle. No matter what you do with the job, they'll say you are overqualified or under-qualified. Your wife doesn't even think you are trying hard enough, so in a sense nobody's giving you much credit. You feel unappreciated.

CLIENT: Maybe what I need is a mentor. I think people that get places are the ones that have mentors. The college students have a teacher who says, "I'll help you." Most of the books say that if you are 45 years old and all the bosses at the place that you're at are all 30 you don't have a very good chance because somebody 30 does not like to hire somebody older than themselves.

COUNSELOR: So you are facing age discrimination and that hurts too. Also, you're feeling cheated that what you did for younger people is not available to you because of your age. Can we explore the age issue a little bit?

CLIENT: I'd like to think that it really doesn't matter. I look at people, and I know I've worked with people that have been fired from other jobs because of their age, and know that I can do better at my age than many who are younger. I feel confident, but you have to have somebody who will at least let you in on the payroll to show that you are competent.

COUNSELOR: You really need somebody to believe in you—your wife to believe in you, a mentor to believe in you, an employer to believe in you, somebody to believe in you.

CLIENT: Right.

COUNSELOR: And hopefully, I can believe in you.

CLIENT: Right. I took a job last summer driving a cab. I thought I would have somebody who could say that I am reliable, that I show up for work and am not a drunkard. But this is not enough. Potential employers want several personal references.

Content/process comments: Understanding. The counselor is trying to understand, in collaboration with the client, the assets and liabilities the client brings to this transition. First, a look at the character of the transition reveals that the trigger—deciding to leave Cleveland—had consequences that were assessed as negative by the client. Although the timing was good regarding the hyper-active son and need for parent involvement in the school, it was bad for the marriage, especially in regard to his self-esteem and his perception that his wife saw him negatively. What comes clear is that the trigger was positive, the timing both positive and negative, the role change negative (he took up housework but has no job), and concurrent stress great. In terms of the characteristics relating to his support, he clearly sees his wife as nonsupportive. He also sees his former contacts in the job world as having disappeared, and further, he sees that professional career counselors are not helpful. Thus he would rate his supports as negative. His options are both plus and minus: He wavers between giving up and taking hold. In regard to his psychological characteristics, the only assessment possible after such a short interview is that he seems very fragmented yet uses a variety of career strategies. Therefore, although his basic psychological resources seem low, his strategies are a plus.

The counselor engaged in identifying themes, interpreting and focusing on some of the assets and liabilities. The counselor did not confront, based on the assumption that at this point he needed support and could not yet take confrontation.

The counselor could have been more effective if she had focused more systematically on the three clusters of variables and summarized each with the client by saying, "Looking at the transition, let's identify your resources" and then together with the client summarized assets and liabilities relating to the transition, the client himself, and his environment.

Influencing Phase

COUNSELOR: So wherever you are turning, it's like you are beating your head against a brick wall. It really is important to try to figure what is the issue you can work on. I don't know whether in the next few minutes we can do a little brainstorming about what kinds of things would be most useful and helpful to you. We can talk about the external career or the internal career.

CLIENT: I think the external career—I have wide interests, you know, and I am willing to do lots of things, and I'm not waiting around for the ideal job. It is hard to get my wife to understand that.

COUNSELOR: Do you think it might be most helpful to talk to somebody who is knowledgeable both about what goes on with the people inside themselves as well as the world of work? In other words, it might be possible to talk to somebody over a period of time while you are continuing to explore different job opportunities. I guess what I'm wondering is whether you would consider some career counseling with somebody who isn't necessarily an employment counselor. Is that something you would see as helpful?

CLIENT: I would think so.

COUNSELOR: That would involve talking about yourself, what is going on inside of yourself, at the same point that you are exploring all these various career options.

CLIENT: Right now I would be willing to go in any direction. Again, I am here for your advice too.

COUNSELOR: Well, I guess my own advice, based on what you have been saying is that you are hitting a lot of barriers which are very hard to deal with. It is not easy, what you have been going through. There is a lot of pain involved. On the other hand, you've got a lot of strength, a lot of resourcefulness, and you are willing to work hard to get yourself a job. So, one of the things that I was throwing out as a possibility is locating a counselor with whom you could review what has been going on, what the different avenues are you've tried, and make some sense out of it. Have you thought about this?

CLIENT: Well, I paid a lot of money, probably to do this exact same thing. But if you have another suggestion, I want to hear it—as long as it is not a fancy agency with lots of phonies.

COUNSELOR: Well, I have two men in mind who do see people privately, who are experts in career development and are also psychologists.

CLIENT: O.K., fine.

COUNSELOR: They are really sensitive to the issues that you are going through. If we work out a referral, which is really what has been going on between us, I'd like to have you come back and get me up to date on how it all works out. If you wish, you can see me as somebody you can kind of come back to so this doesn't have to be the end.

CLIENT: Let me say one thing—I was no way forced out of my previous job. You get to a time. I had benefits. If I had stayed another five years, I could have capitalized on a partial retirement which would help. I left before I had any of these benefits, and it puts increasing pressures on you, too.

COUNSELOR: Yes, the timing of when things happen is important in how you feel about who is controlling you life.

CLIENT: It's nice to be able to control your life but not everybody can. You know, to control your life you pretty much have to stay single, or be able—if any opportunity comes—to grab it. You can't do this if you have kids in school.

COUNSELOR: So there are a lot of what if's, if only's, and that is discouraging too. How shall we leave this? Let me talk to both people and see if they have any time and what their fees are. I will get back to you. Then if it doesn't work out, see me as sort of a backup person that you can come and check in with and talk to because I feel that, a lot of times, as adults are struggling with the kinds of issues that you are talking about, they feel so alone. It is nice to know that there are some people in your corner. So, see me as somebody in your corner, let me be a referral agent for you and see if I can't get you connected with somebody.

CLIENT: Fine. Thank you very much.

Content/Process comments: Influencing.   As the interview comes to a close, the counselor attempts to influence the client to take action which would benefit him. Knowledge of the transition process helps the counselor: For example, he is pervaded with his geographical move and job loss. As time passes, he stays stuck in a very disruptive situation with no visible movement toward integration. The counselor is aware of this "stuckness" and feels that the man is his own worst enemy. If the client's assets and liabilities are charted, it is clear that he is low on transition, self, and environment. He seems out of balance, and to have the cards stacked against him.

The counselor is, therefore, more directive and attempts to structure support by referring him to a trained counseling psychologist expert in both individual and career counseling who can integrate internal stuckness with the world of work.

To summarize: This case is interesting. The client has a number of problems. Although he is scattered and rambling—and could obviously benefit from psychotherapy—he also needs immediate support, linking, and brokering. If, in fact, he can be helped to temporarily connect and be hired, he can be freed to work on some underlying issues. Underlying his situation are the sex role expectations he and his wife have, his feelings of powerlessness, and the interrelationship of home and career. An overriding problem is age bias which makes his situation seem more difficult and reinforce his feelings of powerlessness.

Further, it is interesting to see how one issue—securing a job—is related to many other issues. In this case, a dual-career family has moved, a son has school problems, the wife and husband are both disappointed in the husband's ability to work and meet sex-role expectations. Thus the transition of moving has altered the client's relationships, routines, assumptions, and roles. Note also that the counselor and client disagreed covertly about the nature of the problem.

Workshop Settings

This same three-part interview format, which builds in each variable in the transition, can be used by counselors in group settings as well as for structured individual interviews. An instrument, developed by Schlossberg and Charner (1982) and based on the transition framework, can be filled out and used as a basis for discussing transitions and their management. At this point the instrument has been administered to 50 clerical workers in a university setting. (Further refinements are underway, and a manual for counselors is being written). The first section, which identifies and examines the transition, explores type, context, and impact. Understanding the coping resources—the variables characterizing the particular transition, individual, and environment—is the focus of the second section. The third section looks at the process of coping with the transition itself and includes the individual's appraisal of the transition as well as where he or she is in the phases of assimilation.

The importance of developing structured, time-limited groups around particular transitions is supported by Weiss's work (1976) with individuals or groups in transition. Weiss identifies "a thread of symptoms" characteristic of people in new situations:

- They have an inadequate grasp of the situation because it is new. They do not understand the implications of the situation and they underestimate enormously how long it takes to recover, adjust, and/or integrate the new status.

- They experience self-doubt because they feel they are not handling the situation as well as they "should"; therefore, they lose confidence, which is often reflected in erratic behavior.

- They feel isolated because they often keep their feelings to themselves, not wanting others to think they are exaggerating and are not able to cope.

When the transition begins as a sudden, severely upsetting event (an accident or the sudden onset of a major illness in the family), people are frequently emotionally numbed, their feelings suspended. Support seems to be the only effective kind of help. The helper, who may or may not be a professional person, needs to communicate empathy, understanding, and a readiness to provide whatever service is possible to help the individual. (Such support is, of course, also helpful to individuals at all points in the transition process.)

But, over time, the individual attempts to deal with the upset, grief, and other disruptive emotions and to find new sources of support, and is often confused and uncertain as he or she tries to rearrange his or her life. People in this phase are particularly likely to benefit from programs of individual or group counseling help because they must find new ways of managing their lives and because the decisions they make at this point can profoundly affect the course of the rest of their lives. For instance, the new widow or widower needs a cognitive framework for understanding his or her emotions in the new situation as well as help in managing finances or in locating child-care services. In some cases, short-term help is of little value. Establishing support groups is useful for such groups as the bereaved, who may find that the social network they shared with their dead spouse is gradually disappearing and that they are becoming socially isolated. Making it possible for them to become acquainted with other people in the same situation as themselves is of practical as well as psychological value, as mutual problems and possible solutions can be shared. Or the widows or widowers find that they have continuous difficulty in raising dependent children without the aid of another adult and need a continuing, problem-focused support system.

Weiss's work (1976) with people in transition indicates that in programs set up to assist individuals to resolve their confusion and take the steps necessary to move through the transition, there are two important components: structuring support systems, and providing cognitive information. Leibowitz and Schlossberg (1982) have added planning as a third component. A successful counseling program, then, emphasizes working with homogeneous groups, in which all participants face the same type of transition, and offering these groups support systems, cognitive information on the issues and feelings associated with their specific situation, and planning strategies.

• *Component 1: Structuring support systems.* Although many psychologists and helpers talk about the importance of support as a buffer to stress, Weiss differentiates among types of support: support from peers (others negotiating the same transition), support from veterans (people who have successfully negotiated the transition), and support from a leader (who has a cognitive framework or understanding of the underlying issues represented by the transition). This means that, for example, with a group of newly separated individuals who are dealing with attachment/bonding issues the leader might give a talk on attachment—the antidote to loneliness. The explanation may help the newly separated individuals understand why they cling to each other, even after the decision is made to separate. The group can then react with their own experiences and process it in small groups, each of which includes a veteran. Thus the three kinds of support that need to be built in are:

Support from other participants who are experiencing the same type of transition, which means that program or workshop participants are from homogeneous groups.

Support and encouragement from trained leaders/facilitators.

Support from veterans, that is, from those who have transcended similar experiences and can share these experiences as well as describe helpful strategies.

• *Component 2: Providing cognitive information.* Cognitive information about the issues and problems related to the particular transition the group is anticipating or experiencing needs to be provided. For example, in a career transition workshop, those making the transition to management need to talk about the issues of competency and about the shift from technical to people skills that a move into management necessitates. Or those who have lost their jobs need to learn about the psychological stages associated with job loss, such as denial, confusion, anger, and resolution (Schlossberg & Leibowitz, 1980a). This kind of cognitive information creates a mind set. Program participants begin to understand better what they are presently experiencing and they can prepare for future problems.

Emphasis needs also to be placed on helping group members with anticipatory socialization, that is, helping them learn the rules, norms, roles, and expectations of their new (or aspired-to) roles. In discussing the training of medical students, Merton (1957) talks about the acquisition of new roles and divides role acquisition into two classes: direct learning and indirect learning. By providing cognitive information to individuals undergoing transitions, indirect learning—which involves attitudes, values, and behavior patterns associated with certain roles—can turn into direct learning.

Veterans are particularly valuable in determining what cognitive information is most useful. They are most aware of the issues they faced, what was helpful, what was not helpful, and what they wished they had known.

One way to provide cognitive information is by placing some of the key psychological issues associated with the type of transition along a continuum and discussing these issues. For example, "moves into new roles" can be characterized at one end by "feeling marginal" (lack of norms and behaviors) and at the other by "feeling competent." Individuals in nonevent, nonoccurrence situations can be characterized as "feeling boxed in" (futility and depression) at one end and at the other by "achieving renewal." Those who have lost jobs can be characterized at one end by "losing control" (denial, anger, depression) and at the other by "uncovering new options."

• *Component 3: Planning.* Included here are the activities and strategies which help those undergoing transition to assess their own strengths and weaknesses, to assess their options, and to construct viable action plans. This component is particularly important in pretransition programs, such as for career develoment and for those soon to retire. (Outlines for career transition workshops for preprofessionals, midlevel professionals, and retirees, which use all three components and emphasize action plans, are included in the appendix.)

Of course, all planning activities and strategies must be customized to each group. For example, those making the transition to retirement need to identify what elements of their work life are important to them and how those elements can be replaced if they choose a nonwork environment after retirement. Those making the transition to management need to assess themselves against a profile of management competencies, refine their profiles by interviewing successful managers, and then—as a group—extrapolate the competencies that led to the success of those managers. Those women making the transition of returning to school need to understand that such factors as timing and support (or nonsupport) may affect their academic careers.

In summary, counseling programs and workshops can be developed around any transition in whatever context—personal, career, health, or employment. The components that need to be included are as follows: structuring the support system to include peers and veterans, providing a cognitive map to help those in transition better grasp what they are experiencing, and offering help in planning for next steps.

Summary: The Importance of Integrating Content and Process

Actually connecting the theories and knowledge of adult development to the helping skills has been the focus of this chapter. The knowledge base is linked to the selection and use of interventions by integrating the transition framework (content) and a helping model (process) with goals of exploring, understanding, and coping.

The helper's effectiveness rests both on knowledge of adult development and on selecting and using the appropriate skill or strategy. According to Holland, Magoon, and Spokane (1981), in a review of the effectiveness of career interventions, there is no evidence that one type of intervention or strategy is consistently better than others. They do, however, identify four key elements which, when present, lead to effective behavior change:

1. Giving accurate information about self, resources, and opportunities to clients.

2. Providing clients with a cognitive structure to organize this information. (If clients just obtain information about their interests, with no patterns or groupings, they may not be able to act.)

3. Providing cognitive rehearsals of aspirations, that is, ways to see or project the self into the future.

4. Providing support.

These elements emphasize, once again, the importance of integrating adult development knowledge with process skills.

So far we have primarily examined how counselors can help people as individuals and in groups. A more comprehensive, ecological view of intervention will be suggested in the next chapter.

5

The Many Ways of Helping: People and Environments

All through life people continue to develop, question, and reassess—and can be helped in a variety of ways to love, work, and play. We have looked at what helpers can do to encourage adults to explore their situations, at what helpers need to know to understand better what adults are experiencing so they can help their clients understand the events, and at what helpers can do to bring about more effective coping by their clients.

Everything we have said so far is predicated on the assumption of a direct relation between helper and client or client group. However, it is important now to broaden this perspective by considering that people can and do function more effectively in a supportive environment; the same individuals in a restricted, negative environment can perform poorly. Any book on helping adults needs to take account of an ecological perspective; helpers should redefine "behavior not as sick or well, but as an outcome of interaction between a person and the social system" (Rappaport, 1977, p. 153). The helper with an ecological perspective is thus "interested in change at multiple levels of society" and requires "Conceptions that go beyond the individual." He or she will see that "individual change is not necessarily the most useful target . . . organizational changes, as well as the creation of parallel institutions and programs of social advocacy, are often useful" (p. 157).

James Coleman, the sociologist, refers to the imbalance between the individual and organization as asymmetry.

The principle problems [are] . . . the asymmetry in power that stems from the size disparity. Ordinarily the organization can mobilize far more resources to further its interests than can the individual . . . . It has enormous economies of scale, since it is involved in similar relations with many individuals. In employment, this power differential made possible the numerous methods of worker exploitation that were characteristic of the early part of this century. Since that time, the power imbalance has been redressed through the construction of countervailing organizations, labor unions. In consumption, an exploitation of gullible consumers by sophisticated marketing organizations has occurred through a similar discrepancy in size and thus resources. Unlike workers, consumers have had little success in developing organizations that can balance the power-centered research organizations to balance market research of firms, and organizations to assess the reliability of business, to balance the credit bureaus used by retail firms (1970, p. 19).

Argyris takes a slightly different approach when describing the individual in relation to organizations. He points out that healthy individuals tend to be independent and active, but formal organizations place people in "work situations where they are dependent, subordinate, and submissive" (1957, p. 119). He hypothesizes that the healthier the individual, the less likely he or she will be congruent with the organization, and there are basic incongruencies between the growth trends of a healthy personality and the requirements of the formal organization, whose prime concern is productivity (1957, p. 66). People have many ways to adapt: They may leave, climb the organizational ladder, become apathetic, create opposition groups. Can there be a resolution of the conflict between organizational demands and the desires and concerns of the man who says:

> I'm 45 years old . . . . But I'm not a happy person. The money doesn't mean a goddamned thing. If I could find something else, I'd love to get out of it. Let's say I'm a successful failure. I'm bored with the routine of it all. Basically, it's the same routine (Chiriboga & Thurner, 1975, p. 71).

Kanter's book *Men and Women of the Corporation* (1977) approaches this very problem. She demonstrates that the problems of human beings can basically be solved by structural change in contrast to individual solutions.

Many individuals are powerless, that is, they are unable to "mobilize resources." Kanter's analyses and recommended interventions are designed to "enhance opportunity, distribute power more broadly, and help balance numbers" (p. 7). Her solutions are designed to change the system rather than change the individual. As she states, "This book . . . locates a large measure of the responsibility for the behaviors people engage in at work and their fate inside organizations in the structure of the work systems themselves. Life does not consist of infinite possibility because situations do not make all responses equally plausible or . . . available" (p. 10).

Kanter descibes approaches to person/environment improvement: One set deals with redesigning "boring, meaningless jobs to make them more challenging and meaningful. . . ." The other is the encouragement of more "participatory . . . team centered organizations" (p. 255). Although Kanter applauds these efforts, she sees them as limited. She argues that "repair programs for women who recognize their personal 'deficiencies' in job-market terms . . . [on] how to be more assertive, how to be a manager . . . though useful, do not address the basic problem—enlarging and changing the opportunity structure." She condems these narrow efforts as confirming "the old American notion that money and time is best spent remaking the person" (p. 262). She continues, "Feminists and men in dead-end jobs have a stake in seeing that organizations change to open opportunity channels and decentralize power. . . . Use of individual models of change are likely to prevent people from seeing their joint interests in system-change; rather, they pit groups against one another in the competitive struggle for advantage in situations of scarcity" (p. 264).

Often counselors and other helpers approach an adult's concerns as something to be primarily understood and clarified. The onus is often on the individuals to understand and clarify, to change perspectives, to identify options where none were previously envisioned. In short, a client's perspective is at stake: Change it and everything will fall into place. However, instead of, for example, helping a preretiree and spouse see retirement as an opportunity for new directions, Kanter's approach—more in line with Claude Pepper's legislative program—would be eliminating retirement policies, eliminating age as a variable in institutional decision making. That is, she would change the system.

Clearly the need exists to work on both the individual's perspective and the institution's opportunity structure simultaneously. Often adults feel boxed in because they face internal limitations—"I can't do it, I can't change, I can't"—as well as external, often covert, bureaucratic barriers. Even when a 60-year-old person says "I can," the organizational opportunities often do not exist.

This point is emphasized by Rosenbaum's explanation of what is termed the midlife crisis (1980). He challenges the growing body of literature which attributes the midlife crisis to the individual's confrontation with biological decline, mortality, and aging, and provides an alternative view based on research about the impact of organizations on individuals. Specifically, he plotted a single cohort's pattern of promotional mobility from 1962 to 1975 and studied the relation between promotion and age, controlling for sex, race, education, and level in hierarchy. He found that for those without baccalaureate degrees promotion chances increase gradually until age 35 to 40 and then decline gradually. For those with baccalaureate degrees promotion chances reach a peak of over 60 percent at about age 35 and then decline abruptly to less than 20 percent five to ten years later. The selection system tends to withdraw active considerations from those with baccalaureate degrees after age 40: "A college-educated employee under age 35 can expect to continue advancing while the same employee who holds this expectation five years later is bucking the odds and is very likely to be disappointed" (p. 9). Such precipitous declines in promotion chances are inclined to be traumatic and conducive to the psychological reactions attributed to midcareer, midlife crises. Rosenbaum suggests that counseling to adjust to the situation may be harmful to individuals' self-esteem and sense of control and that it would be far better to design different career systems, particularly ones which make the greatest demands of employees not when family responsibilities are greatest (before 35) but when they had begun to lessen (after 40).

Because it seems that today the isolation of the individual from decision making and power is prevalent, the problem for helpers is twofold: They need to help and protect the rights of persons in these asymmetrical situations, and they need to modify the system to make it more symmetrical.

Ideally, for all situations, all parts of an environment, including the individuals within the environment, should be targeted by the helper for interventions; but in reality helpers and agencies usually have to at least begin by targeting a part. Therefore helpers must make decisions on which individual or group is to be targeted. At the same time, decisions need to be made about the purpose or goal: Is the intervention to prevent a problem from occurring, to treat or remediate, to rehabilitate, to enhance, to make life more meaningful? At the same time, decisions need to be made about the level of the intervention: Are we targeting the individual or group in transition or the setting in which the individual or group operates? Is it the workplace that needs humanizing, or the worker that needs retooling?

The overriding point to remember in choosing or planning any intervention is that people are tied to each other and are part of a system. The issue of spouse abuse offers one example: In one agency the focus has been on the abused (mostly women), but some psychologists in the agency are also experimenting with groups of abusers (mostly men) by teaching the abusers communications skills with the goal of helping abusers learn to express in words what they have been expressing physically. For the issue of parent care, we can work with an individual family or groups of families about appropriate arrangements, and/or we can focus our energies on changing funding for residential homes for ill older people or on reforming nursing homes and changing their images. In the event of an unanticipated heart attack, we can work with the spouses of heart attack victims, and/or we can design preventive programs to eliminate the occurrence of heart attacks through planning work settings which encourage exercise and jogging.

In some programs helpers will deal directly with the individual (the retiree, the abused, the new parent, the newly disabled, the older person having to make living arrangements); in other programs helpers will deal with a significant other (the spouse of the newly disabled, the adult children of the aging person, the abuser); and in still other programs helpers will deal with the system in which the individuals and significant others operate (an organization's retirement plan, a state's policy on housing for the elderly).

In short, all aspects of an issue should be addressed simultaneously so that we can help the individual in transition as well as change the system to enable persons to express their potential, and to achieve or increase their capacity to love, work, and play; but often, depending on our resources, we have to decide to begin by working with the individual, the group, or with the system, and identify and aim at a particular goal.

A helper's orientation will influence his or her analysis of any issue and suggestions for interventions. In the case of Rosenbaum's employees at the midcareer transition, if the helper sees the issue of further promotion as the individual's responsibility, the suggested intervention might be therapy or retraining. If the helper sees the issue of further promotion as a function of the group, suggested interventions might include job redesign, communications skills development, training, consultation on leadership. If the helper sees the issue of further promotion as a result of the organizational climate, the suggested intervention might be a new promotion system for older workers. In reality, all three sets of interventions may be needed.

Caplan's identification of three different types or goals of intervention—primary, secondary, tertiary—is useful. Primary intervention refers to elimination of the problem by changing or modifying the environment so that the problem does not occur or recur. Secondary intervention shortens the duration of the problem or treats it more effectively; thus its goal is to treat the problem before it gets out of hand. Tertiary intervention deals with rehabilitation, as when someone is suddenly disabled. Primary intervention, for example, focuses on requiring seat belts; tertiary intervention focuses on rehabilitation of individuals injured in car accidents (Caplan & Grunebaum, 1970, pp. 61–62).

Similarly, Danish, Smyer, and Novak discuss remedial interventions "designed to alleviate already existing problems"; intervention for the "early detection and treatment of a population 'at risk' "; intervention which "involves counteracting harmful circumstances . . . directed at the total population or community"; counseling "designed to help the individual grow from the experience"; support, intended to "alter the quality of the critical life events"; and enhancement, especially to help people "anticipate an event prior to its occurrence" (1980, pp. 351–354).

In addition, Baltes and Danish emphasize "enriching intervention," which "not only connotes a concern with dysfunction and its prevention or correction, but also states explicitly a counterpart orientation—that of maximizing human potential (1980, p. 60). For example, helping adults more creatively tackle such transitions as birth of a first child, retirement, and promotion enriches their lives. At the same time, prevention of problems associated with new roles can be alleviated with preparatory programs, while other interventions can be designed to alleviate problems already incurred in the new role. The current rhetoric is pro-prevention; however, often people deny the possibility of a problem and can deal with it only after the fact. For example, many people facing retirement eagerly grab on to preretirement planning programs; others deny that any problem will occur and can face it only after six months of retirement.

An illustration will serve to summarize: Today society is witnessing an increase in divorces and an increase in single-parent families, especially those headed by women. This issue can be addressed by focusing on the individual in transition—the new single parent, the children, the in-laws—or by focusing on the system. A deeply intertwined issue is child care and substitute care as an entitlement. Clearly child care is not a national priority today; but without this quality care, children may be emotionally and physically neglected. Again, do we decide to focus on trying to change the system? Or do we focus on the individual, the children, and/or the supports? Are our major goals to alleviate the stress or enrich? We need to remember that focusing on both the individuals and the system will produce the most effective help.

Examples of Institutional Programs

Following are descriptions of several institutional—or system— programs which address in some fashion the twofold problem of protecting the rights of and helping individuals in asymmetrical situations and of modifying the system to make it more symmetrical, and which aim toward improvement of both person and environment.

Work-Redesign Programs

As one possible solution to the discontent of American workers, both blue-collar and white-collar, the authors of *Work in America* (U.S. Department of Health, Education, & Welfare, n.d.) suggest that the workplace be redesigned. In an appendix, the book lists companies that have been experimenting with work-redesign programs. We can see here a continuum of reform from programs based primarily on organizational needs to those based on human needs. Three examples will highlight different approaches along the continuum.

The first example—where organizational needs have priority— is the well-known work-redesign program initiated at AT&T over ten years ago. Its purpose is to give the individual a greater sense of control. Its method is referred to as "functional completeness." According to the personnel director, the program arranges work so that only one particular person is identified with a given piece of work. For instance, instead of having 20 people work on one directory and complete the job in a month, the entire job is given to one person. Or a single individual is given responsibility for installing or repairing the telephones in an entire apartment complex or at an airport. Thus, one person is responsible for making the decisions and carrying out the operations associated with a job; presumably, he or she thus derives a greater feeling of satisfaction and content with the work situation.

At the other end of the continuum—emphasis on individual needs—is the pilot project at the Lawrence Laboratory (University of California) in Livermore. Each year, 250 workers are helped to assess their interests, abilities, and values and to anticipate and make plans for the future. The aims of the organization itself play little part in this process; the person is the focus.

A project now in its sixth year at the National Aeronautics and Space Administration (NASA), Goddard Space Flight Center, represents a midpoint on the continuum. In addition to being given career counseling, men and women just below the middle-manager level have a chance to work for a limited time in a different work setting. This project, coordinated by the University of Maryland, is designed to reenergize these adults and increase their feeling of control. The growth of counseling/support/career services for adults in industrial settings indicates two trends: the newly acknowledged need for assistance and the general community unavailability of such support. The program at NASA, funded by the organization, is a prototype of the new wave of industrial counseling.

Education Programs

Many higher education institutions are experimenting with different structures designed to facilitate the adult's return to education, for example, part-time, evening, and weekend programs. Many others have introduced innovative curricula. Such programs contribute to strengthening and increasing options and enrichment for workers.

The College Board, with funds from the Office of Career Education, has been developing and testing the notion of "study organizer" centers. This approach is designed to improve worker access to educational opportunities by providing a study organizer as well as materials and products in a location close to industrial settings where workers can seek advice and information on a regular basis.

The American Center for the Quality of Work Life (ACQWL), with support from the Fund for the Improvement of Postsecondary Education, is adapting the educational brokering concept at two industrial settings. The ACQWL approach argues that the workplace can become the locus for the development of learning activities and that educational brokering is a service that can assist workers in becoming the principal organizers and promoters of increased continuing learning activities in their own work setting.

These intervention programs are aimed at improving information and providing educational brokering/counseling to workers in an attempt to overcome problems associated with worker participation in education programs. Additional modifications and adaptations of these approaches need to be developed to provide information and brokering services to larger numbers of adult workers (Charner, 1980, pp. 57–58). It seems likely that more institutions will join the movement, especially as academic institutions seek to survive in the face of declining enrollments on the part of the "typical" undergraduates. The American Council on Education has charged a commission to identify ways to change or modify higher education so that it is more open to adults. The issue that needs continuous assessment is this: Do educational policies and programs enable adults to move freely, or do they restrict, bind, and box them in?

Faculty Development Programs

The emphasis on faculty development designed to counteract the low morale on many campuses is also an example of increasing awareness of asymmetry. When confronted with a faculty member whose morale is low, the problem again is whether to focus on helping the individual or on changing the environment. We need, of course, to look at the problem from both sides.

Faculty morale has become a major problem on today's university campuses. Kanter (1977) points to the increasing number of persons in academia who find themselves among the "stuck." Because of the "pyramid squeeze" and the difficulty of changing jobs within the present academic marketplace, persons perceive less opportunity to advance professionally. With the decrease in available resources, they simultaneously find themselves less able to perform at the level expected by themselves and their superiors. As with Rosenbaum's midcareer crisis adult workers, lack of opportunity and lack of power lead to low morale. Kanter concludes, "When people see growth prospects close to them in their institutions, they start disengaging" (p. 5). Faculty find themselves caught in the bind of being expected to produce more at a time when research funds and support services are being cut back and when the rewards for effort are less evident and less predictable. At the same time, departments are expected to upgrade their faculties and their graduate programs although there is little money for either new positions or support for graduate students. The temptation is for faculty to despair, to be pessimistic, to become alienated from the university and critical of its administration, and to invest increasingly less energy and time in the university community.

Traditionally, faculty development has focused on providing an opportunity for faculty to increase their subject matter competency. This was, and probably still is, thought to be best accomplished through providing support for sabbaticals, travel to professional meetings, and research. During the past decade, however, faculty development efforts have focused primarily on the improvement of teaching, on the assumption that teaching is the central role of faculty even though it has been ignored in the training of faculty. Activities have included the establishment of teaching improvement grants, instructional support and consulting services, and various superficial attempts to elevate teaching within the reward system (e.g., teaching excellence awards which carry no release time or other tangible reward).

Although most of the programs which fit under the loose rubric of "faculty development" have, as their basic goal, the improvement of teaching, approaches to the achievement of this goal vary considerably. According to Gaff (1975), these approaches can be classified into three categories: individual faculty development, instructional development, and organizational development.

● *Individual faculty development* seeks to help faculty explore their attitudes toward teaching, develop teaching skills, gain insights into the learning process, and improve relationships with students and colleagues. The intellectual basis for this approach is in clinical, developmental, and social psychology, and development activities often take the form of seminars and workshops.

● *Instructional development* focuses on the content and process of instruction. Typically, faculty members are helped to do such things as design appropriate learning experiences for students, specify course objectives, and prepare instructional materials.

● *Organizational development* is based on the assumption that the academic organization needs to be more sensitive to faculty and must therefore change the organizational climate to value faculty.

An example of a faculty development program combining these categories is the activities of a faculty development committee at the University of Maryland which was initiated by the provost of the Division of Human and Community Resources to address the issue of low morale within the division and to suggest programs which might be developed to alleviate the situation (Faculty Development Committee, 1981). To facilitate the committee's efforts, the division allocated a limited amount of funds to support faculty development activities geared to enhance the well-being of division faculty while being supportive of the stated mission of the university.

The committee recommended that the issue of faculty development be addressed in three ways: from the perspective of the division (what the division could do to create a climate more conducive to scholarly achievement and high faculty morale); the department (what the department could do to facilitate better faculty and departmental functioning); and the individual faculty (what could be done to assist individual faculty who wish to work on their own personal or professional development). Efforts focused both on restructuring the environment so that it would be more facilitative of faculty growth and achievement and on providing assistance to individuals who wanted help in assessing and meeting their professional goals. The recommendations, which follow, were divided into those which involved some restructuring at the division and department levels and those which involved increased assistance to individual faculty, thereby attacking the problem of faculty morale by focusing on the institution as well as the individual.

At the division level:

● *Faculty development coordinating committee.* A team composed of one faculty member from each of the four colleges in the division should develop and administer faculty development activities within the division on an ongoing basis.

● *Discussion and redefinition of the mission of the division.* A series of structured discussions within the division concerning its current and future mission within the present university setting should be initiated.

● *Division scholar program.* Each term, four division faculty (one from each of the units) who have made outstanding contributions as teachers and scholars should be designated as division scholars and granted release from all teaching and committee responsibilities so that they may concentrate on on-campus creative productivity.

● *Faculty career counseling.* The career development center should be given university funds to purchase materials and assign a counselor the task of developing and servicing a career counseling center for faculty.

At the department level:

• *Annual chairperson workshops.* The provost's office, in concert with the deans, should take responsibility for providing annual training for departmental chairpersons in the basic principles and techniques of department administration, resource management, curriculum planning, and faculty development.

• *Annual department planning sessions.* Department chairpersons should set aside a concentrated period of several days at the beginning of each spring term, during which the department faculty should meet as a unit to review departmental goals, establish clear priorities and objectives for the next two years, and determine in detail how these should be met.

At the individual level:

• *Liberal faculty leave policy.* Faculty should be encouraged to take leaves without pay for off-campus experience in between earned sabbatical leaves.

• *Funds to facilitate faculty productivity.* Small grants should be made available to aid faculty in professional development and to promote research, scholarship, and publication.

Career Programs

Effective interventions, as based on the work of Weiss (and described in Chapter 4), have three major components: support from others in the same situation and from veterans who have successfully negotiated the transition, a cognitive framework for understanding the underlying issues facing the client, and help in planning for the next steps.

The actual content of each component will depend, of course, on the goal and level of intervention and on the particular persons and environments. For example, a program for college freshmen to prepare them for transitions including retirement will be different from a program designed for retirees. A program designed for an individual will differ from a program designed to target an organization so that it will provide retirement planning for all its employees. The design will also differ depending on whether the intervention strategy includes, for example, a television panel or face-to-face counseling.

One intervention strategy which clearly incorporates the three components is an institutional support program for employees who lost their jobs as a result of a reduction in force (RIF) necessitated by programmatic and organizational changes at NASA's Goddard Space Flight Center. The program, initiated shortly after the RIF was announced, targeted 53 men whose positions and grade levels varied, ranging from nonprofessional support (such as a grass cutter) to professional/managerial (such as a manager of a communications operation). Experts from an outplacement counseling agency and members of the personnel staff who worked with RIF'd employees after the outplacement counselors left provided leadership.

For the first component, others in the same situation and veterans who had successfully negotiated such a transition provided support in a week-long workshop for the RIF'd group.

The second component, a cognitive framework to help the RIF'd employees understand what they were experiencing, was also provided during the workshop, with emphasis on the changing reactions—numbness and disbelief, followed by a sense of betrayal, then panic, then anger, and finally resolution—that could be expected over time.

For the third component, two kinds of planning for next steps were provided: job leads, whereby technique personnel within the organization used their professional contacts to locate appropriate job openings and passed this information on to the displaced employees, and job-finding training, based on the assumption that employees facing termination need a systematic process to help them absorb the trauma of displacement and mount a successful job search. The training (conducted by an outside consultant group) took place through individual counseling activities and in the workshop. During the half-hour counseling sessions—which started shortly after the RIF notices had been sent out—employees were given a chance to express their feelings about being RIF'd. At the same time, they were told how to prepare for the workshop by developing autobiographical data. Parts of the workshop aimed at helping employees to sell themselves effectively in the job market. To this end, they were instructed in methods for identifying their skills and abilities, for developing an attractive resume, for interviewing prospective employers, and for going after jobs. A total of 20 hours was devoted to these group activities during the week of the workshop. In addition, each person met for half an hour a day with a counselor for the purpose of refining his job-search campaign.

Participant reaction to this institutional support program was overwhelmingly favorable. (The men were surveyed by means of a questionnaire mailed out three months after the RIF was announced; in addition, eight of the men were interviewed in depth immediately after the RIF was announced and three months later.) Virtually all the men said that the outplacement and counseling support had given them confidence and hope. Equally important, the program was effective in helping most of the RIF'd employees find new jobs; in virtually all cases they seemed to have positive feelings about their new situations, and most seemed to have adapted to the transition of job loss.

One positive result of the program on the organization's environment was the assurance that it gave to coworkers who were not affected by the RIF. The 53 men who lost their jobs continued to work in the organization for one month after the RIF was announced and, of course, continued to have daily contact with other employees. Because of the job-finding training and the outplacement service, the organization projected an image of being socially conscious and committed to helping the terminated employees find new jobs; this image helped to minimize the potentially detrimental effects of the RIF on other employees and to bolster worker morale.

Other positive effects on the environment for organizations which offer such support programs for terminated employees—in addition to a better image—are a lower risk of litigation for illegal practices, shorter severance payment, and better management of human resources. The cost of such programs can also be weighed against the costs to the taxpayers of unemployment compensation and the costs to society at large of having large numbers of disgruntled and unemployed citizens.

Programs designed to help terminated employees find new jobs represent only one type of institutional career support that can be designed and that corporations can offer to meet transition needs, to promote person/environment fit. Other institutional programs include career development programs for prospective managerial-level employees, retraining programs for lower level workers whose jobs have been eliminated by technological advances, programs to update the knowledge and skills of technical and professional personnel, and programs for employees (and their spouses) who are required to make residential moves.

Examples of Strategies

Too often helpers have considered counseling as the major, if not the only, strategy for helping, whatever the purpose or level of helping. Recent times have witnessed the growth of many innovations in strategies as well as settings, such as telephone counseling, storefront counseling, bibliotherapy, consultation, outreach, computers for career guidance. The tests of a particular strategy's effectiveness are: Does it help the individual explore, understand and cope? Does it also help modify the system so that greater numbers of people can live more effectively?

Two strategies which seem new on the horizon are discussed in this section: the media and computers. Consultation, a strategy growing in importance, is also touched upon, as are the roles helpers can use in both individual and system interventions. These strategies are illustrative and only suggestive of alternatives to face-to-face interactions. The strategies which can effectively and appropriately facilitate exploring, understanding, coping—and symmetry—are endless.

The Media

As more adults watch more television, the relationship between the media and adults emerges as a significant issue requiring the raising of pertinent questions. Who controls the media? What are the cultural values of those in charge? What are their attitudes and the state of their knowledge? What messages are sent to the consumers?

Are the media agents of social change, reinforcers of the status quo, or mirrors of reality? What agenda about adults does the media reflect, and who sets this agenda?

Because the media reach and affect a large portion of the popuation, it is not surprising that educators and psychologists are seizing the opportunity to use media to reach and influence people. The media, which can link people and available resources, can also affect adult socialization, the process through which adults learn to perform the roles and behaviors which they expect of themselves.

Although television generally stresses entertainment, both network and public television and radio have begun to address and incorporate principles and issues of mental health and education. A range of programs has experimented with psychological subject matter and has included direct interaction between psychologists and viewers in call-in shows, talk shows focused on topics of interest (such as the "Phil Donahue" show), and more didactic educational shows that feature lectures on specific topics.

This trend has great potential—but it needs to be carefully evaluated. It is one thing to incorporate mental health principles in programming; it is another to attempt therapy for individual consumers. The ethics of engaging in psychological work on television and radio are now being debated by the American Psychological Association's ethics committee and by media psychologists who are organizing to examine appropriate ways to use television as a mental health tool.

More subtle is the impact of network dramas or daytime soap operas, particularly when they deal with important human issues like homosexuality, prejudice, job loss, physical disability, and death. Advertising provides still another forum.

To understand the full impact of the media requires a systematic study of the total mass communications system. Here we will take a look at the media in terms of the views of aging it is perpetuating and at an example of a television series based on the transition framework.

The media and older adults. Gerbner, Gross, Signonelli, and Morgan (1980) developed a method to examine the "aggregate system of messages" that the media communicates about adults. They juxtaposed the messages from 1,300 programs and 16,600 characters of prime-time and weekend daytime television programming and advertising from 1968 to 1979 ("message system analysis") with social reality as reflected in the 1977 census data ("cultural indicator analysis"). They found many distortions, among them that almost four out of ten elderly characters were likely to be victimized. This compared to less than one in 100 elderly citizens who actually became victims of criminal violence, robbery, or assault, a rate lower than that for other age groups. They found both the young and the old grossly underrepresented. Half of the people in television dramas were between ages 25 and 45 but that group makes up only one-third of the population. Of more than 300 speaking characters weekly in prime-time, only seven were over 65, the study found. In short, except for soap operas, the elderly are dramatically underrepresented.

Further, adults in general are ignored or stereotyped in portrayal. A survey of 899 characters portrayed in 300 television commercials concludes that "as the age of a female character increases, the likelihood that she will sell a digestive aid, a laxative, a pain reliever, or a denture product increases" (Jamieson & Campbell, 1983).

Other studies conclude or corroborate that:

- The elderly are underrepresented.

- Older men outnumber older women three to one.

- Proportionately fewer older characters are "good," while the proportion of "bad" older characters, especially men, is larger than in the younger age groups.

- When the success of characters is measured, more older women are unsuccessful than successful.

- Elderly women are more often portrayed as victims, and/or in poor health (White House Conference, 1981).

Gerbner's studies also looked at how television messages about older people affect viewers' "conceptions of social reality." They concluded that the more people watch television, "the more they tend to perceive old people in generally negative and unfavorable terms." Heavy viewers believe "old people are a vanishing breed" and that women age faster and earlier in life than men. Increased viewing seems bound to increase the television audience's generally negative views of older people. Watching television does not promote "*any* positive images of older people," according to Gerbner's study. Constant watchers are said to believe that the elderly are unhealthy, financially distressed, sexually inactive, stubborn, and intolerant (Gerbner et al., 1980).

But even though they are slighted, neglected, and insulted, older Americans are faithful television watchers. Television particularly attracts four groups: women, blacks, the poor, and the elderly. "Females typically view more than males . . . of all ages . . . . Viewing is inversely related to social class . . . Blacks typically view more than whites . . . and elderly persons typically view more than . . . younger" (Comstock, Chaffee, Katzman, McCombs, & Roberts, 1978, p. 293). By contrast, the dominant figure portrayed by television is the youthful, white, male adult. Portrayals of the four groups of heaviest viewers is stereotypic, according to Comstock.

The current state of affairs may be characterized as one in which young adults, especially male, are the producers, writers, distributors, and stars while older adults are the viewers, vicariously watching the life of the vigorous young and the disintegrating old. The message is clear. The message needs changing.

Thus, because the mass media currently delivers a distorted picture of older adults, television does not reflect what has happened or what is likely to happen. I suggest that its message needs changing. But how will these changes occur? How can the influence agents be influenced? As more attention focuses on older adults, what form will the attention take? The view of older adults presented by the mass media reflects the assumptions and prejudices of advertisers, writers, and producers that may or may not be clearly articulated but inevitably reflects an untested, unformulated, and biased view of aging. It seems appropriate for helpers to force the issue, to argue for enlightenment, to show how opinion makers, influence agents—the captains of consciousness—are not conscious of their own biases and assumptions. Their lack of knowledge, sympathy, and empathy of adults and their development are plain— plain enough to dictate a remedial course of action.

Although there are no easy answers, a national policy on mass media and aging is beginning to take shape as indicated by the work of the 1981 White House Conference on Aging and in funding by the Annenberg School of Communications to the Corporation for Public Broadcasting. For those concerned about the media, the White House Conference provided both good and bad news. For example, a technical committee on the media was established in preparation for the conference, but the committee's report, *Creating an Age-Integrated Society: Implications for the Media,* was not distributed to delegates with other technical committee reports. The media report was available at the conference, but delegates were never informed of its availability. Further, the issue of the media and aging was ignored at the conference. Nevertheless, even though the technical committee's major recommendations never surfaced at the conference, they exist and can provide a basis for future policy and action.

One of the technical committee's recommendations was for the formulation of a National Council for Mass Media and Older Persons in order to promote more honest portrayals of older people. Goals of the recommended council were to "promote research on media portrayal and program activity; explore developments in media industries; promote access to emerging technologies and establish priorities for their use; and promote advocacy efforts in media of assistance to older Americans" (White House Conference on Aging, 1981). Thus, the council would be able to serve as a watchdog and advocate and insure that decision makers—especially writers, directors, producers, and advertisers—were encouraged to portray older adults accurately—in complex, interesting, hopeful ways that reflect the best data available on adult development.

This recommendation and others stemmed from the work of the

Gray Panthers' Media Watch Task Force, which set criteria for monitoring television and trained volunteers to carry out the work. Two encouraging results so far have been that groups for media watching are springing up and the National Association of Broadcasters' Television Code has been changed to include age along with race, sex, and creed as an area "to be treated with sensitivity."

The technical committee also recognized the potential of new technology "for improving the quality of life for the nation's 24 million older Americans" through offering "innovative services that can help solve problems faced by older Americans" (White House Conference, 1981). Older people face many situations which seem unmanageable, confusing, or unexpected; they, like other adults, need to be helped rather than anesthetized by the media.

A television series based on the transition framework. The way television can be used to help adults is illustrated by the five-part "Caught-in-Between" series developed around the recurring issues of adulthood and produced for NBC's Knowledge Series (Schlossberg & Leibowitz, 1980). Based on the knowledge that adults can benefit from cognitive information about what they are experiencing as well as from the support of others going through the same transition, each of the five programs presents one of the transitions most adults normally undergo. The transitions are highlighted through discussions by psychologists, discussions by people experiencing the transition, audience participation (in three shows), and resource suggestions for viewers.

The shows, however, address a paradox: Although adults like to feel unique and special, they also feel relieved to find that others are dealing with similar concerns. The challenge for the producers was to select and present relevant issues—and to provide help—within five half-hour shows.

The first segment, "When Was the Last Time You Called Your Mother?" reflects the fact that people continue to work on the issues of maturity and autonomy throughout their lives, that (to paraphrase Gould) adult development is the process of liberating oneself from the constraints of childhood, freeing oneself from parents. The second show, "Second Time Around," discusses the concerns of blended families—second marriages that involve his, her, and their children—and indicates some of the complexities of instant intimacy throughout the life course. The third show, "Starting Over," illustrates that choosing a career is not a once-and-for-all matter, that every time an adult resolves some major issue, he or she has to start all over again. Two retired football players and their wives and four women with home and family responsibilities who had returned to school make it clear that adulthood is a series of transitions between relatively stable periods. Viewers at home are invited to join in a structured exercise often used as a first step in planning career change.

The fourth show, "Looking at Parent Care," investigates the issues that arise when caretaking roles are reversed, when adult children find it necessary to offer help or assume responsibility for parents who once took care of them. Among problems discussed are how adults are caught in between their own needs, the needs of their children, and the needs of their older parents; how sibling rivalry can recur in middle age around the issue of parent care; and how middle-aged women are often the most stressed because they are the ones responsible for older parents—whether their own or in-laws.

The last segment in the series, "Fun and Friends," points out the difficulty of finding time for recreation and friendship in the demanding years of middle adulthood, the importance of fun and friends as buffers to life stress, and the different types and purposes and numbers of friends through the life course.

Computers

In the fall of 1966 a proposal to the Illinois board of education for a small grant to study the use of computers in vocational guidance was noteworthy (Harris-Bowlsbey, 1983). In the 1980s, national magazines regularly discuss the computer revolution and how it assists, for example, in shopping, in home protection, in helping paraplegics to exercise and walk.

Harris-Bowlsbey, who initiated the 1966 grant, has now with others developed Discover III as a computer strategy to facilitate adult career development (Harris-Bowlsbey, Leibowitz, & Forrer, 1982). The program has five modules which can be used in sequence or entered by the user at any place in the system:

• *Module 1: Understanding career develoment and change.* The computer helps individuals define the types of career decisions they are facing and look at their own readiness for change.

• *Module 2: Self-assessment.* Through three assessments of their interests, skills, and work-related values, individuals obtain from the computer a graphic and in-color "map" of their own personal characteristics and how those qualities relate to specific careers.

• *Module 3: Information gathering.* Individuals learn several techniques for gathering the information they need on organizations, the work environment, and specific careers or jobs so that they can make further career plans.

• *Module 4: Decision making.* By integrating the information acquired in preceding modules about interests, skills, and values with specific organizational and career information, the computer helps individuals to find out how they make decisions and to develop concrete short- and long-term career goals.

• *Module 5: Action planning.* Computer graphics present a model action plan and help individuals take the steps necessary to develop their own career plans.

Harris-Bowlsbey (1983) predicts that the move from information systems to more comprehensive guidance systems (which will include a total package for helping individuals become aware of career planning) is the direction for the future in career planning. By promoting awareness of alternatives and knowledge of the decision-making process, as well as by providing "easily accessible banks of information" and individualized delivery, computer programs like Discover III offer the potential for helpers to deliver "high quality, sophisticated, and individualized counseling and guidance at a relatively low cost." As in all fields, such programs can free professionals from routine and repetitive tasks.

Harris-Bowlsbey also sees a continuing move from single-user large computers to multi-user microcomputer systems, many of which will be in the home and which will make heavy use of audio and visual materials to enhance their programs.

Consultation

Increasingly, counselors, social workers and other professionals are called upon to consult—to advise school systems and hospitals, industry, even whole communities. The ecological perspective becomes even more important in consulting, for consulting gives helpers the opportunity to promote symmetry and person/environment improvement on many levels in many areas.

Approaches to consultation differ, ranging from expert advice on an identified problem to collaboration in the process of uncovering the problem (Schein, 1978, p. 340). Whatever the goal or purpose of the consultation, the helping consultant usually engages in the following steps: "(a) building a working relationship, (b) gathering information, (c) identifying the problem, (d) exploring possible solutions, (e) implementing an intervention, and (f) evaluating the effectiveness" (Kurpius & Robinson, 1978, p. 322).

In consulting with institutions and organizations about, for example, ways to develop preretirement programs, knowledge of transitions provides an essential base. Knowing that individuals' reactions change over time, consultants can perform needs assessments of people before retirement and a year after retirement, and thus insure effective, timely programs. Further, consultants are often able to set up programs aimed at both people and systems. For example, a program of direct service to an organization's preretirees and recent retirees can be complemented by a program changing the system by initiating flexible employment policies for people of any age.

Roles

Helpers use many techniques and strategies in promoting exploring, understanding, and coping—as well as person/environment fit—for individuals, groups, systems. One way of looking at what makes helpers effective in their work with both individuals and systems is to examine specifically the roles they utilize. The roles in the following list, based on incidents of "effective helping" identified by a group of employees and supervisors (Leibowitz & Schlossberg, 1981, 1982), can be used in a wide variety of situations and settings, and need to be included in helpers' repertoires of behaviors.

- *Communicator.* One who promotes a two-way exchange between himself or herself and the client.
- *Counselor.* One who helps the client to clarify goals and identify steps to take in reaching these goals, whether or not they relate to the present setting or organization.
- *Appraiser.* One who evaluates a client's performance, gives feedback to the client, and helps to work out a development plan so the client can negotiate the goals and objectives specific to the current situation.
- *Coach.* One who gives instruction or skill training to enable a client to function or to do his or her job more effectively.
- *Mentor.* One who serves as a sponsor to facilitate a client's personal or career growth.

- *Advisor.* One who gives information about opportunities both within and outside the situation or organization.

- *Broker.* One who serves as an agent (go-between) for the client and appropriate resources (such as people and institutions) for information.

- *Referral agent.* One who identifies resources to help a client with specific problems.

- *Advocate.* One who intervenes on behalf of a client for benefits and elimination of obstacles.

- *Consultant.* One who helps diagnose a problem, usually organizational, and develop alternative solutions, and assists or advises in implementing solutions and evaluating success.

Summary: Connections

This chapter's look at the ecological perspective has emphasized that there are many ways we can help people, that helping is complex, that no single approach or strategy is "the answer," and that considering both individuals and systems is essential. Take the example of the woman who confessed, "I feel selfish. Mark and I were finally alone. The kids are married, and we were able to pick up and go bowling, forget to cook, or just do what we wanted when we wanted. I was even beginning to think of leaving my boring job and exploring other possibilities; maybe even returning to school. Then my mother, who is widowed, became ill; and I was the sibling who had to have her live with us. I resent her presence, but see no alternative. I feel selfish, angry, even cheated."

The interventions we might make for her are numerous. We can help the woman, the couple, or all three with individual or family therapy. We can suggest participation in one of the currently existing groups which help families resolve the balance between individual and family needs. We can suggest participation in one of the support groups made up of others in the same boat in which mutual sharing brings relief, alternatives are generated, and new perspectives are gained from others' experiences. Another possibility for an intervention is the television series already described which deals with issues in adulthood, particularly the segment focusing on issues of parent care. Also possible is intervention through organizational career development programs which support individual exploration even for those with family and economic constraints. Additionally, we can advocate for the expansion of facilities and programs for the ill elderly.

Clearly, there is no best way to help normal adults face their inevitable crises and transitions, particularly since what is a crisis for one may be an opportunity for another; what is on time for some may be devastating and off time for others. Helpers whose goals are to shift the balance from problems to possibilities, to help people move from feeling boxed in to seeing new options, to help adults achieve or maintain their ability to love, work, and play, need to intervene in many creative ways. Our efforts to help adults renew themselves and face transitions and crises positively or relieve them of the burden of feeling alone can range from individual therapy to organizational change, depending on our diagnosis of where the problems lie. The interventions we plan can be as varied as the many adult development theorists and can be based on, for example, Danish's claims that inadequate coping stems from lack of skill, knowledge, or risk assessment; on my transition framework, which indicates that problems are often related to the nature of the transition as well as the individual's support system, options, or self; or on Kantor's indications that the system itself needs changing.

But all our interventions need to be based on knowledge of adult development; as the knowledge base expands, we, too need to expand and revise our repertoire of helping skills and interventions, keeping in mind our goals of freeing people—which comes when they see new or alternative options—and opening the system up so adults can function and grow—which comes with advocacy and opportunity.

This has been a book connecting knowledge to skills, showing how the knowledge base of adult development can be connected to helping skills so that those working with adults can be more creative, more tuned in, more connected, and have more ways of helping available to them.

To recapitulate: Many theorists explain adult behavior. I suggest linking helping skills with those theorists like Neugarten who emphasize the "fanning out" of the individuality of adults during the lifespan. Furthermore, I suggest using transition theory as a basis for helping. Transitions occur in many varieties throughout life, but probably most salient for helpers is the degree to which they are anticipated or unanticipated. Transition theory explains that how an adult copes with transitions depends on—and is mediated by—the variables characterizing the particular transition, the particular individual, the particular environment.

By connecting this view of adult development with different ways of helping and by combining the knowledge base with helping skills, professionals, paraprofessionals, and friends can help adults explore, understand, and cope; help people change the situation when that is called for; change the meaning of the situation when that is called for; handle the stress that accompanies a transition when that is called for. For example, using such techniques as reflecting, open questioning, and focusing is useful in exploring and uncovering how the particular transition is altering the person's life. If helpers are to help the individual understand the situation and develop a new perspective which in turn can stimulate more options, it is imperative for them to listen to the particular adult and identify the underlying themes and problems so interventions can be suggested. To illustrate, many techniques exist for overcoming writers' blocks and for stress reduction. In listening to one writer describe his particular anxiety, it became apparent that what underlay his problem were pervasive fears of being found out, of being incompetent, of being a disappointment to his parents; and further, that his current effort signified for him his magnum opus. Once he and the helper understood these underlying issues, options for dealing with the block became evident. In listening to another writer who said she had no time to write, it became clear that it was because she was barraged by household and child care activities. The solution was the banding together of a group of women and renting a house for "quiet space."

But no longer is a counselor merely a good listener; he or she must also be a broker, an advocate, a linker. The helper with a broad view will take the initiative depending on the needs of the particular adult or group of adults, in changing, for example, the university's rules on financial aid, on part-time students, or on credit for life experience. The helper of adults needs to function in a number of ways; particular situations need particular kinds of help; and helpers armed with knowledge and a multiplicity of roles can be more flexible and helpful, and able to put it all together more effectively.

Helpers need to ask, "Am I helping adults to live fuller lives? To achieve and maintain their ability to work, play, and love?" Politicians, legislators, citizens need to ask, "Are we promoting a country where people from all walks of life can live decent, worthwhile lives?" Helping is not an isolated activity only available to those professionally trained in credentialed programs. Help can come in many forms from many sources. All of us have within ourselves the potential for unleashing talents in others—and ourselves.

Appendix:
Career Transition Workshops

In these transition workshops, participants design individualized plans. In the followup sessions, progress on plans is discussed, ways to overcome any obstacles that have emerged are brainstormed, and continuing support and motivation are built. Evaluation data demonstrate that a clear majority of participants do engage in behaviors consistent with their action plans.

1. The Next Step Management

Goal: To assist technical specialists, generally engineers or scientists, considering the move into management

Format: Six 2-hour sessions; one 3-hour followup session

Component 1: Support System: Support is offered to the group in the following ways:

- The group is homogeneous.
- Trainers promote discussion and interaction.
- Guest lecturers—in-house effective managers who have made the technical-to-management transition themselves—are used as resource experts.
- Participants are encouraged to maintain informal contact with one another after the seminar is concluded.
- A followup session is scheduled three months after the workshop.

From "Critical Career Transitions: A Model for Designing Career Services" by Z. B. Leibowitz and N. K. Schlossberg, *Training and Development Journal,* 1982, *36* (2), 12–19. Reprinted by permission.

Component 2: Cognitive Information: The following key issues are shared and discussed within the group:

- Shift in emphasis from technical skills to interpersonal skills.
- Shift from individually completing work to delegating work.
- Shift from judging success based on their own work to judging success based on the performance of others.
- High-risk decision making—having to make decisions before all the data are in.
- Control—shifting from hard-data decision making to soft-data decision making.
- Competence—"If I was a successful technical specialist, will I be successful as a manager?"
- "Is a management career the only success model at Goddard?"
- Political skills needed to obtain and control resources.
- "If I choose a management path, where will I wind up?"

Component 3: Planning: The following topics and tools are used to help participants plan:

- Career development is presented as a lifelong process.
- Self-assessment of managerial characteristics, values, interests, and skills is conducted.
- A profile of a successful manager at Goddard is compiled by participants.
- Individual managerial skill-deficit areas are targeted for further work.
- Decision-making concerning making or not making the move into management is encouraged.
- An action plan of future career goals, to be reviewed with their supervisor, is encouraged.
- Guidelines for discussing the reality of future plans with their managers are provided.

2. Seminar in Career Perspectives of Midlevel Professionals

Goal: To assist employees who have reached a plateau in their careers in reappraising their current situations and establishing work/life goals.

Format: Three 3-hour sessions; one 3-hour followup session.

Component 1: Support System: Support is offered to the group in the following ways:

- The group is homogeneous.

- Trainers help participants identify and discuss critical issues.

- Participants interact with one another and have the opportunity to feel, "I'm not the only one."

- A followup session is scheduled three months after the workshop.

Component 2: Cognitive Information: The following key issues are shared and discussed within the group:

- The myth that "up is the only way."

- What success is; how others define success; how each participant defines success.

- The discrepancy between aspirations and achievement— "Where am I now compared to where I thought I would be?"

- "Who's to blame for my plight? No one? Myself? The organization?"

- Control—"Who's in control of my career? Me or the organization? How can I gain control?"

- Balance—disengaging from work and seeking payoffs in other life areas.

Component 3: Planning: The following topics and tools are used to help participants plan:

- Information on aspects of adult growth and development as well as change strategies which impact career growth are presented.

- A framework for understanding "stuck" vs. "moving" employees is provided.

- Participants engage in planning by gathering data, brainstorming alternatives, developing goals and objectives, setting target dates, and evaluating.

- Mutual career concerns and strategies are discussed.

- Balanced career/life goals are emphasized.

- Networking and the mentor concept are discussed.

- Guidelines for generating feedback from supervisors, colleagues, and family are provided.

- Internal/external obstacles to change are discussed.

- Activities for developing individualized action plans are provided.

3. Building the Future: A Retirement Planning Seminar

Goal: To assist employees in designing meaningful, realistic preretirement and postretirement plans.
Format: Five 3-hour sessions; one 3-hour followup session.
Component 1: Support System: Support is offered to the group in the following ways:

- Guest lecturers—retirees who speak firsthand of the experience—are used as resource experts.

- Participants share their concerns and experiences.

- Trainers foster discussions and assist participants in focusing on key feelings and issues.

Component 2: Cognitive Information: The following key issues are shared and discussed within the group:

- Anxieties associated with retirement.

- Stages of retirement—high anxiety, denial, "honeymoon stage."

- Issues of change—moving from being pervaded by the change through adapting to it.

- Replacing work needs through nonwork or new-work areas.

- Renegotiating relationships—"married for better or for worse, but not for lunch."

- Fear of aging.

Component 3: Planning: The following topics and tools are used to help participants plan:

- Issues involved in continued growth and development through the later years are presented and discussed.
- Managing the major transition of retirement is presented and discussed.
- Self-assessment (interests, skills, values, lifestyles) and environment (present, e.g. work and home, and future, e.g. retirement) are gathered as data for planning.
- A planning schema is presented and participants apply it in their individual plans.
- Financial planning in retirement is discussed by a financial consultant.
- A presentation on government retirement is made by Goddard Space Flight Center's retirement representative.
- Retired Goddard Space Flight Center personnel present a panel on their experience of retirement.

References

Adams, J., Hayes, J., & Hopson, B. *Transitions understanding and managing personal change.* London: Martin Robertson & Company, 1976.

Alexy, W. O. Dimensions of psychological counseling that facilitate the grieving process of bereaved parents. *Journal of Counseling Psychology,* 1982, *29* (5), 498–507.

Argyris, C. *Personality and organization: The conflict between the system and the individual.* New York: Harper & Row, 1957.

Aslanian, C. B., & Brickell, H. N. *Americans in transition: Life changes and reasons for adult learning.* New York: College Entrance Examination Board, 1980.

Baltes, P. B., & Brim, O. G., Jr. (Eds.). *Lifespan development and behavior* (Vol. 3). New York: Academic Press, 1980.

Baltes, P. B., & Danish, S. J. Intervention in lifespan development and aging: Issues and concepts. In R. R. Turner & H. W. Reese (Eds.), *Lifespan developmental psychology intervention.* New York: Academic Press, 1980.

Barton, P. *Worklife transitions: The adult learning connection.* New York: McGraw-Hill, 1982.

Baruch, G. K., & Barnett, R. C. On the well-being of adult women. In L. A. Bond & J. C. Rosen (Eds.), *Competence and coping during adulthood.* Hanover, N.H.: University Press of New England, 1980.

Beeson, D., & Lowenthal, M. F. Perceived stress across life course. In M. F. Lowenthal, M. Thurnher, & D. Chiriboga (Eds.), *Four stages of life: A comparative study of men and women facing transitions.* San Francisco: Jossey-Bass, 1975.

Brammer, L. M. *The helping relationship process and skills* (2nd ed.). Englewood Cliffs, N.J.: Prentice-Hall, 1979.

Brammer, L. M., & Abrego, P. J. Intervention strategies for coping with transitions. *The Counseling Psychologist,* 1981, *9* (2), 19–36.

Brammer, L. M., & Shostrom, E. L. *Therapeutic psychology* (2nd ed.). Englewood Cliffs, N.J.: Prentice-Hall, 1977.

Brim, O. G., Jr. Theories of the male midlife crisis. *The Counseling Psychologist,* 1976, *6* (1), 2–9.

Brim, O. G., Jr., & Kagan, J. (Eds.). *Constancy and change in human development.* Cambridge, Mass.: Harvard University Press, 1980.

Brim, O. G., Jr., & Ryff, C. D. On the properties of life events. In P. B. Baltes & O. G. Brim, Jr. (Eds.), *Lifespan development and behavior* (Vol. 3). New York: Academic Press, 1980.

Caine, L. *Widow.* New York: William Morrow, 1974.

Campbell, A. *The sense of well-being in America.* New York: McGraw-Hill, 1981.

Campbell, A., Converse, P. E., & Rodgers, W. L. *The quality of American life.* New York: Russell Sage Foundation, 1976.

Campbell, M. D., Wilson, L. G., & Hanson, G. R. The invisible minority: A study of adult university students. Final report submitted to the Hogg Foundation for Mental Health. Austin: Office of the Dean of Students, University of Texas, 1980.

Caplan, G. The family as support system. In G. Caplan & M. Killilea (Eds.), *Support systems and mutual help: Multidisciplinary explorations.* New York: Grune & Stratton, 1976.

Caplan, G., & Grunebaum, H. Perspectives on primary prevention: A review. In P. E. Cook (Ed.), *Community psychology and community mental health.* San Francisco: Holden-Day, 1970.

Caplan, G., & Killilea, M. (Eds.) *Support systems and mutual help: Multidisciplinary explorations.* New York: Grune and Stratton, 1976.

Cattell, R. B. Theory of fluid and crystallized intelligence: A critical experiment. *Journal of Educational Psychology,* 1963, *54,* 1–22.

Charner, I. *Patterns of adult participation in learning activities.* Washington, D.C.: National Institute for Work and Learning, 1980.

Chiriboga, D. Perceptions of well-being. In M. F. Lowenthal, M. Thurnher, & D. Chiriboga (Eds.), *Four stages of life: A comparative study of men and women facing transitions.* San Francisco: Jossey-Bass, 1975.

Chiriboga, D., Coho, A., Stein, J. A., & Roberts, J. Divorce, stress, and social support: A study in helpseeking. *Journal of Divorce,* 1979, *3,* 121–135.

Chiriboga, D., & Gigy, L. Perspectives on life course. In M. F. Lowenthal, M. Thurnher, & D. Chiriboga (Eds.), *Four stages of life: A comparative study of men and women facing transitions.* San Francisco: Jossey-Bass, 1975.

Chiriboga, D., & Lowenthal, M. F. Complexities of adaptation. In M. F. Lowenthal, M. Thurnher, & D. Chiriboga (Eds.), *Four stages of life: A comparative study of men and women facing transitions.* San Francisco: Jossey-Bass, 1975.

Chiriboga, D., & Thurhner, M. Concept of self. In M. F. Lowenthal, M. Thurnher, & D. Chiriboga (Eds.), *Four stages of life: A comparative study of men and women facing transitions.* San Francisco: Jossey-Bass, 1975.

Chodoff, P. The German concentration camp as a psychological stress. In R. H. Moos (Ed.), *Human adaptation: Coping with life crises.* Lexington, MA: D. C. Heath, 1976.

Cicirelli, V. G. Sibling relationships in adulthood: A lifespan perspective. In L. W. Poon (Ed.), *Aging in the 1980s: Psychological issues.* Washington, D.C.: American Psychological Association, 1980.

Coelho, G. V., Hamburg, D. A., & Adams, J. E. *Coping and adaptation.* New York: Basic Books, 1974.

Cohen, F. Coping with surgery: Information, psychological preparation, and recovery. In L. W. Poon (Ed.), *Aging in the 1980s: Psychological issues.* Washington, D.C.: American Psychological Association, 1980.

Coleman, J. S. The principle of symmetry in college choice. In Commission on Tests, *Report of the Commission on Tests II Briefs.* New York: College Entrance Examination Board, 1970.

Comstock, G., Chaffee, S., Katzman, N., McCombs, M., & Roberts, D. *Television and human behavior.* New York: Columbia University Press, 1978.

Cousins, N. *Anatomy of an illness.* New York: Bantam Books, 1979.

Cross, K. P. *Adults as learners.* San Francisco: Jossey-Bass, 1981.

Danish, S. J. Lifespan human development and intervention: A necessary link. *Counseling Psychologist,* 1981, *9* (2), 40–43.

Danish, S. J., & D'Augelli, A. R. Promoting competence and enhancing development through life development intervention. In L. A. Bond & J. C. Rosen (Eds.), *Competence and coping during adulthood.* Hanover, N.H.: University Press of New England, 1980.

Danish, S. J., Smyer, M. A., & Novak, C. A. Developmental intervention: Enhancing life-event processes. In P. B. Baltes & O. G. Brim, Jr. (Eds.), *Lifespan development and behavior* (Vol. 3). New York: Academic Press, 1980.

Dimsdale, J. E. The coping behavior of Nazi concentration camp survivors. In R. H. Moos (Ed.), *Human adaptation: Coping with life crises.* Lexington, Mass.: D. C. Heath, 1976.

Dohrenwend, B. S., Krasnoff, L., Askenasy, A. R., & Dorhenwend, B. P. Exemplification of a method for scaling life events: The Peri life events scale. *Journal of Health and Social Behavior,* 1978, *19,* 205–229.

Dyer, E. D. Parenthood as crisis: A restudy. In R. H. Moos (Ed.), *Human adaptation: Coping with life crises.* Lexington, Mass.: D. C. Heath, 1976.

Egan, G. *The skilled helper.* Monterey, Calif.: Brooks/Cole, 1975.

Egan, G. *The skilled helper* (2nd ed.). Monterey, Calif.: Brooks/Cole, 1982.

Erikson, E. H. *Childhood and Society.* New York: Norton, 1950.

Faculty Development Committee, The Division of Human and Community Resources, University of Maryland. *Final Report.* May 1, 1981.

Fiske, M. Changing hierarchies of commitment in adulthood. In N. J. Smelser & E. H. Erikson (Eds.), *Themes of work and love in adulthood.* Cambridge, Mass.: Harvard University Press, 1980.

Gaff, J. G. *Toward faculty renewal.* San Francisco: Jossey-Bass, 1975.

Gallagher, D., Thompson, L. W., & Levy, S. M. Clinical psychological assessment of older adults. In L. W. Poon (Ed.), *Aging in the 1980s: Psychological issues.* Washington, D.C.: American Psychological Association, 1980.

George, L. K. *Role transitions in later life.* Monterey, Calif.: Brooks/Cole, 1980.

George, L. K., & Siegler, I. C. *Coping with stress and coping in later life: Older people speak for themselves.* Durham, N.C.: Center for the Study of Aging and Human Development and Department of Psychiatry, Duke University Medical Center, 1981.

Gerbner, G., Gross, L., Signonelli, N., & Morgan, M. Aging with television: Images on television drama and conceptions of social reality. *Journal of Communications,* Winter, 1980, *30*(1), pp. 37–47.

Giesen, C. B., & Datan, N. The competent older woman. In N. Datan and N. Lohmann (Eds.), *Transitions of aging.* New York: Academic Press, 1980.

Gilligan, C. *In a different voice.* Cambridge, Mass.: Harvard University Press, 1982. (a)

Gilligan, C. Why should a woman be more like a man? *Psychology Today,* June 1982, pp. 68–77. (b)

Gould, R. *Transformations.* New York: Simon & Schuster, 1978.

Gould, R. Discussion of Schlossberg-Brammer-Abrego papers. *The Counseling Psychologist,* 1981, *9* (2), 44–46.

Greenberg, L. S., & Kahn, S. E. The stimulation phase in counseling. *Counselor Education and Supervision,* December 1979, pp. 137–145.

Gutmann, D. C. The cross-cultural perspective: Notes toward a comparative psychology of aging. In J. E. Birren & K. W. Schaie (Eds.), *Handbook of the psychology of aging.* New York: Van Nostrand Reinhold, 1977.

Hall, E. Acting one's age: New rules for old? Interview with B. L. Neugarten. *Psychology Today,* April 1980, pp. 66–80.

Harris-Bowlsbey, J. A. A historical perspective. In C. Johnson (Ed.), *Microcomputers and the school counselor.* Washington, D.C.: American Personnel and Guidance Press, 1983.

Harris-Bowlsbey, J. A., Leibowitz, Z. B., & Forrer, S. *Discover III: The computer-based career development system for organizations.* Towson, Md.: Discover Foundation, Inc., 1982.

Harrison, L. R., & Entine, A. D. Existing programs and emerging strategies. *The Counseling Psychologist,* 1976, *6* (1), 45–49.

Heffernan, J. M. *Educational and career services for adults.* Lexington, Mass.: D. C. Heath, 1981.

Heilman, M. E. Sometimes beauty can be beastly. *New York Times,* Sunday, June 22, 1980, p. 16E.

Hennig, M., & Jardim, A. *The managerial woman.* New York: Doubleday, 1977.

Hill, R. *Families under stress.* New York: Harpers, 1949.

Hill, R. Generic features of families under stress. In H. J. Parad (Ed.), *Crisis intervention: Selected readings.* New York: Family Service Association of America, 1965.

Holland, J. L., Magoon, T. M., & Spokane, A. R. Counseling psychology: Career interventions research and theory. *Annual Review of Psychology,* 1981, *32,* 279–305.

Holmes, T. H., & Rahe, R. H. The social readjustment rating scale. *Journal of Psychosomatic Research,* 1967, *2,* 213–218.

Hopson, B. Response to the papers by Schlossberg, Brammer, and Abrego, *The Counseling Psychologist,* 1981, *9* (2), 36–39.

Horowitz, M. J., & Wilner, N. Life events, stress, and coping. In L. W. Poon, (Ed.), *Aging in the 1980s: Psychological Issues.* Washington, D.C.: American Psychological Association, 1980.

Huizinga, J. *Homoludens: A study of the play element in culture.* Boston: Beacon Press, 1950.

Ivey, A. L., & Simek-Downing, L. *Counseling and psychotherapy: Skills, theories, and practice.* Englewood Cliffs, N.J.: Prentice-Hall, 1980.

Jamieson, K., & Campbell, K. *Interplay of influence: Media and their publics in news, advertising and politics.* Belmont, Calif: Wadsworth, 1983.

Janis, I. L. (Ed.). *Counseling on personal decisions: Theory and research on short-term helping relationships.* New Haven, Conn.: Yale University Press, 1982.

Johnson, C. (Ed.). *Microcomputers and the school counselor.* Washington, D.C.: American Personnel and Guidance Press, in press.

Kahn, R. L. *Memorandum to SSRC Committee on work and personality in the middle years.* Ann Arbor, Mich.: June 2, 1975.

Kahn, R. L., & Antonucci, T. C. Convoys over the life course: Attachment, roles, and social support. In P. B. Baltes & O. G. Brim, Jr. (Eds.), *Lifespan development and behavior* (Vol. 3). New York: Academic Press, 1980.

Kanter, R. M. *Men and women of the corporation.* New York: Basic Books, 1977.

Kanter, R. M. *The changing shape of work: Psychosocial trends in America.* Washington, D.C.: American Association of Higher Education, 1978.

Kaplan, D. M., & Mason, E. A. Maternal reactions to premature birth viewed as an acute emotional disorder. In H. S. Parad (Ed.), *Crisis intervention: Selected readings.* New York: Family Service Association of America, 1965.

Kelley, H. H., & Michela, J. L. Attribution theory and research. *Annual Review of Psychology,* 1980, *31,* 457–501.

Kilpatrick, E. P., & Cantril, H. Self-anchoring scaling: A measure of individual's unique reality worlds. *Journal of Individual Psychology,* 1960, *16,* 158–173.

Kohlberg, L. Stages of moral developent as a basis for moral education. In
    C. Beck & E. Sullivan (Eds.), *Moral education*. Canada: University of
    Toronto, 1970.

Kohn, M. L. Job complexity and adult personality. In N. J. Smelser & E.
    H. Erikson (Eds.), *Themes of work and love in adulthood*. Cambridge,
    Mass.: Harvard University Press, 1980.

Kübler-Ross, E. *On death and dying*. New York: Macmillan, 1969.

Kuhlen, R. G. Motivational changes during the adult years. In R. G.
    Kuhlen (Ed.), *Psychological backgrounds for adult education*. Chicago:
    Center for the Study of Liberal Education for Adults, 1963.

Kurpius, D. W., & Robinson, S. E. An overview of consultation. In *Person-
    nel and Guidance Journal*, 1978, *6*, 320–323.

Lazarus, R. S. The stress and coping paradigm. In L. A. Bond & J. C.
    Rosen (Eds.), *Competence and coping during adulthood*. Hanover,
    N.H.: University Press of New England, 1980.

Lazarus, R. S. Little hassles can be hazardous to health. *Psychology To-
    day*, July 1981, pp. 58–62. (a)

Lazarus, R. S. Stress and coping in aging. Speech given at the 89th An-
    nual Convention of the American Psychological Association, August
    24, 1981. (b)

Lazarus, R. S., Averill, J. R., & Opton, E. M., Jr. The psychology of coping:
    Issues of research and assessment. In G. V. Coelho, D. A. Hamburg, &
    J. E. Adams (Eds.), *Coping and adaptation*. New York: Basic Books,
    1974.

Lazarus, R. S., Cohen, J. B., Folkman, S., Kanner, A., & Schaefer, C.
    Psychological stress and adaptation: Some unresolved issues. In H.
    Selye (Ed.), *Selye's guide to stress research* (Vol. 1). New York: Van
    Nostrand Reinhold, 1980.

Leiberman, M. A. Adaptive processes in late life. In N. Datan & L. H.
    Ginsberg (Eds.), *Lifespan developmental psychology*. New York: Aca-
    demic Press, 1975.

Leibowitz, Z. B., & Schlossberg, N. K. Training managers for their role in
    a career development system. *Training and Development Journal*,
    1981, *35* (7), 72–79.

Leibowitz, Z. B., & Schlossberg, N. K. Critical career transitions: A model
    for designing career services. *Training and Development Journal*,
    1982, *36* (2), 12–19.

LeMasters, E. D. Parenthood as crisis. *Marriage and Family*, 1957, *19*,
    352–355.

Levine, S. V. Draft dodgers: Coping with stress, adapting to exile. In R. H.
    Moos (Ed.), *Human adaptation: Coping with life crises*. Lexington,
    Mass.: D. C. Heath, 1976.

Levinson, D. J., with Darrow, C. N., Klein, E. B., Levinson, M. H., &
    McKee, B. *The seasons of a man's life*. New York: Alfred A. Knopf,
    1978.

Lindemann, E. Symptomology and management of acute grief. In H. J. Parad (Ed.), *Crisis intervention: Selected readings*. New York: Family Service Association of America, 1965.

Lipman-Blumen, J. A crisis perspective on divorce and role change. In J. R. Chapam & M. Gates (Eds.), *Women into wives: The legal and economic impact of marriage*. Sage Yearbook on Women's Policy Studies (Vol. 2). Beverly Hills, Calif.: Sage Publishing, 1976.

Lipman-Blumen, J., Handley-Isaksen, A., & Leavitt, H. J. Achieving styles in men and women: A model, an instrument, and some findings. In J. T. Spence (Ed.), *Achievement and achievement motives: Psychological and sociological approaches*. San Francisco: W. H. Freeman, 1983.

Lipman-Blumen, J., & Leavitt, H. J. Vicarious and direct achievement patterns in adulthood, *Counseling Psychologist*, 1976, *6* (1), 26–32.

Loevinger, J. *Ego development: Conceptions and theories*. San Francisco: Jossey-Bass, 1976.

Lowenthal, M. F., & Chiriboga, D. Responses to stress. In M. F. Lowenthal, M. Thurnher, & D. Chiriboga (Eds.), *Four stages of life: A comparative study of men and women facing transitions*. San Francisco, Jossey-Bass, 1975.

Lowenthal, M. F., & Pierce, R. The pretransitional stance. In M. F. Lowenthal, M. Thurnher, & D. Chiriboga (Eds.), *Four stages of life: A comparative study of men and women facing transitions*. San Francisco, Jossey-Bass, 1975.

Lowenthal, M. F., Thurnher, M., & Chiriboga, D. *Four stages of life: A comparative study of men and women facing transitions*. San Francisco: Jossey-Bass, 1975.

Lowenthal, M. F., & Weiss, L. Intimacy and crisis in adulthood. *The Counseling Psychologist*, 1976, *6* (1), 10–15.

Lynch, J. J. *The broken heart: The medical consequences of loneliness*. New York: Basic Books, 1977.

Maccoby, M. *The gamesman: The new corporate leaders*. New York: Simon & Schuster, 1976.

Maccoby, M. Work and human development. *Professional Psychology*, 1980, *11* (3), 509–519.

Meichenbaum, D. H. Cognitive factors in behavior modification: Modifying what clients say to themselves. In C. Franks and G. T. Wilson (Eds.) *Annual review of behavior therapy*. New York: Brunner/Mazel, 1973.

Merton, R. K. *Social theory and social structure*. Glencoe: The Free Press of Glencoe, 1957.

Miller, J., Schooler, C., Kohn, M. L., & Miller, K. A. Women and work: The psychological effects of occupational conditions. *American Journal of Sociology*, 1979, *85* (1), 66–94.

Moos, R. H., & Tsu, V. Human competence and coping: An overview. In R. H. Moos (Ed.), *Human adaptation: Coping with life crises*. Lexington, Mass.: Heath, 1976.

Neugarten, B. L. Adaptation and the life cycle. *The Counseling Psychologist,* 1976, *6* (1), 16–20.

Neugarten, B. L. Time, age, and the life cycle. *American Journal of Psychiatry,* 1979, *136* (7), 887–894.

Neugarten, B. L., Moore, J. W., & Lowe, J. C. Age norms, age constraints, and adult socialization. *American Journal of Sociology,* 1965, *70,* 710–717.

Ochiltree, J. K., Brekke, D., & Yager, G. E. A cognitive self-instructional modeling approach vs. the Cardhuff model for training empathy. Paper presented at the meeting of the American Research Association, Washington, D.C., 1975.

Parkes, C. M. Psychosocial transitions: A field for study. *Social Science and Medicine* (Vol. 5). London: Pergamon Press, 1971.

Parkes, C. M. Attachment and the prevention of mental disorders. In C. M. Parkes & J. Stevenson-Hinde (Eds.), *The place of attachment in human behavior.* New York: Basic Books, 1982.

Pearlin, L. I. Life-strains and psychological distress among adults. In N. J. Smelser & E. H. Erickson (Eds.), *Themes of work and love in adulthood.* Cambridge, Mass.: Harvard University Press, 1980.

Pearlin, L. I. Life strains and distress in maturity. Speech at the 7th Annual Conference for Helpers of Adults, University of Maryland, May 13, 1982.

Pearlin, L. I., & Leiberman, M. A. Social sources of emotional distress. In R. Simmons (Ed.), *Research in community and mental health,* (Vol. 1). Greenwich, Conn.: JAI Press, 1979.

Pearlin, L. I., & Schooler, C. The structure of coping. *Journal of Health and Social Behavior,* 1978, *19,* 2–21.

Perry, W. G. *Forms of intellectual and ethical development in the college years.* New York: Holt, Rinehart, & Winston, 1970.

Ramey, E. Anatomy-destiny: Is burnout inevitable? Speech at the 6th Annual Conference for Helpers of Adults, University of Maryland, May 6, 1981.

Rappaport, J. *Community psychology: Values, research, and action.* New York: Holt, Rinehart, & Winston, 1977.

Riegel, K. F. Developmental psychology and society: Some historical and ethical considerations. In J. R. Nesselroade & H. R. Reese (Eds.), *Lifespan developmental psychology: Methodological issues.* New York: Academic Press, 1973.

Rosen, B., and Jerdee, T. H. Too old or not too old. *Harvard Business Review,* November-December 1977, pp. 97–106.

Rosen, J. L., & Bibring, G. L. Psychological reactions of hospitalized male patients to a heart attack: Age and social class differences. In B. L. Neugarten (Ed.), *Middle age and aging.* Chicago: University of Chicago Press, 1968.

Rosenbaum, J. E. Organizational careers and life cycle stages. Paper presented to the American Sociological Association, New York City, August 30, 1980.

Rotter, J. Generalized expectancies for internal versus external control of reinforcement. *Psychological Monographs,* 1966, *80* (1), Whole No. 609.

Rubin, L. *Women of a certain age: The midlife search for self.* New York: Harper Colophon Books, Harper & Row, 1981.

Sarason, S. B., & Lorentz, E. *The challenge of the resource exchange network.* San Francisco: Jossey-Bass, 1979.

Schain, W. Conversation with author. Washington, D.C., July 1981.

Schein, E. H. The role of the consultant: Content expert or process facilitator. *Personnel and Guidance Journal,* 1978, *56* (6), 339–343.

Schlossberg, N. K. Adult men: Education or re-education. *Vocational Guidance Quarterly,* 1970, *19* (1), 36–40.

Schlossberg, N. K. A model for analyzing human adaptation to transition. *The Counseling Psychologist,* 1981, *9* (2), 2–18.

Schlossberg, N. K., & Charner, I. Development of a self-help instrument for coping with change. Project in process, 1982.

Schlossberg, N. K., & Leibowitz, Z. B. Organizational support systems as buffers to job loss. *Journal of Vocational Behavior,* 1980, *17,* 204–217. (a)

Schlossberg, N. K., & Leibowitz, Z. B. *Caught in Between: Issues of Adult Development.* NBC Knowledge Series, TV show originally aired in Washington, D.C., October, 1980. (b)

Schlossberg, N. K., Troll, L., & Leibowitz, Z. B. *Perspectives on counseling adults.* Monterey, Calif.: Brooks/Cole, 1978.

Seidenberg, R. *Corporate wives: Corporate casualties.* New York: Am Com, A Division of American Management Association, 1973.

Shanas, E., Townsend, P., Wedderburn, D., Friis, H., Milhoj, P., & Stehouwer, J. The psychology of health. In B. L. Neugarten (Ed.), *Middle age and aging.* Chicago: University of Chicago Press, 1968.

Siegler, I. Conversation with author. Center on Aging, Duke University, June 1981.

Smelser, N. J. Issues in the study of work and love in adulthood. In N. J. Smelser & E. H. Erikson (Eds.), *Themes of work and love in adulthood.* Cambridge, Mass.: Harvard University Press, 1980.

Smelser, N. J., & Erikson, E. H. (Eds.). *Themes of work and love in adulthood.* Cambridge, Mass.: Harvard University Press, 1980.

Spaulding, R. C., & Ford, C. V. The Pueblo incident: Psychological reactions to the stresses of imprisonment and repatriation. In R. H. Moos (Ed.), *Human adaptation: Coping with life crises.* Lexington, Mass.: D. C. Heath, 1976.

Spence, D., & Lurie, E. Style of life. In M. F. Lowenthal, M. Thurnher, & D. Chiriboga (Eds.) *Four stages of life: A comparative study of men and women facing transitions.* San Francisco: Jossey-Bass, 1975.

Spierer, H. *Major transitions in the human life cycle.* New York: Academy for Educational Development, 1977.

Steinem, G. The stage is set: Where are we going from here? *Ms.,* July/August, 1982, p. 77.

Sussman, M. B. An analytic model for the sociological study of retirement. In F. M. Carp (Ed.), *Retirement.* New York: Human Sciences Press, 1972.

Thurnher, M. Continuities and discontinuities in value orientations. In M. F. Lowenthal, M. Thurnher, & D. Chiriboga (Eds.), *Four stages of life: A comparative study of men and women facing transitions.* San Francisco: Jossey-Bass, 1975.

Tiedeman, D. V., & O'Hara, R. P. *Career development: Choice and adjustment.* New York: College Entrance Examination Board, 1963.

Touchton, J. Still room at top at national/state levels. *Comment, A Research/Action Report on Wo/men, 13* (2). Also appears in *Women in Education,* Summer 1982, p. 19.

Touchton, J., & Shavlik, D. Challenging the assumptions of leadership: Women and men of the academy. In C. Foster (Ed.), *New directions for higher education* (Vol. 22). San Francisco: Jossey-Bass, 1978.

Troll, L. *Continuations: Adult development and aging.* Monterey, Calif.: Brooks/Cole, 1982.

Troll, L., & Schlossberg, N. K. How "age based" are college counselors? *Industrial Gerontology,* Summer 1971, pp. 14–20.

Turner, R. R., & Reese, H. W. (Eds.). *Lifespan developmental psychology intervention.* New York: Academic Press, 1980.

U.S. Department of Health, Education, & Welfare. *Work in America: Report of a special task force to the Secretary of Health, Education, & Welfare.* Cambridge, Mass.: MIT Press, n.d.

Vaillant, G. E. *Adaptation to life.* Boston: Little, Brown & Co., 1977.

Vaillant, G. E. Maturity over the life cycle. Speech at the 7th Annual Conference for Helpers of Adults, University of Maryland, May 12, 1982.

Van Hoose, W., & Worth, M. R. *Counseling adults.* Monterey, Calif.: Brooks/Cole, 1982.

Wapner, S. Transactions of persons-in-environments: Some critical transitions. *Journal of Environmental Psychology,* 1981, *1,* 223–239.

Weathersby, R. P. Ego development. In A. W. Chickering (Ed.), *The modern American college.* San Francisco: Jossey-Bass, 1981.

Weathersby, R. P., & Tarule, J. M. *Adult development: Implications for higher education.* AAHE/ERIC/Higher Education Research Report No. 4. Washington, D.C.: American Association for Higher Education, 1980.

Weinberg, S. L., & Richardson, M. S. Dimensions of stress in early parenting. *Journal of Counseling and Clinical Psychology,* 1981, *49* (5), 686–693.

Weiss, R. S. Helping relationships: Relationships of clients with physicians, social workers, priests, and others. *Social Problems,* 1973, *20,* 319–328.

Weiss, R. S. *Marital separation.* New York: Basic Books, 1975.

Weiss, R. S. Transition states and other stressful situations: Their nature and programs for their management. In G. Caplan & M. Killilea (Eds.), *Support systems and mutual help: Multidisciplinary explorations.* New York: Grune & Stratton, 1976.

Weiss, R. S. Attachment in adult life. In C. M. Parkes & J. Stevenson-Hinde (Eds.), *The place of attachment in human behavior.* New York: Basic Books, 1982.

The 1981 White House Conference on Aging. *Report of Technical Committee: Creating an age-integrated society: Implications for the media.* Mimeographed, 1981.

White, R. Strategies of adaptation: An attempt at systematic description. In R. H. Moos (Ed.), *Human adaptation: Coping with life crises.* Lexington, Mass.: D. C. Heath, 1976.

Willis, S. L., & Baltes, P. B. Intelligence in adulthood and aging: Contemporary issues. In L. W. Poon (Ed.), *Aging in the 1980s: Psychological issues.* Washington, D.C.: American Psychological Association, 1980.

Zaleznik, A., & Jardim, A. Management. In P. F. Lazarsfeld, W. H. Sewell, & H. L. Wilensky (Eds.), *The uses of sociology.* New York: Basic Books, 1967.

Index